FEAR
AND
LOATHING
IN
BANGKOK

Also by Christopher G. Moore

Novels in the Vincent Calvino crime fiction series

Spirit House o *Asia Hand* o *Zero Hour in Phnom Penh*
Comfort Zone o *The Big Weird* o *Cold Hit*
Minor Wife o *Pattaya 24/7* o *The Risk of Infidelity Index*
Paying Back Jack o *The Corruptionist* o *9 Gold Bullets*
Missing in Rangoon o *The Marriage Tree*

Other novels

A Killing Smile o *A Bewitching Smile* o *A Haunting Smile*
His Lordship's Arsenal o *Tokyo Joe* o *Red Sky Falling*
God of Darkness o *Chairs* o *Waiting for the Lady*
Gambling on Magic o *The Wisdom of Beer*

Non-fiction

Heart Talk o *The Vincent Calvino Reader's Guide*
The Cultural Detective o *Faking It in Bangkok*

Anthologies

Bangkok Noir o *Phnom Penh Noir*
The Orwell Brigade

FEAR
AND
LOATHING
IN
BANGKOK

CHRISTOPHER G. MOORE

Heaven Lake Press

Distributed in Thailand by:
Asia Document Bureau Ltd.
P.O. Box 1029
Nana Post Office
Bangkok 10112 Thailand
Fax: (662) 260-4578
Web site: http://www.heavenlakepress.com
email: editorial@heavenlakepress.com

First published in Thailand
by Heaven Lake Press
Printed in Thailand

Jacket design: K. Jiamsomboon
Author's photograph: Ralf Tooten © 2012

ISBN 978-616-7503-24-0

For Sainarong Rasananda

Contents

PART I
Where the Wild Things Are

1 I Am Awesome   3

2 Dumb Criminals   7

3 Where the Wild Things Are   12

4 Ghostly Crying Babies   18

5 Fake Shit in the Plantations   22

6 Bangkok's 300 Exits   25

7 The Tragedy of Elephants   31

PART II
Criminal Justice System, Thai-Style

8 Speeding Red Bull's Hit 'n' Run   39

9 The Cell and the Cell Phone: Thailand's 3G
   Prisons   46

10 Reenactment of Crimes: Reality Check   51

11 Omnishambles Thai-Style   56

12 Presumption of Innocence until Executed   63

13 When Godot Is an Assassin and You Don't Have to
   Wait: Thai Hit Men Hierarchy   68

PART III
Crimes without Borders

14 Gun Homicides and the Honor Culture   *77*

15 The Rates of Murder   *83*

16 Illegal Spirit Migrants   *89*

17 Fighting Crime across International Borders   *94*

18 Corporations Carrying out Crime inside Alice in
Wonderland   *101*

19 Organized Crime Building a Supply Chain   *108*

20 We Need to Have a Talk about Greed   *112*

PART IV
Culture and Justice

21 The Shadow of Freedom   *121*

22 Jailing False Prophets   *124*

23 The Sacredness of Justice   *129*

24 Above the Law   *136*

25 Poison   *141*

26 Proportionality and Crime Suppression   *146*

PART V
Government, Crime and Technology

27 He Said, She Said   *153*

28 Forcing People to Shut Up or Throw Up   157

29 Data Mining in the Age of Terrorism   162

30 Big Data Noir   169

31 Inside Galileo's Fear Chamber   178

32 Falling Into The Trap   186

PART VI
Anger and Fear

33 Angrier Thais   195

34 Thai Political Super Storms – Kreng Jai System Under Attack   202

35 Anger and the Medical Solution   210

36 The State of Fear   217

37 Creating Fear   223

38 Counterfactuals and Fictional Worlds   229

39 Parker's Absence of Fear   234

40 Insanity at the Gate   240

PART VII
Brain Games

41 Memory Bottlenecks   247

42 Self-Deception and Self-Forgetting   252

43 Ghost Whisperers in Asia   257

PART VIII
On Crime Fiction

44 Dispatches from the Front Lines of Crime Fiction's
    Extremistan, Part 1   265

45 Dispatches from the Front Lines of Crime Fiction's
    Extremistan, Part 2   271

46 Dispatches from the Front Lines of Crime Fiction's
    Extremistan, Part 3   277

47 Noir Fiction, Part 1: Mind Hacks   282

48 Noir Fiction, Part 2: Barbarians   288

49 Big Ideas in Crime Fiction   294

50 Orwell, Koestler and the Noir Brigade   300

PART IX
On Writing

51 Rolling the Dice   307

52 The Writer as Truth Seeker   312

53 Apophenia   316

54 Words on Walls   323

55 Private Eyes Riding the Time Machine   329

56 The Death of Literary Irony   334

57 Beyond the Lamppost Light   339

58 Author's Muse   343

59 Re-imagining Henry Miller   346

60 When the Cuckoo Calls Your Name: A Lesson in
    Success for Writers   352

Part 1

Where the Wild Things Are

I Am Awesome

Some criminals start out young as they embark on a life of crime. Many reasons can be found to explain why someone turned "bad" and adopted the life of an outlaw. One of those reasons is financial. The criminal wants a certain lifestyle that takes money. He has a choice—find a job, save up for the car, the condo, the holidays, to support his partner and dependents. Or if his plans are grand, then no regular job will finance the structure of a life that only the wealthy are able to afford.

Occasionally, there is a criminal who has a broad vision of his future. His life plan could only be financed by winning a super lottery or by crime.

The *Bangkok Post* carried the photograph and story by ace reporter Sunthon Pongpao about the arrest of the 25-year-old Saichol Mailuan.

Saichol (in Thailand people are referred to by their first name) was cornered in Wang Noi district, Ayutthaya, by the police in a drug sting. The suspect opened up with his .357 hand gun at a number of police officers. The spent shells indicated he fired five times. (Keep that number in mind, we will come back to it.)

The report said that the police were unharmed as they wore bulletproof vests. But there was no mention of whether the shots fired by Saichol struck anywhere near the vicinity of the arresting officers. If they'd bounced off the bulletproof vests, I have a feeling the vests with the holes would have been displayed for the media.

Saichol's shooting skills are a valid subject of inquiry, as one of the five rounds (remember the number five, we are getting there) resulted in a self-inflicted wound to his left leg.

In other words, the suspect shot himself in the left leg while resisting arrest by a small army of policemen.

That degree of accuracy doesn't suggest he was a trained marksman or professional gunman. In the photograph accompanying the article (you'll have to search online to see it, as it is copyrighted, and we wouldn't want to breach a copyright), Saichol is seated at a table, a crew of non-smiling Thai police officers standing behind him and at his side, the .357 handgun on the table and box of shells spread out so everyone can see exactly what a .357 round looks like.

Saichol was photographed wearing a T-shirt with the words—**I Am Awesome**. That may seem like a young man's bravado. It would have been quite wrong had the T-shirt said—**I Am a Crack Shot**. Awesomeness is something few people can rightly claim at any age, while anyone can learn to shoot a gun.

What did the police discover in their investigation of the suspect's background?

First, he's quite young: 25 years old. I know I said that before. How much living did you have behind you at 25? I'd wager a bet it doesn't come close to Saichol.

Second, he'd already done five years in prison for attempted murder as well as drug dealing and theft (as also reported by Thai-language newspapers). Matichon reported that Saichol confessed to having been to jail five times. The fact that he's a lousy shot may explain the prior *attempted* murder conviction.

Third, his ability as a drug dealer rivals his shooting ability. He sold *yaba*: methamphetamine pills, a.k.a. "crazy drug."

Fourth, and here comes that most auspicious number five in Saichol's young life, he had five wives. The wives lived in five different households. Five houses. Five rice cookers, Five TV sets, Five sets of dental and medical bills, five motorcycles or cars, five wardrobes. Married life times five takes some serious cash. Economies of scale aren't in favor of such a person. Note to Ministry of Education—mathematics courses ought to teach scaling, power laws and how to buy food and other stuff in bulk.

Fifth, there is no mention as to which of the five shots hit his leg. Was it the first shot? That may explain why he squeezed off four more shots without hitting any of the cops. Was he trying some kind of fast draw and pulled the trigger before removing the .357 from his holster? Or was it his fifth shot, and that ended his shooting spree?

Odds makers in Saichol's hometown are offering higher odds for the self-inflicted shot coming from rounds two, three or four. Another question: was he left-handed or right-handed? If the cops are standing in front of you, how do you shoot yourself in the left leg? It's this kind of question that you'd think someone would put to the suspect. Perhaps has done, but the answers have never been reported. Why is that? Maybe the order of the rounds will come out in the evidence at his trial. Though he will likely cop a plea and there will be no trial, and the mystery of the number of the round that hit his leg will remain.

Let's summarize what we know so far: Saichol is a high-testosterone 25-year-old who is a bad shot. His left leg suffered a self-inflicted .357 hole from one of five rounds he fired. He was nabbed red-handed with 1,000 *ya ba* pills.

On his earlier conviction Saichol spent five years in the monkey house. He supported five Thai wives in five different households. He's been in jail five times.

Karma and the number five are finely woven into Saichol's life.

One would have to begrudgingly concede that Saichol has earned the right to wear his T-shirt in his meet-the-press, with the police glowering in the background.

Rumor has it that all of the underground lottery tickets in Ayutthaya with the number 555 in them were quickly snapped up after the news of his most recent arrest broke. There has been no word on how his five wives will support themselves as their common husband returns to prison. Note to the press: Visitation rights should be an interesting story to follow up. Will the gang of five wives have to draw straws or can they visit as a group? The BBC, CNN and others would follow like a pack of hungry wolves should they appear together wearing T-shirts—**He's Awesome**.

The question is whether Saichol will again get another five-year stretch in the big house and at age 30 emerge a changed man. Can he go straight? Will he have learned his lesson? Which of the five wives will be waiting to greet him upon his release? Can this be turned into a reality show?

As for that T-shirt message—**I Am Awesome**—it might be the one shirt that he doesn't want to wear inside the big house. He might think about a tattoo instead.

Just saying.

Dumb Criminals

The murky world of criminals has its fair share of morons. In the noir world, criminals are aggressive, sinister, violent and unstable. In the real world there are are all kinds of people who aren't good at their chosen occupation. Some people don't have what it takes to be a criminal.

Though 2012 has yet to end, people are already drawing up lists of the stupidest criminals. Here are some examples:

1. Diminished Capacity as a Result of Being Involuntarily Made a Werewolf in Germany

No one bothered to inform Thomas Stroup of the limitations of such a defense. Ohio police arrested Thomas and charged him for underage drinking. The evidence was reasonably clear. Thomas passed out in a trailer encircled by swords. Other residents in the trailer park had complained that Thomas started fights and was otherwise a nasty character. When confronted by the police, Stroup said he was sober. Though he admitted his behavior had been strange, he said it was beyond his control as he'd been scratched by a wolf in Germany, and this wolf-like spirit had motivated him to kill the officer's cousin, named Keith. Only the officer had no cousin named Keith.

2. The Dude Abides. At home only.

Christopher Jansen was on trial in March in Pontiac, Michigan, for drug possession. Young Christopher claimed that he had been searched without a warrant. The DA countered that the arresting officer acted properly without a search warrant as he had probable cause. He saw a "bulge" in Christopher's jacket and thought it might have been a gun. Christopher objected to that conclusion. It turned out he was wearing the same jacket that day in court. He removed the jacket and handed to the judge for inspection. The judge removed a packet of cocaine from the jacket pocket. The judge laughed so hard he needed a five-minute recess to get a grip on his giggles before the trial could resume.

3. Having Too Much Fun as a Legal Defense

Closer to home there are endless examples of foreign tourists who arrive in Thailand having left their thinking mind at home and who then discover ... like everywhere else, there are laws here.

Take, for example, a couple of Indian tourists who decide to get drunk and then at some stage also decide either to have some fun or else head back to their hotel—but then, it's a holiday after all, so why not do both? So they steal a motorbike owned by a taxi driver who works at a taxi queue in South Pattaya. It seems that Mr. Govind Lal, age 43, and Mr. Varun Kumar Guel, age 28, just couldn't pass that motorcycle without noticing the key had been left in the ignition. There is no explanation of what distracted the other motorcycle taxi driver in the queue. The motorcycle owner, Moragot, age 32, later admitted his bladder had been killing him so he'd rushed away to use the toilet, leaving the key in the ignition. When he returned, his bike was gone.

But with the bamboo telegraph in hyper mode, the missing bike and the two Indians are spotted on Second Road in Pattaya. Friends of Khun Moragot force the bike to stop and take the two Indians to Pattaya Police Station. The suspects' defense was was they only intended to borrow the motorcycle and have some fun, and besides, they were far too drunk to have the criminal intent to commit a theft. Khun Moragot, the crime victim, must have been quite upset to hear the Indians prattling a defense reserved only for Thais caught in these circumstances. That is the only explanation for his refusal to accept a financial compensation package by the two suspects. No way these guys were going to pay their way out of justice. The two Indians were remanded for trial.

4. Tug of War with an ATM

Tourists not only get drunk and commit stupid crimes, but when they stay longer than their bankroll, the real fun begins as they formulate stupid plans to replenish their wallets. And what better place to get money than a bank? Why not rip an automatic banking machine off the wall, cut it open like a mad beast and drain out the money? You have now entered the chain of reasoning that makes desperate men into morons. In June 2012 in Chon Buri, Alexander Milbourn, 25, and Shaun Edward Tracy, 34, had a brilliant plan to attack an ATM at the Bank of Ayudhya's Laem Chabang branch. The local police said the two hit the ATM late at night on June 21.

The two Britons groused out a third man they called Richard (a popular name among British expats in Pattaya). Richard was on the lamb. One wonders which one of these guys was the ringleader. They've got a map. Or maybe not. They just decide on impulse to hit the ATMs in Si Racha district, which include Bangkok Bank's Bo Win branch, Bank of Ayudhya's Laem Chabang branch and Bo Win branch. There was a slight preference for Bank of Ayudhya ATMs.

This is where it is gets interesting. If you are going to steal something built into a wall to prevent theft, you have to respect that whoever installed it will have made it difficult to easily pry loose. Or so you would think. But you're not out of money and desperate in Pattaya like these three Britons. Their plan was to tie a tow sling around the ATM and attach the other end of the sling to their car's bumper. Both ends secure, ATM to car bumper, driver gets in and pushes the accelerator to the floor. It didn't work. In all three attempts, the tow sling failed to pull the ATM loose. One might think after the first failure, the gang might have a rethink of their technique. But no, they tried a second time. By the third time they must have been resigned to touring ATM machines by the thousands in Pattaya in hopes there was at least one that would prove they were right, and the first three machines were just flukes of bad luck. What would a reasonable thief do? Change cars. It must be the car's fault.

It also might occur to most people (especially Britons) that banks have significantly more CCTV cameras than tellers and other staff. They are watching you. Not these boys. It took them three failed attempts to get the attention of the police who gradually became aware that someone was attempting to steal ATM machines. The point is the tourists got caught and were probably just as surprised at being arrested as they were when the second and third ATM machines failed to pop out of the wall.

The police took into custody the tow sling and the two cars used in the attempted thefts and are still looking for Richard. Personally, I think the Indians could have handled it much better—with their imaginary friend Richard, they could have claimed they were very drunk and had mistaken the ATM machines for paragliding docking stations and had no idea they had anything to do with banking. It might not have worked any better for the Britons than it had for the Indians. Yet the Thai justice system has a lot of tolerance for drunks. It has very little for sober tourists tying tow slips to their ATMs.

Here's some advice: When you're on holiday, don't commit a crime. If you decide to break that rule, think about how dumb your plan is, borrow the money from mum or dad or a friend, and go back home. Because none of your friends are going to tie a tow sling to your cell bars and clear a path for your freedom.

Where the Wild Things Are

Bangkok this week has secured its reputation as the place (to borrow Maurice Sendak's book title) "where the wild things are." Wild things, as in wild, feral animals, are a good place to begin a Conrad-like journey into the heart of urban darkness.

Noah, according the myth, collected a pair of each animal and loaded them onto an ark as he had advanced warning that a flood would wipe out life on the planet. This week a modern version of Noah was busted in Bangkok, although no ark was found on the premises. But that is a minor detail, as no self-respecting face-displaying local would be caught dead shoving animals into a wooden boat. The new ark is an imported luxury car.

Before we move on to the animal selection process for filling up an ark, let's start with the noise animals make. Noah must have had neighbors too. We never heard their side of the story. Noah didn't work in silence. He banged nails day and night to construct the ark, while his animals, caged up, no doubt kicked up a chorus. Never heard that part of the story? Right. That merely proves that some great background stories never are told, or if told, are remembered and passed down from generation to generation.

In Bangkok, after a drinking session, the music is usually turned up ... and up ... and at some point it blares through the neighbor's walls. The racket leeches through the floors and ceiling and sucks you dry. Welcome to the neighbor from hell. The one with the teenager who has formed a rock band with his buddies but no one has ever taken a music lesson. The wannabe rock stars bang away on electric guitars and drums from midnight to four in the morning. You complain to the police. They do nothing. Thailand is a fount of unconventional stories about hellish neighbors, but at last there is a story where the police actually came, saw, held their noses and returned with very large trucks to remove the source of the noise. Only in this case, it wasn't loud music that caused the misery.

In one of the remote neighborhoods in Bangkok, Khun Lek bolts up in bed as he tries to awake from a nightmare of roaring lions and a distant chatter of pigs and peacocks. He is now awake but the sound of the jungle hasn't disappeared. And then he smells something foul, as if a hundred sewers have backed up and overflowed in his bedroom.

The police discover that the neighbor, a Mr. Montri, runs a pet shop at the Weekend Market also known as Jattujak or JJ Market. He's previously been convicted of trading in wildlife and has gone back to his old ways, the evidence of which officials soon find: 14 white lions, 4 otter civets, 1 oryx, 23 meerkats, 1,000 sugar gliders, 12 peacocks, 13 turtles, 6 minks, 4 miniature pigs, 17 marmosets, 2 hornbills, a number of other birds and some stuffed animals. It seems the police got tired of the census after the ordeal of counting 17 marmosets (those little buggers race around like rats on speed and all look alike, making counting an ordeal), and the quantities grew vague when it came to the birds and stuffed animals. There it is. After the great flood, the world starts over with this population of animals.

Mr. Montri tells the police that he has the paperwork to legally import the lions from South Africa. Apparently a lion costs 200,000 baht wholesale or about $6,700.00. There is a slight problem with the papers. The import documentation shows 16 lions coming into Bangkok, and there are only 14 in the cages on Mr. Montri's land. The paperwork hasn't stopped the police from charging Mr. Montri with offenses that could delay the sailing of the Mr. Montri's ark by up to four years.

Where were the missing two lions? That question is one Mr. Montri's neighbors are seeking answers to as they gingerly rush from their front doors, climb into their cars or onto the seats of their motorcycles and get out while the getting is good.

The rich in Thailand apparently have a strong desire to own unusual pets. There is also a dark side, too, as the delicate bits from some of these animals are also made into medicines. The secret sex lives of some old men require harvesting organs from rare, large African animals. Others go for luxury sports cars.

This leads us back to the ongoing investigation by a large number of agencies into the smuggling of luxury cars into Thailand. The 300 percent import taxes are staggeringly high for someone using the normal import channels. That provides an opportunity for someone who can figure out a shortcut. Somehow 2,000 luxury cars were smuggled into Laem Chabang port in Chon Buri and stored, making it one of the world's largest luxury car parking lots in the world. As one would expect, cars began disappearing from the port as importers began selling them off at bargain prices.

The Department of Special Investigation (DSI) is looking into 600 luxury cars to see if they were legally imported. DSI has impounded 100 of the cars so far this year.

News reports indicate that 90 percent of the luxury cars imported into Thailand have entered the country illegally. That is more than just a little leakage in the system. That's the sound of Niagara Falls roaring next to those missing lions. Like the prohibition of alcohol or the criminalization of drugs, a 300 percent tax on a luxury item is guaranteed to fuel a grey and black market, to corrupt officials and to create a wealthy criminal class of middlemen. In the case of Thailand, the grey and black markets are the lion's share of the luxury car market.

The grey market includes luxury cars used abroad by students and imported into Thailand when they return. Just think about it. You come home from a year of study abroad with a half-million-dollar car that slides in under the tax regulations. Or if you have a luxury car assembled in Thailand, another free pass—even though the assembly of such cars requires technicians and facilities that rival NASA, and the local "assembly" shops appear to have no more than the usual screwdriver and hammer. And the luxury car has to be registered. Basically the luxury car market is a legal mess with many fingers pointing and many more fingers in the pot.

The owners of luxury cars are a who's who of "hi-so" personalities, senior government officials and even an abbot. Their sons and daughters also have a taste for the exotic import that distinguishes them from the lower orders running around town in their government subsidized locally assembled cars that cost less than the upholstery on a Bentley.

You need vitality to drive one of these babies. With a white lion in the passenger's seat no one—I repeat, no one—is going to have a larger face than the man behind the wheel. Most humans are status obsessed, and the Thais are no exception to the rule. Face is important. What you drive, what you wear and the animals you collect, if of the right sort, can create a face the size of the moon. Capitalism in its full glory has provided a mechanism to achieve the elevated heights undreamed of in Noah's day of mere ark builders.

If we stand aside from the personalities and the distracting images, we can see more clearly what is at stake. The lions and the luxury cars are really a story about our uneasy, troubled relationship with nature and each other. Our problem has caused a problem with nature once it became apparent that there is vastly more profit in destruction than in maintenance of natural resources.

We are a species of Deceptive Apes—Killer Apes—and we are a danger to ourselves and all other species. Our ancestors passed laws and wrote constitutions to protect us against ourselves. In the digital age we have found those in power have discovered new and powerful ways of deception, means far beyond the imagination of prior generations.

We deceive ourselves that nature can absorb our rapacious behavior. We deceive ourselves that those who collect information will never use it for their benefit rather than our own.

We deceive ourselves into believing that the rule of law will continue to protect us like a dyke against the rising tide of government intrusion. Apathy is the bedfellow of deception. We are enablers of the worst excesses, things that should worry us but don't. A majority of Thais accept corruption as part of the system. A majority of Americans don't object if their government accesses, stores and analyzes their emails, Amazon purchases, Google searches, Facebook likes and posts, and telephone calls.

Collectively we've fallen into a state of denial that a price is paid for deception, and that we are the ones who pay it. Our minds fill with the soma of the media and the government officials, and we miss the context and the larger issues. Like the audience of a great magician who knows how to distract, we are easily fooled. We focus our attention on the slightly amusing personal stories that limit the damage to a couple of dodgy schemes that the authorities are investigating. Imported lions and luxury vehicles are a good laugh. Until we realize that we are laughing when we should be weeping.

We live in a time of great loss—nature, privacy, freedom, honesty and fairness. One by one, these values are dying. Like Old English words, one day no one will remember what such words meant back in our day. The natural habitat of the Deceptive Ape is in transition. What will that new space look like? Perhaps our descendants will occupy a mental cage with as much space to roam as the cages in which the Bangkok-residing white lions were housed.

We can only guess. The new "Where the Wild Things Are" is just beginning to unfold.

Ghostly Crying Babies

Last week I discussed the way writers, among others, can gather up unconnected events, people and things and find an underlying theme that binds them together. The mental process involved, sometimes known as apophenia, also explains the human infatuation with shamans, gurus, fortunetellers, palm readers and crystal ball gazers—those who claim access to the hidden forces of the universe. Their coupling of unrelated events lends a magical quality to their promises of success in love and business.

It can also be a good term to examine a police case.

Last week in Bangkok, the police received a complaint that a hotel guest had heard the sound of "ghostly" babies crying from a room. That's right: babies. Not just one baby crying. The police immediately dispatched their ghostbuster unit to investigate. It might seem strange that the police would rush to a hotel because someone heard babies crying. Babies are known to cry. At any given time, there must be thousands of crying babies in Thailand. Some of them may even sound ghostly.

But in this case, the ghostly crying babies launched something not unlike a ghost busting SWAT team to the scene.

The Crying Baby Unit discovered that the hotel guest wasn't in the room where the reported crying had been heard. They couldn't hear any ghostly crying babies, either. The babies had apparently stopped crying, or maybe there was a more sinister reason. Not satisfied they had an adequate answer, the police returned to the hotel several hours later. This time they found a British national, a twenty-eight-year-old ethnic Chinese man named Choe Hok Kuen, in room 301. (That could be a lucky number for those who connect numbers associated with accidents, deaths, suicides and other misadventures with the numbers on lotto tickets.)

The police search earlier hadn't turned up one crying baby that sounded like a ghost. Not even a non-ghostly crying baby could be heard. Hotel rooms tend to be small in size. I imagined the police looked around the room, maybe knelt down and had a look under the bed, checked out the bathroom. They found no sign of a baby, crying or otherwise. Room 301 was baby clean. But there was something new to search this time. Mr. Choe's shoulder bag became the focus of attention. Inside, like a clue in a good mystery, was a key to another hotel.

One of the police must have reasoned, "Could the suspect have stashed the crying babies in another room, in another hotel?" There was only one way to find out. The police escorted Mr. Choe to the second hotel.

The police likely tossed the second room looking for crying babies and had no more luck than in Mr. Choe's first room. Someone decided it would be a good idea if Mr. Choe opened his luggage, just to be on the safe side, as that was the only place left they hadn't search for crying babies. After all, they had found a key in his shoulder bag. The MO of this criminal suspect was to keep incriminating evidence in some kind of a bag.

Instead of a crying baby, the police discovered as they opened Mr. Choe's luggage, according to the *Bangkok Post*, "six fetuses wrapped in gold leaf and tied with religious threads."

Rather than a crying baby, the police announced, "I believe it's the world's first body snatcher bust involving the commercial trade in fetuses."

Following this investigative coup, the police interrogated Mr. Choe about the six dead babies in his luggage. He confessed to the police that he was a Master of Witchcraft. He didn't say which university had conferred the master's degree, or whether he had obtained it through a correspondence course at a polytech in the East Midlands. Mr. Choe said he also had a website where he offered black magic and divination services, which could be ordered as easily as biscuits and a cup of tea from room service.

After Mr. Choe's promotional and marketing statement was recorded, the police steered the conversation back to the six fetuses in his luggage. He must have raised an eyebrow and stared at them as if only a child could ask such a silly question. The babies—called *kumarn thong* ("golden baby" in Thai)—were essential elements in a black magic ritual. And he sometimes sold one or two fetuses to believers who wanted one for home ritual use. He bragged he sold one for a million dollars. It always comes down to money.

This hadn't been Mr. Choe's first shopping expedition for *kumarn thong*. Since 2007, he'd been shopping in Thailand 16 times for dead babies. The police speculated Mr. Choe's supply chain likely led to abortion clinics. An investigation is being launched to determine which clinics might be in the fetus selling racket.

Returning to the beginning of this essay, the market for *kumarn thong* is a classic example of apophenia. The gold leaf, the religious threads, Khmer writing on the dead babies— all unconnected items are vested with a magical über-connection empowering a person to succeed in business and love. This is the kind of connection that requires "faith" or belief. It is without any testable foundation. No experiment can confirm or deny such claims. They stand outside science, logic or reason.

Kumarn thong exists at the mad, extreme end of superstitious human belief systems. Who doesn't wish for success in business and love? The answer—there are enough rich people willing to believe that a dead baby, a shaman and a ritual will bring such success to keep Mr. Choe returning to Thailand 16 times in five years.

As for Mr. Choe, he faces charges of concealing human corpses, and could face up to one year in prison and a 2,000 baht fine. Only our black magic ghost story doesn't end there. The six fetuses found in Mr. Choe's room have been stored in the evidence cabinet at Plabpachai Police Station, where a woman police officer made an offering of red Fanta soda and yogurt. Afterwards, several police officers at the station claim to have heard a whispering voice saying, "The white chubby lady is very kind." Stay tuned for a follow up report on whether the ghostly whispering and crying is next heard in the courtroom as part of the testimony in this case.

Previously published as "Black Magic Karma Changing Crimes" on June 1, 2012.

Fake Shit in the Plantations

Governments in most places want to help citizens who struggle to make a living. Thailand is no exception. The law of unintended consequences unfortunately comes into play when government policy attempts to control market forces. Greed is a bulldozer that ploughs through Wall Street; it also rolls through the rubber plantations and rice fields of Asia.

In the South of Thailand there are many rubber plantations. Rubber trees require fertilizer. The essential ingredient of fertilizer? One assumes it is poo. The people who make fertilizer, like all good capitalists, seek to maximize their profits from every bag. If this becomes a highly regulated business where the government sets the price, then one way to boost the profits is to sell the farmers "fake" fertilizer. It is difficult to believe that there are cheaper substitutes for poo, but apparently that is the case.

What the English-language newspapers in Thailand fail to say is that the "fake" fertilizer story has shit hitting the fan in more than one ASEAN country. What seems to be an eccentric story from Thailand is actually a story that is spreading through the region. America had the subprime mortgage meltdown in 2008, while Asia has a subprime fertilizer story in 2012.

Vietnam also has bad boys diluting the fertilizer in their country. In Vietnam, tests showed that rather than 20 percent organic content, the fertilizer had less than 15 percent. What's a farmer in a remote area without testing to do? That's the problem. Remote areas where the fake fertilizer is used won't really know the problem until their crop yields tell them. The Vietnamese authorities responded with a crackdown, raiding five companies selling the fake shit. But with fines being on the light side, the crackdown won't solve the problem. The Vietnamese solution is for the state to get into the shit business. They're building a huge fertilizer factory. I am certain we can revisit this story in a couple of years to see just how well that solution worked.

Not to be left out of the biggest shit story to hit the region in years, the Philippines is also investigating fake fertilizer in Mindanao. The police seized thousands of bags of fake ammonium sulfate, ammonium phosphate, urea, muriate potash and monosodium sulfate salt. This happened after the cops found the safehouse where the fake fertilizer gang had warehouses.

Tempo reported, "The suspected leader of the gang, Edgar Calledo, and seven of his workers were caught mixing, rescaling, and resacking ... suspected adulterated fertilizer products inside a warehouse in Maa, Davao City."

They were caught red-handed. It would be good if the local reporters kept us informed about the trial of that gang of corporate thugs. How this is any different from activities of the average derivative trader on Wall Street is a subject that would require a separate essay. But I am certain by now you can see the general theory is roughly the same. Only on Wall Street, they mixed shit in with the good stuff, while in this region, to save on the cost of shit, they put in the fake stuff.

The problem can be traced to governmental capping of the price of fertilizer. That is called a price control. It means that to keep farmers and producers of agricultural products contented voters, the price of shit has to be kept below market price. If the manufacturer is a state enterprise, then the taxpayers subsidize the true cost of shit. But if the price control is on private manufacturers, and the cost is rising, you would expect one of two outcomes: (1) the use of fake materials that cost much less, or (2) a refusal to manufacture and sell their product at the controlled price. The first is fraud, the second is civil disobedience.

According to *The Nation*, in Thailand fertilizer producers and retailers have put the government on notice that they won't be selling any more of their shit under the government's current price structure. The national stocks of fertilizer are dwindling. The government is looking to import fertilizer from Malaysia to fill the gap. The government is caught between farmers who want cheap fertilizer and fertilizer companies that want a profitable return on their investment.

The lesson is that even shit has a market price, and when the government policy is that the private sector has to bear the cost of production even though this not only wipes out their profit margin but puts them in a loss position, something has to give. The alternatives aren't pretty: fake fertilizer, fraudulent fertilizer gangs, black market fertilizer and damaged crop yields.

Wall Street bankers and Southeast Asia fertilizer manufacturers have more in common than anyone would have thought. They could recruit from the same pool of executives who know the best techniques of getting people to believe that a little fake shit doesn't spoil the crop yields.

Previously published under the title "When Poo has the Wrong Bad Smell" on May 18, 2012.

Bangkok's 300 Exits

Some weeks provide an avalanche of events—enough to fill a book of essays. For example, a German national who'd finished serving a prison sentence in Australia for theft and drug law violations escaped his private security guards at the Bangkok airport and had a two-day holiday in Bangkok before the police caught up with him. Carlo Konstantin Kohl, age 25, a German national with an Australian accent (and a contemporary of Mr. I Am Awesome, the 25-year-old Thai drug dealer with five wives I wrote about a couple of weeks ago) was being extradited to Germany.

Mr. Kohl's escorts were two private security personnel whose task was delayed at Suvarnabhumi Airport due to bad weather. The security detail had decided to wait for the onward flight to Germany in the transit lounge with Mr. Kohl. It was a long overnight wait, and the guards fell asleep, according to the *Bangkok Post* (although the Australians denied that). Mr. Kohl decided he wasn't all that anxious to return to Germany, where he was wanted on parole violation charges. According to local reports, he wandered around the airport for hours.

His escape from the airport confirmed that it has more exit doors than Bangkok's illegal gambling casinos—300 doors—and is far less secure. Any one of the airport exit doors, apparently, can be easily disabled by snipping an electric wire.

Rumors are unconfirmed that Immigration—having discovered all of these doors may be in surplus for emergency use—might convert a half dozen of these surplus exits into Fast Track lanes for those willing to pay an extra fee. Of course, I made that up, but anything you can conceive in your imagination just might have a counterpart in reality in Thailand.

Thais love stories about handsome young rogue *farang* giving the authorities in Australia and Thailand a dual set of black eyes. Kohl was bound to endear himself to a Thai audience by stopping at the airport for a foot massage before hightailing it to Soi Cowboy. The local press played the *sanuk* angle of the story as if Mr. Kohl's visit to Bangkok's hot spots was a blend of *Home Alone* and *The Hangover Part II*—a handsome young rogue for a star; fumbling, sleeping Australians; and a tour of the hot spots of Bangkok.

Establishing the facts has been a challenge. Like objects in zero gravity, facts in Thailand have a habit of floating free, bouncing off the shell of reality. Untethered, they remain fluid and forever just out of reach. The Thais have a way of dealing with facts that appear to incriminate someone important—those facts fall into the category of insufficient evidence. In Kohl's case no Thai officials of rank were incriminated (that was news in itself). His romp through Bangkok was an adventure, and besides, everyone was quite happy to lay the blame on the Australian security detail—including the Australians. Falling asleep on the job? That could never happen in Thailand. What about all of those doors Mr. Kohl rattled? Some of the doors had been kept open for the convenience of airport staff. A bolt hole might be useful when the time comes to sneak a cigarette, to hide from the boss or to find a cozy spot for a quick nap.

Even the circumstances of Kohl's capture/surrender/ ambush—take your pick—are unclear. He was arrested in the vicinity of the German embassy. One press report said Kohl had applied for a replacement passport two weeks earlier. That was the first clue that he'd been enjoying himself in Bangkok for some while, flying under the radar.

Hadn't anyone notified the Germany embassy in Bangkok to be on the lookout for him? Apparently not, but facts, like elementary particles in physics, apparently only allow you to measure location or velocity. I'd hazard a guess that Heisenberg's head would have been spinning to explain the facts in this case. Was Kohl on his way to the German embassy to pick up his replacement passport? Did he suddenly have a pang of guilt and then walk up and turn himself in to a Thai cop? We don't know those facts. You can't find them anywhere in the press accounts.

In one week Carlo Konstantin Kohl managed more front page coverage in the English language newspapers than the Prime Minister or her brother—the one who was prime minister when the airport with the 300 exit doors opened, and who used one of them to exit the country some years ago. This was exactly the kind of story the local media love—a bankable Hollywood-style rogue, private Keystone Cop foreigners, and no one of importance had been accused of corruption, thuggish behavior or a display of gross arrogance. Allegations of negligence, well, to complain about that is to complain about the oxygen we breath. Though it's true the Thai press had a report that the taxi driver who drove Kohl from the airport into Bangkok charged him 3,000 baht for a ride that normally would cost under 300, it's not certain Kohl was aware that he'd been grossly overcharged. I suspect he gave the driver a hundred dollar bill. Unless, after his foot massage, Kohl had made a trip to one of the airport exchange booths.

With a bit of time to reflect, the *Bangkok Post* ran editorial suggesting that if Kohl could use a coin to open a security door at the airport, then terrorists well-trained in escape and evasion skills could easily have popped open all 300 doors at once.

Kohl, who was fined 6,000 baht ($200) and given a two-year suspended sentence for illegal entry, later conducted what appeared to be a workshop in front of about 50 officials who watched Kohl show how he had used a coin to open a security door and how he had cut the wire. It was less a reenactment of the crime than the usual photo op that the local papers run of a foreign guest speaker or a guru from abroad, holding one of those seminars at a five-star hotel, lunch included, for the purpose of professional development and the transfer of foreign know-how and technology.

This tale of Kohl's fun holiday in Bangkok overlooks one or two issues that I've not seen raised in the press accounts. Shouldn't someone be asking the question of whether there are protocols that require foreign police agencies or private security firms used by law enforcement to transport prisoners to other countries, to notify local authorities that a criminal will be passing through as a transit passenger? Wouldn't the Thais like to know in advance of arrival of someone like Mr. Kohl at their airport? Would they have rules to be observed, such as not to fall asleep in the transit lounge while escorting a prisoner? Can any serial killer show up in the custody of a couple of sleep-deprived private security guards, take a power nap in the transit lounge and allow their charge to depart on a tour of the city? What other people or things are going on in transit lounges that Thai officials might be interested in as a matter of public security and safety?

Or is the international transport of prisoners one of those black boxes, like the renditions the Americans ran out of Thailand for some years, where flights come and go out of a shadowy world with a wink and a nod? Do other countries have procedures that set out what notice and process must be complied with in flying prisoners in and out of their country?

The problem with such questions is they take the fun out of Kohl's story. Better to keep a lid on the broader implications of what happened by limiting attention to the official response, which is to send a crew around to rattle the 300 security doors at the airport. The questions are also embarrassing to both the Australians and the Thais. Asking why the Thai authorities didn't receive advance notice of Mr. Kohl's arrival raises the uncomfortable possibility that the Australians were under no obligation to give the Thais any such notice.

Credit must go to Mr. Kohl was exposing the security problem at the airport. Additional credit is due for establishing the abiding metaphor whenever an influential person is facing a "fact" that causes a major loss of face and serious criminal charge—he will find 300 exit doors, and one of those doors will allow him to escape. Call it the "insufficient evidence" door.

The more interesting story this week was the explosion and fire that destroyed a carrier lorry loaded with six foreign luxury cars that somehow had entered the country and avoided import duties—interesting especially because the parties involved have links to major politicians and government officials.

The six luxury cars have caused a turf battle between the police, customs, the revenue department and the anti-corruption agency, and no doubt other agencies will seek to have the cars and jurisdiction under their authority as well.

Doors, 300 of them, and the question is which doors will open and close before the mystery of who owned and imported the six luxury cars is revealed. Next week, reading the local press will be an exercise in observing multiple doors opening and slamming shut like the doors of nineteenth century prison cells. Could the Australians take the fall for those luxury cars? Did someone fall asleep again? Somewhere, official wheels are turning, and doorknobs to power are being tested.

The Tragedy of Elephants

One of George Orwell's most enduring essays is titled "Shooting an Elephant." In the 1930s Orwell served as a colonial official in Burma. He was a sub-divisional police officer. Young Orwell's hatred of the idea of empire was matched only by his brutal contempt for the unfortunate souls who were the subject of the imperial occupation of their homelands.

His iconic essay about an elephant goes to the heart of imperialism—the linkage of the despot with the expectations of those exploited. The story begins when the narrator received a phone call about an elephant on the rampage in a bazaar. He brings his old .44 Winchester, knowing it is too small a weapon to down an elephant, but as a means to frighten the beast. The elephant is in musth and the mahout has taken a wrong turn, ending up twelve hours off course.

All the weapons in the empire are with the authorities. The locals have no weapons and as a result are "quite helpless" against the raging elephant. They can only stand to the side and observe as the elephant destroys a hut and fruit stalls, eats produce, overturns a van and stomps a "black Dravidian coolie" to death in the mud. And wait for the British colonial officials to handle the problem. The locals are victims. They are passive. Their only choice is to wait for those with guns to arrive and save the day.

Seeing the dead man, the narrator sends a servant to a friend's house to borrow an elephant gun. Once he has the elephant gun, the mood of the crowd changes from indifference to an expectation of harvesting the elephant's meat once it had been shot. A small army of locals follows on the heels of the official to the paddy field where the elephant is found quietly eating grass.

The danger has gone out of the situation. The elephant is calmly feeding itself and no more dangerous than a cow. The official has no desire to kill the elephant and sees no compelling reason to do so until he considers the crowd of 2,000 Burmese watching and waiting. It is not idle interest that has drawn them to the field. He represents authority. He has an elephant gun. They have only their hands. "A sahib has to act like a sahib…" He has no choice but to act out his role; it is impossible not to kill the elephant, not because the elephant poses a danger any longer, but because an armed man without resolution will no longer be feared. He must never show fear to the natives. A fearful man without resolve would no longer project that he is the legitimate master of their destiny. Though he might be despised for killing the creature, he would be feared, and that is the framework on which empire rests.

The killing of the elephant is a messy affair, with multiple shots and great suffering by the beast, which takes a good half an hour to die. Afterwards, opinion is divided about whether the official has done the right thing by killing the elephant. What makes him happy is that the "coolie" has been killed, for his death has justified the death of the elephant, even though it was no longer a danger to anyone. The shooting has been almost like the execution of a murderer. No one could deny that murder had happened. While an elephant couldn't form the intent to kill as a human being could, nonetheless, with view of the human corpse, no one could say that the shooting was wrong.

Orwell's parable about an elephant can't be disconnected from the context of empire. A modern version of the story happened last week in Thailand. A Thai nurse and her husband visited Lae Paniad Elephant Kraal in Ayutthaya. The nurse offered an elephant named Plai Big some food. The elephant grabbed her arm and pulled her toward him, stomping on her with his foot. Her husband rushed to help his wife. Plai Big gored him. The nurse died from massive injuries to her internal organs. The husband was seriously injured.

As in Orwell's "Shooting an Elephant," an elephant, a 27-year-old three-tonne male, had killed a human. In this case the dead woman was a nurse. She was hardly a member of the "coolie" class that featured in Orwell's story. No one ran to the authorities and asked that a police official be dispatched to shoot the elephant. The Thai resolution had a different outcome. A ritual was performed at the elephant kraal. The ends of the elephant's tusks were sawed off by 20 centimeters. The purpose of the ceremony was to free the elephant of the spirit of the dead woman. It was reported that Plai Big would never work with the public again. Plai Big's fate will be to spend the rest of his days in solitary confinement.

In Orwell's story there was a tragedy. In the contemporary Thai story is a similar tragedy. When foreigners occupy another land, the need to maintain fear and authority rule out any other option. It was never about the elephant; it has always been about the monopoly on violence as the means to show resolve. For Orwell, nothing short of pulling the trigger to kill could establish that such resolve was beyond question. To maintain order was to show that resolve, even though the shooting wasn't otherwise necessary. And maybe that is the point of Orwell's story. Indecisiveness in the exercise of force would have been a sign of weakness. One man in a crowd of 2,000, if weak, would not survive. He would be laughed at. And the last thing a man with a gun can allow is laughter at his expense.

In Thailand the dynamic is different. By not shooting an elephant, no official would be exposed to belittling laughter. The elephant didn't have to die to maintain authority and the right to use force. Rather than violence as a response, a ritual was held to free the elephant from the spirit of the dead woman. A metaphysical resolution rather than physical violence ruled the day. Also in the Thai story, the elephant has a name, an age and an identity. In the Orwell story, the elephant, like the locals and the dead "coolie," are nameless.

The tragedy of elephants doesn't stem from the fact that they sometimes kill people but rather from the expectations of the survivors and the critical detail of who is in charge of the weapons. The elephant in both cases acted out of hormonal heat, a moment of rage. Compare that compulsion with the choice given the very human foreign armed policeman who, when pressed by the size of the crowd around him, kills the animal in cold blood. The premeditation, the thought process, the politics—these are what is disturbing and haunting about these stories. The elephants shame us by showing how we calculate in our killings, and how the rituals of healing are available only once a community draws upon its own traditions without interference from the outside.

From Syria to the West Bank to Pakistan, Iraq and Afghanistan, the expectation that killing the elephant is required has not changed from Orwell's *Burmese Days*. The lesson is clear that occupiers use fear to maintain control over local populations. It is also clear that Orwell's lesson hasn't been learned, as the forces of imperialism are tested today just as they were in his time, and those who are occupied welcome the raging elephant because he provides thousands with an opportunity to witness the first signs of weakness that will embolden them to take up weapons against the elephant killers who is not one of their own.

Part II

Criminal Justice System, Thai-Style

Speeding Red Bull's Hit 'n Run

At five in the morning of Tuesday, September 4, 2012, 27-year-old Red Bull heir Vorayuth Yoovidhya was driving his million-dollar Ferrari on the road in a fashionable area of Bangkok when he hit a policeman on motorcycle patrol. The driver failed to stop after the impact. From the look at the damaged Ferrari in the press photo, it appears to have been driven fast.

How fast was the Ferrari going before the accident? Did the policeman suddenly cut in front of the Ferrari, as claimed by the Ferrari driver? Did the accident happen while the driver was sober, as his family lawyer claimed? The press reports from the English-language papers add new details daily and contradict earlier reports. The basics are reported in *The Nation*. The Ferrari was estimated to be traveling at 200 kph when the accident happened. As with many crime and accident scenes, the press leaked information. Whether this information is accurate is another question. What we know from the press is this: "Impact traces show that the Ferrari crashed straight into the rear of the motorbike, leaving an imprint of the bike's exhaust pipe on the car's front."

The body of the policeman appears to have somehow stuck on the bonnet; his motorbike was dragged 200 meters before the Ferrari finally drove clear of the wreckage. Some time before that, the policeman's body fell from the car onto the street, where he was left to die with a broken neck and multiple broken bones.

Was the driver drunk at the time his car rammed into the back of the police motorcycle?

According to the *Bangkok Post*, Vorayuth's alcohol level exceeded the legal limit. As the test was taken hours after the accident, it might be assumed that at the time of the accident it was higher. Why the delay in testing for alcohol in a hit-and-run case involving the death of a police officer? Because the police were refused access to the Red Bull family compound where the driver was hiding after the accident. The family driver, or a family retainer, falsely claimed that he had been driving the Ferrari.

Influential, wealthy people don't like inconvenient facts or evidence. One of the hugely important aspects of great wealth and power is the ability to control information, to make certain that information channels pitch your story in the best possible light and ignore facts or evidence that might discredit that story.

We also have a story to tell of the driver, the grandson of a wealthy family, who drove his heavily damaged million-dollar car away, leaving behind like bread crumbs a trail of engine oil all the way from the accident scene right to the family house and underground garage. There he parked the car and went into the house.

Shortly after 5:00 a.m., at the moment of impact, everything changed for the two men involved. One was a cop who died. The other was a rich kid who chose to do what rich kids do—seek refuge in the family mansion. Vorayuth could have stopped his Ferrari and gone to the aid of the police officer he had struck. It is impossible to know whether it was the initial impact or the subsequent dragging of the officer that resulted in his death. However small the chance, it might have made a difference. At least to the driver's humanity.

What happened next is revealing on a number of cultural, social and political levels. Let's be honest. People panic. People make mistakes. People exercise poor judgment in a crisis, and, at crucial times such as this, the cultural training of a lifetime comes into play as they go into automatic pilot. These are the moments when what people are taught by their parents, schools and others in their lives can be understood more clearly.

If you live in a place where the default is to game the system, you couldn't ask for a better case study.

The initial contact at the family mansion was by the local police, who showed up at the door and were denied entry—by a maid. The door was shut. The police walked away. Yes, an officer has been killed, and the servant at the wealthy person's door has said they could not enter. Wealth and influence induce fear, and the police, rather than pressing ahead, did the expected. They found a "middle way"—meaning a way to fix the problem. A senior police officer from the local district police station (the one where the dead officer was assigned) apparently made a deal with a servant of the family to let someone else in the household (another servant of course) to take the fall for Vorayuth. They went in the side door.

This was a hard switch to make plausible. It wasn't as if the driver had taken a second-hand pickup out for a run. Maids, gardeners and drivers normally aren't given the keys to million-dollar sports cars to have a spin around the neighborhood. The setup smacked of desperation or arrogance, probably a bit of both.

I want to pause for a moment and ask you to consider how culture comes into play in such a tragedy. Privilege, entitlement, influence, connections are words we all know.

They are abstract concepts but with real consequences. The default action of the family and the police was to game the system.

That's how immense power works everywhere, and it is why the rule of law is the only mechanism we have to restrain those with such power from running us over and pushing a servant forward as the "cutout" or "fall guy" so that the heir to the family fortune can have the Ferrari repaired and ready to drive another day.

After hours of negotiation between the police and the family and their lawyer, the 27-year-old heir was taken to the police station and promptly released on a $16,000 bail.

One of the saddest aspects of the case is the likelihood that money will talk and punishment will be reduced to compensation for the victim's family. It has happened before. After enough incidents of this kind it is difficult not to conclude that this is how the system works. It's not a freakish outcome but a normal one, where officials and someone in a rich family work out a corrupt solution to "fix" the problem. If the servant of the Red Bull heir had taken the place of the driver, an innocent man would have been sent to prison to serve the time for the wrongful death. This is the heart of corruption, of the system gamers, the flaw of the patronage system—all of it played out on Sukhumvit Road, inside a mansion, the parties locked in the embrace of cover-up and corruption.

It's not necessarily that Thais don't have a sense of justice, but they have seen too many examples of impunity enjoyed by the rich and powerful when they break the law. This Red Bull heir case came just a few weeks after a "hi-so" teen driver, daughter of a high-ranking official, was given a two-year suspended sentence after having been found guilty of reckless driving causing nine deaths. She was just 16 and driving without a license when the fatal accident happened on an expressway two years ago. Besides the suspended sentence, the punishment included 48 hours of community service and a ban on driving until the age of 25.

Thais are asking: Will the Red Bull heir join the long list of Thailand's privileged youths who have killed ordinary people with their cars and then served no time? Actors, singers, celebrities and children from well-connected families with influential surnames and ranks are often given a "Get out of Jail Free" card.

In this case the wealthy family lost control of the information. The evidence was overwhelming, and it was obvious who the driver was and who was lying to protect him. The senior police officer involved in the failed cover-up was soon transferred to what is called in English an "inactive" post. Unless you've lived in Thailand, you might not be familiar with inactive posts. Think of an inactive post as a secular purgatory where cops, bureaucrats and other public servants are sent. It is a temporary limbo existence that serves as punishment for those who have been caught taking bribes, fiddling with the books, planting evidence, abusing their authority or otherwise breaking the law.

The official in the inactive post continues to draw his salary and stays at home or catches up on his golf game, waiting until the scandal blows over. At that point— weeks or months after the incident—the official is quietly eased back into service. People forget about it. There is no memory. No follow-up in the press. It is as if it never happened. The inactive post is what passes for punishment and justice in cases such as this one.

In other legal systems, a cop who has conspired to subvert justice would be deemed to have committed a serious crime. His actions would be seen as undermining the rule of law, and he would be arrested and charged with a crime and, if found guilty, sent to prison. The use of the inactive post is a telltale sign that the rule of law is not a justice system that applies equally to all citizens. In this Orwellian world of fixers, the money card trumps the justice aspiration. What happened in the Ferrari hit–and–run case is not unique. If you live abroad, you know about this case because the weight of Red Bull fortune puts the family on the radar screen of the richest people on the planet. People take great interest in the lives of the rich and famous especially when they run afoul of the law. They want to know how that person will be treated, knowing the outcome will speak volumes about the strength of the legal system against the weight of money and influence.

At the time of this writing, to settle the public outrage, the Red Bull heir may face a manslaughter charge and a drunk driving charge. And a senior police official is at risk of being sacked.

The Bangkok city police general has assumed control over the investigation, saying that he would see the driver in the dock or he would resign. In reality criminal cases like this one often drag on for a long time. It is not uncommon for years to pass before there is a verdict. Most Thais are skeptical. Following this case, Reuters published a piece on impunity for the rich and famous.

"Jail is only for the poor," said one of a stream of comments posted on the popular Thai website, Pantip.com. "The rich never get punished. Find a scapegoat."

Another comment on the news site Manager.co.th read: "He'll probably just get a suspended sentence. What's the cost of a life?"

Suspended jail terms do seem to be the norm for politically powerful or well–connected Thais.

There is a chance the family driver might go to jail for his willingness to take the fall for the family. The senior cop who had conspired to help the family might also suffer more than the usual punishment of a couple of months in an inactive post. They are the little people in this drama. What will happen to the driver? The Reuters report gives a hint of what most Thais believe to be the outcome.

The rule of law protects the ordinary man or woman, but inside a system of titans who are viewed as being blessed by their good karma—blood money exchanges hands. Such big people are to be respected and deferred to and never challenged. When you live in a position above the law, you and your family can commit crimes knowing that at the end of the day you can't be touched personally so long as you open your wallet. The amounts paid in such cases by Western standards are very small. And that's the way things are. In a few weeks, other news will overtake this story. It will be buried. Like the dead police officer, the Red Bull Ferrari story will rest in a forgotten grave that only a few people will visit.

The Cell and the Cell Phone:
Thailand's 3G Prisons

The idea of prison is that a convicted criminal is removed from society and locked in a facility where his freedom of movement and freedom of association are limited. A prisoner occupies a cell. Unless he's in solitary, the prisoner also has access to other facilities such as a dinning hall, a library, an exercise room and a TV room. Punishment means removal from society. Loss of freedom. Loss of liberty. And loss of opportunities to conduct a business or trade.

Then came the cell phone. Given recent events in a Thai prison, it might be argued that "cell" phone is a good description of the mobile phones with cheap SIM cards that can put a drug dealer in contact with his organization. Add an iPad, an iPhone and a hard drive for backups, and being in prison doesn't really mean the same thing as in the old analog world where a man had to be physically present to oil the machinery on the illegal treadmill that sent drugs in one direction and received money from the other.

If you are going to run a home office out of your prison cell, the first thing you need to do is find a partner or two in authority. These are prison staff, officials and guards whose job is to make certain the prisoner is kept out of circulation for the term of his sentence. When most people think of prisons, if they think of them at all, the image is of a tattooed murderer, rapist, robber or pedophile. The violent, twisted, dangerous dregs of society belong behind bars. It satisfies the human need to avenge the harm to victims and also protects the members of society from suffering a similar fate at the hands of such predators.

Most prisons are filled with people from the illegal drug trade. They are more like businessmen than the general population. Thugs, gangsters, ruthless and law-breaking businessmen, to be sure. Given the overall ethical quality of workers in the finance and banking industry, these prisoners share more with the members of the board of directors of Goldman Sachs than with the child killer waiting for his day of reckoning on death row.

These are prisoners with organizational skills, employees and expertise in paying off the right people. Well, just *some* expertise in paying off the right people, or they wouldn't be in prison. They can develop their payoff skills with some years in prison. They have an entire prison staff to practice on. The guards and staff are paid peanuts. The drug lords inside are making large profits and can offer incentives that would take an ordinary life of guarding prisoners and getting by in near poverty on a quantum leap into a better life of fancy houses, cars and holidays.

You take something that millions of people want and make it illegal, creating a small class of people willing to break that law to reap the profits, and then you have a perfect storm that produces a new wave of convicts who in turn, rather than being punished in prison, move their operations inside as joint ventures with the officials running the place. Think of it as renting office space with bars on the windows and your own private security operation to protect you.

Cell phones for cells. That could have been the lead in a recent *Bangkok Post* report on a statement by the police chief at Nakhon Si Thammarat prison that prisoners in his jail were working drug deals with prisoners at another prison, Bang Khwang Central. How did the police chief figure this out? He conducted a raid last Sunday. The raid yielded "284 mobile phones, 1,700 methamphetamine pills, or *ya ba,* and 50g of crystal meth, or *ya ice*, in prison cells." In a second raid on Monday, officials seized more than 10 phones and more than 100 inmates tested positive for drugs.

The betting money is that officials inside the prison tipped their paymasters in advance of the raid, meaning that what was seized was only what couldn't be hidden or taken out of the prison in advance of the raid. One general went on record to admit his frustration that some prisoners had advance warning of the raid. It's hard to be surprised by their loyalty.

The prison officials take a hard look at their monthly government paycheck. Then they have a long look at the revenue steam they could be getting from convicted drug dealers inside the prison. The choice is drawing water from a leaky old tap or dipping over the edge of Niagara Falls. If water were money, where would you fill your bucket? All those extra zeros are bound to tip the scale of loyalty. Follow the money, as they say, and you can pretty much guess where a man's loyalty lies.

It seems the men inside the joint had been running a large drug network, with the digital trail running through the back jungle lanes in Laos and Myanmar. Meanwhile, the policy of dealing with illegal drugs hasn't changed. The current government has sent the cops to arrest and if need be shoot drug "dealers" (along with occasional innocent bystanders as collateral damage) as a public show of how they are cracking down on the illegal drug racket.

But the recent prison raid demonstrates that the authorities may have been looking in the wrong place. This puts the spotlight on an uncomfortable thought: that the people who are driving their pickups with a stash of drugs hidden inside are as much the problem as the convicted drug dealers who continue to run the business from behind bars.

The Justice Ministry has announced a crackdown on the drug trade in prisons. If you think that's going to work, please raise your hand. As I thought, I see no hands raised. Doubling the pay of prison staff and officials isn't going to help. The illegal money is far too much. Jam the cell phones; someone will sell an anti-jammer device. Conduct more frequent raids; they will be scheduled to make certain the main business isn't inconvenienced too much. Lock up inmates in bare cells with the lights on 24 hours a day; human rights organizations will descend along with camera crews and you will face charges of human rights violations.

Here's an idea. Why not reconsider the notion of criminalizing drugs? We assess how we characterize victimless crimes and addicts, and develop policies that reflect a difference between treatment and incarceration. That might just put the current crop of drug dealers in prison out of business and return prison staff and officials to their duties where they'd relearn the art of living on a civil servant salary.

Otherwise, the government can pretend, as governments do in most places, that they are cracking down on illegal drugs and protecting society. When in reality the official policy effectively has moved the headquarters of the drug business off the streets and into a secure facility where the cops can't ambush them and shoot them dead and claim self-defense.

The new globalized set of high tech savvy drug dealers who now live in prisons would be the first to resist decriminalization. If they had a lobbyist in this capital or another and made large campaign contributions, they would be the first to support the current system of extra-judicial killings (a good way to teach the non-jailed drug dealers to stay out of their territory), occasional raids and crackdowns. It is a great cover for their operations. It allows politicians to stay popular by methods they insist are winning the war on drugs.

When we know that the war has already been won. Just visit a prison and you'll find a band of the winners of the current policies. This elite class of prisoners are building themselves nice little nest eggs for the day they walk out of the prison gate. No doubt, once out, they will miss the freedom they had on the inside. The outside world is far more dangerous and expensive.

Reenactment of Crimes: Reality Check

Theatre since the time of the Greeks has produced plays as a mirror to hold up to society to see the reality of their existence. We are accustomed to the division of drama into the two different aspects of our lives—comedy and tragedy. We respond with laughter or tears as the emotional chords are played on our heartstrings with the virtuosity of the great dramatist. Not all cultures draw their dramatic heritage from the Greeks or Romans, nor are all dramas the product of professional stage producers, scriptwriters and directors.

In Thailand the police have an exclusive on the right to stage the drama of a criminal reenactment. A number of times a year it is show time in the Land of Smiles.

The police reenactment of crimes has been refined over many years in Thailand until it has reached the level of an anticipated theatrical event. The reconstructions of actual crimes might be thought to be closer to carnival or street theatre than to tightly scripted plays in the vein of Shakespeare. The police, having caught the criminal, arrange for him or her (most of the time it's him) to appear in front of the media and show how the suspect committed the crime. The police are cast in the role of heroes, the villain (sometimes there are more than one) is the real-life suspect, and everyone plays their role before news reporters and TV cameras.

This is a different concept from a TV show like *Crime Stoppers*, where to catch a criminal, the police reenact the crime to engage the public with a request for information to assist in identifying and arresting the suspect.

In Thailand the police arrest the suspected criminal who has "confessed" to the crime. What follows the confession is a media presentation where the suspect, actors, and the police stage a reconstruction of the crime.

Reenactments can carry a light note, a hint of comedy with a suspect who has the media spotlight. That certainly proved to be the case with Carlo Konstantin Kohl, a German national who escaped from the airport where he'd been held in the transit lounge on his journey from Australia to Germany.

Sometimes the "theatre" moves from the realm of controlled drama, produced and directed by the police, to live drama, which shows just how badly things can go wrong with a staged reenactment of a crime.

In a recent criminal case, a Vietnamese national, a suspect in an abduction case, was on his way to a crime scene reenactment when he escaped out of the back of a police van.

When a 17-year drug addict reenacted the vicious stabbing of a maid in Phuket—she was stabbed 80 times and her throat slit—relatives and neighbors tried to beat up the suspect, and the police had to intervene to protect him. As he was a minor, his face was covered by a balaclava.

In the case of the sexual assault and robbery of two Russian women, the police had Thai actresses play the role of the Russians in the reconstruction of the crime. Obviously a "reconstructed" crime doesn't actually reproduce all the crime's elements. It is more like a PowerPoint presentation of how to fly an airplane than actually getting in the cockpit and taking off.

The Nation recently reported the police rationale for reenactments of crime:

A Metropolitan Police specialist said a reenactment is important for an investigation because each criminal or each gang behaves differently in committing a crime. Details on how criminals commit each crime help the police understand the pattern of a crime. This can help them track down other criminals showing the same behaviour pattern and help reduce the loss of life and property.

The use of reenactments as police-school training for crime investigators strikes me as an interesting, though implausible, heuristic tool. If the police explanation is correct, perhaps the reenactments ought to take place in an actual theatre or classroom. I think the jury is out on exactly how such reenactments expand the range of knowledge about criminal behavior. Watching Superman in *Man of Steel* might impart some knowledge about criminal conduct as well.

Crime reenactments, in my view, touch on a much older idea about communities gathering to witness a wrongdoer repent, confess his crime and show his contrition by assisting the authorities in demonstrating what he did. Reenactments are a ritual, like the rituals surrounding birth, marriage and death. The ritual of crime reenactment—with the police acting as representatives of the justice gods—allow the victim's family, friends and neighbors to witness the suspect confess his sin.

Another point, which also isn't explained, is why the press is invited to attend these performances, along with large numbers of police officers and onlookers who are allowed to watch the whole proceeding up close. Could it be that the reenactments are also an effective way of communicating with the public that the police not only have solved the crime but are busy protecting them, and by locking this man up they are keeping them safe? As we've learnt with recent events in the intelligence community in America, the desire to feel safe is a license to do whatever is necessary to accomplish that goal. Reenactments are hatched from a primordial fear of the dangers posed by other people.

Western lawyers have argued that the Thai police reenactments would be illegal in most countries. Recently a member of the National Human Rights Commission, Paiboon Warahapaitoon, requested that the police take into account the human rights implications arising from staging crime reenactments. Even under Thai law, the accused can't be convicted solely based on a confession. A reenactment is no more than a dramatization of a confession that cannot be used to convict without support from independent evidence.

Most of the supposed criminals featured in these reenactments are young Thais with little education and from poor families. The rich and well-off are not actors in these dramas. They have their lawyers and their day in court, but are usually to be found out on bail, denying the charges against them.

Last week a Thai diplomat stationed in Cairo was involved in an altercation in a luxury hotel. The facts are yet to be finally established, but the preliminary reports have the young Thai woman diplomat kicking, scratching and biting an Egyptian lawyer in front of her husband and other witnesses after a round of insults at Egypt and Egyptian people. The diplomat has claimed self-defense but offered no details of what caused her to feel threatened. The Thai Ministry of Foreign Affairs has recalled her to Bangkok and said it will investigate the matter. Whatever is found, one thing that you can be assured won't happen is a reenactment of the incident.

If you want to see how the rich carry on, watch primetime Thai TV *lakorn* (soap operas) on the free TV channels. They are the next best things to crime reenactments of the assaults and other crimes that the privileged commit. *Lakorn* are wildly popular amongst a large segment of the population. This fact shows that there is a popular appetite for reenactments of crimes, nasty and anti-social behavior which don't quite rise to crimes but nonetheless inflict a fair measure of emotional damage to the victims.

For this reason I think it is unlikely that the popularity of the Thai *lakorn* will wane any time soon. And the same can be predicted for criminal reenactments starring members of the underclasses. All societies need a way of staging drama. Each culture evolves a set of expectations, roles, producers, directors and media stars. The Thais give the starring roles to the poor in reality news entertainment in crime reenactments, and the rich get theirs in soapy primetime TV dramas. Thai audiences are as entertained as any member of the old *Globe Theatre* in London. The show must go on. And when the price of admission is free, and the villain at center stage performs his role, for that moment, he achieves a moment of fame. And the police reinforce their image as heroes, defenders, protectors against the "others" who are out there waiting to kill, maim, rob, rape or assault.

Shakespeare in *Richard II* wrote: "As in a theatre, the eyes of men, after a well-graced actor leaves the stage, are idly bent on him that enters next." And who enters next may well be someone caught on a video camera. Digital video recorders in cell phones have the potential, over time, to replace the police reenactment. The purpose of the reenactment is for the suspect to show how he committed the crime. Videos such as those found on YouTube eliminate the need for reenactments.

Omnishambles Thai Style

he *Oxford English Dictionary* has included a new word in their 2012 edition—"omnishambles," which is defined as "a situation that has been comprehensively mismanaged, characterized by a string of blunders and miscalculations." In Thailand it is a linguistic tradition to shorten long words. There is a good chance that "omnishambles" will enter the Thai vocabulary as something like "om." The shortened word in this case has the sound of a chant, the kind that takes you into a meditative state.

Last week provided a good example of "om" in overdrive as the Thai authorities sought to limit the damage of the alleged rape of a young Dutch tourist.

The cover-up or denial of unpleasant facts by local officials was immortalized in Thomas Mann's *Death in Venice*. In that case it was the mysterious outbreak of disease that officials feared would harm tourism if known. In an economy dependent on tourism, when there is a crime against a tourist or an outbreak of a communicable disease, an important question arises: how should the police, courts, prosecutors and other government officials respond?

Do the local officials cover up? That is the *Death in Venice* solution.

Do they blame the tourist? That was recently the Thai solution to an alleged rape committed by a Thai tour guide against a 19-year-old Dutch woman in July 2012. The facts at hand (remember facts reported in the local press are often only distantly related to what actually happened) indicate the following. The young woman had been on holiday with her boyfriend on the Island of Krabi. On the evening of her birthday, she went to dinner with her boyfriend and a tour guide. The boyfriend then departed, leaving his girlfriend in the company of the tour guide. On the way back to the hotel, the tour guide allegedly raped the young Dutch woman. I use the word "allegedly" because the tour guide hasn't been tried and convicted of the crime, and until that happens, no matter how damning the evidence (and in this case from the press reports, it seems the evidence is strong), we must remember that he's not guilty of the crime.

That said, the evidence—doctor's medical report, victim's statement, suspect's confession, photograph of the victim's bruised face—suggests a strong case against the suspect, who ran away after the incident. He either went into hiding or managed otherwise to avoid the police for a couple of months. The police finally caught him (or he voluntarily turned himself in, according to some news reports). When a court released the suspect on bail, the victim's father made and released a video on YouTube, which has gone viral with over 400,000 views. His anguish and despair over what happened to his daughter and the release of the suspect on bail pulls at the heart.

From politicians to the police the response has been devoid of anything approaching compassion for the victim or expressions of sorrow and regret over what happened. Krabi police uploaded two YouTube videos, but the second video was removed. According to the *Bangkok Post*, the police video that was removed, titled "The Truth from Krabi," had around 50,000 views, 24 likes and 355 dislikes. It wasn't a hit and became another example of the "om" factor.

But the YouTube video by the victim's father remains online with an approval rating that is the opposite of the Krabi police videos. Meanwhile, the media heard a number of officials resort to the kind of rationalizations, justifications and frankly ugly statements, such as that because the rape victim had gone to dinner with the suspected rapist, she got what she deserved. "Omnishambles" is the correct description of the various statements and counter-videos made by the police. If you read the comments following the "Evil Man From Krabi" YouTube video, an overwhelming number of Thais seem to have come out in support of the victim and are shocked and disgusted by the official reaction to the rape suspect's being released on bail.

When the police finally caught up with the suspect, he confessed to the charges, then retracted the confession and was bailed. The case against granting bail was a good one. The suspect already had shown through his previous conduct that he might flee to avoid being prosecuted for his crime. Also, the suspect is a tour guide alleged to have committed an act of violence against someone who'd hired him. He's free to return to his work for tourists who likely would not know he's facing rape charges. His being out as usual puts other tourists at risk. Would you allow your teenage daughter to use this tour guide knowing he's a rape suspect? This is strange way to encourage tourism.

In sum: the suspect confessed to the crime, which had been well documented by the doctor who examined the victim. The suspect did a runner. He physically beat up the victim. He raped her and left her on the road. The attending doctor said it looked like she'd been in a motorcycle accident. Despite these facts, the suspect, who confessed to aggravated rape, was released on bail. He's back on the streets and beaches of Krabi and presumably free to continue his line of work.

We learn a lot about a culture by examining the degree of transparency and openness in the process in which it seeks to gather evidence, evaluate the evidence and base their decisions on the evidence. We learn a great deal about notions of justice and the equality of treatment without consideration of ethnicity, nationality or social status. The Krabi rape case is a classic text, like *Death in Venice*, which shows the operation of law enforcement and the administration of justice up close and personal.

Consider the first Krabi police video posted in response to the "Evil Man from Krabi," also posted on YouTube. Unless you are fluent in Thai, you won't follow what the policeman on this video is saying about the incident. That may be just as well. The explanation is rambling, defensive and not terribly coherent. This isn't a parody; it is an inside glimpse of the subculture and attitudes of law enforcement officials. There are no subtitles for the video. It doesn't seem to be have been produced for an international audience.

You may note the inflection in the voice when he uses the word "*farang*" and then substitute "Jew," "Latino," "gay" or "black." You don't need to understand the language to understand the underlying attitude. The tourist is the "*farang*," the *other*, not one of us.

The "official" response to the criminal case by those in authority (as opposed to thousands of Thai citizens) exposes a number of important attitudes. First, sensitivity to the suffering of someone who is the victim of a violent crime is not acknowledged. There is no sense of the huge physical and psychological damage suffered by the victim. Instead there's a jackboot mentality—we are the boss and we do no wrong. The authoritarian mindset is tailor-made for enhancing the omnishambles. The police don't come across as serving justice or helping the victims of violent crimes.

They are simply scary men who can do whatever they want, and whatever they say is the law.

Second, the only way to get the attention of people who run their own little nasty local empires of impunity is to expose them: put them in the spotlight, and let the world judge for themselves whether going on a holiday to a place with police officials with these attitudes and priorities is worth the risk. If something goes wrong and you're a tourist on holiday, then it is likely your fault. You will be left chanting "om."

Third, police reform has been the subject of many commissions and committees, but nothing has ever been done about it. It's always business as usual. Part of the reason that reform is so difficult to achieve is illustrated in this case. Reform is not about changing a procedure, training in the latest detection techniques or new uniforms. The aftermath of handling the rape case shows the deep-rooted culture of impunity, a top-down military command culture and a culture with a warrior mentality, and anyone who doubts, criticizes or complains is attacked.

"Evil Man from Krabi" is an attack against a legal system that is perceived to have committed an injustice. You can see and hear the full arsenal the authorities bring to media. They alternate from justifying their handling of the case to pointing the finger at others, to attacking the victim, to looking into blocking the YouTube video, to concentrating on how to limit the damage to their face and the tourist industry.

Resort locations like Krabi have developed a local economy based on tourism. Millions of dollars have been spent to create an international image of Thai fun, hospitality and service. But the PR machine explodes once the monkey wrench from the dark side is thrown into the works. The Thai authorities, based on statements and videos they've released, suggest that tourists are a commodity, something to be bought and sold, to be marketed to, managed, relieved of money. No one in power was reported as speaking of the violation suffered by this young woman, her loss of dignity or her right to respect as a human being.

The case also exposes the knee-jerk reaction of the police and other government officials that it is the foreign woman who is at fault because of the clothes that she wore or that she had dinner or a drink with the rapist. In other words, foreign women get what they deserve. This "evolved" feudalistic worldview is one where the police, in their mind, are always right. They close ranks. They have the power. You have none. They issue rambling statements of justification. They aren't used to someone challenging their version of events. When it is exposed that what they claim are the facts are distortions and lies, the fallback position is usually along the lines of a "misunderstanding."

What the officials and police fail to understand is with social media networks across the world, the old true and tested tactics that once worked to shut up the locals no longer work. They no longer control the information or the message. Millions of people can watch, read and listen and more importantly question, judge and criticize the officials and police. They seem unable to understand the new world of information which exposes cant, hypocrisy, lies, obfuscation and excuses for what they are. Omnishambles exposes them. They have no place to hide.

The danger exposed in Krabi isn't the suspected rapist who is on bail, but the officials who are in charge of the security of the thousands of tourists who flock to the beaches of Krabi and elsewhere in Thailand. The message can get out that their safety and welfare are not priorities, and that message has registered loud and clear in this case. When reform finally comes—as it will—the agency behind the reform will be the outward pressure from millions of Thais who take heart that the attitudes of those in power will ultimately change.

Presumption of Innocence Until Executed

The lag between penning an editorial and breaking news can seem an eternity even when the two appear in the same edition of the newspaper. A Thai death penalty case has created a perfect journalistic storm, with editors praising something while reporter updates undermine and destroy the basis of such praise.

On August 1, 2012, the *Bangkok Post*, in an editorial titled "Sending the Right Signals," supported the court decision to impose the death penalty on three police officers convicted of the murder of a 17-year-old twelve years earlier.

"They clearly thought they were so far above the law that they had the power of life and death," the editorial concluded.

On another page of the *Bangkok Post* we are informed that the three cops sentenced to death have been released on bail. Altogether six police officers were charged with crimes related to the killing. One defendant was acquitted. Aside from the three officers sentenced to death, one officer was sentenced to life in prison and another to seven years. They are all now out of jail.

A casual search of the history of the law of bail from 18th-century English and American law discloses no bail provision for someone convicted of murder and sentenced to death. The idea of someone condemned to death being set free on bail is not one that is common. Granting bail is mostly done prior to a trial. Once the accused has been convicted of the crime, the normal reasons for bail no longer apply, i.e., the ability to assist defense counsel in countering the Crown's case.

The presumption of innocence is lost once the court convicts the accused. While the convicted criminal may argue he has a continuing need to assist his legal counsel in the appellate process, the assistance is no longer that of a man presumed innocent.

A conviction by a court is the ultimate assignment of guilt and responsibility. Allowing bail for non-violent convicts might be justified, but the grounds quickly vanish when the convict has been found guilty of murder.

The handing down of the death sentence upon conviction makes the granting of bail a case few lawyers will have encountered. In a bail assessment hearing, the court must assess the likelihood that the party requesting bail will jump bail and flee from prosecution. The Crown argues (inevitably) that the applicant is a high-risk case and the application should be denied, while the applicant proposes that that his family, community and work history suggest that he will submit to the court and not seek to escape.

It comes down to the discretion of the court to decide: what are the chances the applicant for bail will skip town and not appear at his hearing? That is a reasonable inquiry. When you ask a man who has been convicted to show up for his hanging, you know there will be a little voice inside him that will scream "Flee!" Where the law of probabilities needle starts to point to one-hundred percent, the question should be asked, not whether the man with the death sentence will flee, but when and where this will happen.

Thus, once a man has been convicted and sentenced to death, it is difficult to think of a stronger case for the prisoner to run away as fast as he can. He has nothing to lose. He's no worse off trying to escape once he's been released from prison than if he never tries. He's hanged in any event. As a matter of game theory, he'd be a fool not to make an attempt to escape, and he has nothing to lose trying to settle scores with those witnesses who were responsible for his conviction and death sentence.

The crime in question goes back to Thailand's War on Drugs in the early 2000s. Officially by the time the killing was called off, 2,500 extrajudicial killings had occurred throughout the country. The idea of the War on Drugs was to rescue children and communities from the evil of drugs. And the best way to rescue them was to suppress and terrorize people involved in the drug business. Police were given a free hand to deal with suspected drug offenders, making no real distinction between users, dealers or petty criminals. It is never a good idea to issue 007 license-to-kill permits to law enforcement officers. Unlike the carnage in a James Bond movie, the casualty rate has a way of skyrocketing as the police fall into the routine of manning the roles of the prosecutor, judge and executioner. There were bound to be abuses.

Reports have circulated from that time (though no independent investigation was conducted) mentioning a range of victims who were innocent (at least of drug crimes) as well as casual drug users; these people were murdered during the dark era of the War on Drugs. The police said the deaths were the result of drug gangs going to war with each other. Others proposed the involvement of the police. Calls for an outside investigation and accounting of the actions of law enforcement officials largely went unanswered. The inability to bring to justice government officers responsible for the killings has often been cited as evidence of the culture of immunity and impunity that applies to government officials.

On Monday of this week (July 31, 2012), a Thai criminal court took the bold step of convicting five police officers for their roles in the death of Kiattisak Thitboonskrong, a 17-year-old boy in upcountry Thailand who allegedly had stolen a motorbike. The killing of the boy, for which three of the policemen were convicted and sentenced to die, had no real connection with the War on Drugs and highlights the mission creep that often occurs once official lawlessness is sanctioned.

During the proceedings the murder victim's aunt and two other witnesses were put under a police witness protection program. With the conviction of the officers, that protection automatically lapses. In normal circumstances that would make sense. After the conviction the criminal is not on the street and not a threat to the witnesses. The aunt and witnesses now face the prospect of going about their business without protection against the convicted police officers whose convictions were aided by their testimony, and those death sentence convicts are now out on bail.

The court decision to grant bail to convicted criminals sends contradictory messages. On the one hand, the conviction suggests that the criminal court is ready to hold the police officer to account for murder. That is a significant shift to the rule of law and accountability, requiring institutional courage by the court. At the same time, assuming the press reports are accurate, by releasing the three police officers sentenced to death, the conviction has been undermined and the lives of witnesses placed in possible harm's way.

In most places in the world, when an accused has been convicted of an offense punishable by death or life imprisonment, he is not eligible for bail. In the days that come, there will be explanations, justifications and finally the usual official stonewalling over the bail decision.

The bottom line is "Sending the Right Signal" might prove to have been a premature caption for the editorial applauding the conviction of the cops implicated in the boy's murder. At best the five convictions and grant of bail applications fall should under the heading of "Sending a Confused Signal," to summarize to the way the state deal with its officials who commit murder or other serious crimes. At this juncture it is impossible to know what conditions were attached to the bail, the reporting obligations, the restrictions on contacting witnesses, the handing over of passports, the attachment of electronic monitoring bracelets, etc.

What is clear is the signal that for cops convicted of capital murder and sentenced to die for their crimes, their right to liberty exceeds the right of movement and safety of the witnesses who testified against them. On the scale of justice, that is an odd weighing of the interests of the parties, not to mention the interest of the public. How the risks will play out in the days to come is difficult to assess. But the people who testified against the cops in the murder case and the cops who were convicted and sentenced to death share a common bond—they want to stay alive.

When Godot Is an Assassin and You Don't Have to Wait: Thai Hit Men Hierarchy

The 2013 Thai Most Wanted Hit Men list has 100 names. The 2011 list had only 75. That's a 33 percent productivity and employment increase in two years. If this were the economy, people would be in the streets celebrating. This list is not Thai companies on the stock exchange but a list of Thai hired killers who are in a bullish occupation.

Like the "long-list" of Booker Prize nominees, the 2013 Most Wanted list is a long one. We'll get to the short-list and the machinery to choose the winner a bit later. No literary award I am aware of has ever announced a long list with a name of 100 authors. In the real world, down those mean streets walk not writers taking notes for a great crime novel but hired killers whom the police would like to catch. And there are at least 100 of them, which works out about five or six hitmen for each author on a typical crime fiction award long-list.

Authors must choose their hit men carefully. It seems there are difficulties in apprehending the Most Wanted Hit Men—they are even more careful than most authors. After all they have a lot more at stake, and more to lose.

Thailand law enforcement challenges aren't unique (though what country exists where the citizens in huge numbers don't believe this?). The police in every country face the same set of problems—suppressing crime and capturing criminals who refuse to be suppressed. Techniques of crime suppression and catching the bad guys are glimpses into the culture of the legal justice system and the social system.

In the past the Thai police have used the Most Wanted list to produce what translates as *"criminal suspect calendars,"* featuring photos of the bad guys (or bad women). Maybe the photographs were old, blurry and badly lit, with horrible angles—the usual things people say about my photos. In any event these calendars (we're not told where they were displayed) failed to bring phone calls from the public with information that they just saw what looked like #73 eating *som tum* at a food stall on Sukhumvit Road. The police phone didn't ring. Or if it did, the caller wasn't reporting the location of a wanted hit man.

Faced with the bold facts—can't suppress them, can't catch them—the police decided on a new campaign to hunt down the gunmen for hire in Thailand. Social hierarchy is the lifeblood of Thai society—and the building blocks are the Lego-like tropes of family names, titles, rank, private schools and private clubs. A Thai can step back in any social scene and immediately experience another person's place on the pyramid grid as though equipped with a sonar system to pick up frequencies that foreigners simply don't perceive.

Why not rank hitmen? That seems like a logical extension to the normal way people perceive themselves and others— they are either above or below you. This genius for ad hoc hierarchy-making as a blueprint for a hit men pyramid is far more impressive than anything you'll ever find in Egypt. If you are raised and educated in seeing social relations as pyramids, why not adapt that idea to how you design your Most Wanted list?

Here's how the new Most Wanted Hit Men list will work—according to the Thai police.

Level 1

Level 1 is for the top gun. The Professional. A Level 1 hit man has proved himself capable and reliable, with many successful assignments on his résumé. The assassins on this list are not limited to those wanted under an arrest warrant. Apparently just because you've committed an assassination doesn't automatically mean you will have an arrest warrant issued. The example given by the authorities is the hit man who has just been released from prison having served time for his last job. Apparently the concept of double jeopardy gives way to preventive action. Once you've done your time for a hit, you are a Level 1 guy who is wanted by the authorities.

The Hired Gunman Pro who is always wanted by the police, arrest warrant or not, is at the top of the hierarchy. It is important to emphasize this point so no one is confused or walks away from a citizen's arrest of such a hit man who might argue there is no outstanding warrant. Get the guy. Bring him in. If you're working at Level 1, the police want you even if there's no paperwork other than the list. The privilege of the top rank is to be always wanted.

Level 2

There's always some new guy breaking into the game. Same as in sports. One day you're kicking in goals, and the next day you're on the bench because some new kid can kick the ball better and farther than you. These are the semi-pros looking for the chance to play in the PGA-level hit men's league. They are still building the résumés showing their wins. The police warrant these are the most dangerous players—young, hungry, trigger-happy and as résumé obsessed as a student trying to get accepted for a Harvard MBA program. The police statement was silent as to the necessity of any outstanding arrest warrant before arresting such a person. It might be that the arrest warrant exclusion is for only Level 1—give them a bit of hierarchy pride. As it is unclear, no doubt it could lead to arguments, and—just to remind you—these people are heavily armed. That is never a good thing in Thailand.

Level 3

Level 1 and Level 2 are your pro or semi-pro freelance, free agent players. They take assignments from anyone with the cash and the desire to see someone dead. The Level 3 hit men are a different breed. They fit the mode of the in-house lawyers. They work for an influential figure or the mafia. Yes, in Thailand there is apparently quite a distinction between the two categories worth an essay on its own. The third-level players raise an interesting policing issue. Why not check with the godfather:

"Seen #43 recently?"

"No, he's been on the sick list," says the godfather, or, "No, he's been transferred to sales and is attending a seminar in KL."

"Well, if you see him, give us a call."

"You'll be the first to know."

Level 3 is the place where no one ever seems to find any relevant evidence of a crime. It all disappears down that Alice in the Wonderland rabbit hole without leaving a tiny, bitty trace. The gunman signs on for the usual company benefits and enters the workplace where whatever evidence he leaves behind will magically disappear, and he draws a regular salary. The police admit Level 3 is the toughest nut to crack.

Level 4

We are at the bottom of the pyramid on a dark night. In a sandstorm. In the desert, looking for whom? These guys are not yet qualified to be hit men. No, they've not earned their stripes. The most you can say for them is they've murdered people in a conflict. That's not what professional killers do, who have no emotional connection with the victim or conflict. The police want to put a lid on the possibility that these hot-headed, hot-blooded killers, who get into lethal fights and arguments, don't suddenly become cool under fire, chilled water running through their veins and climb up to either Level 2 or 3. The greater fear is a lateral entry into a Level 3 position with a godfather.

Supposedly 30 percent of the Level 4 killers have contacts with the Level 3 players and bosses. This assumes that bosses at Level 3, given a choice, would take a Level 2 or Level 4 guy. In a pinch a Level 4 guy might be given a chance to see if he can kill someone he doesn't hate without first punching him out. As a general rule, it's horses for courses in the playbook for most godfathers.

The Thai police, despite the limitations of the list, have an ace up their sleeve. Thais are highly sociable. They are hard to separate from their parents, friends and relatives. The police have figured there is no level of assassin that can sustain isolation. The loneliness of being on the run is too much for the Thai hit man, who will sooner or later head to his parents' house, his favorite *mia noi's* room or the hangout where he drinks and sings karaoke with his friends. The idea is the police will look for clues among the hit man's relatives and close associates.

Cost

No discussion of hit men can be separated from the price for their services. A no-frills, basic-level hit of an ordinary person starts at 50,000 baht (or roughly $1800 US). Most of the hits at the low end of the market are the result of love affairs that implode like ancient stars. Only in this case, the black hole is between the eyes. If the target is a "somebody" in one of the other social hierarchies, the price can shoot up.

How have the Thai police been doing in catching the professional killers included on the 2013 Most Wanted list? Six months into 2013, they've arrested four, and two have died. There is no report on what level these six hitmen came from. The main takeaway is that your risk of being arrested for being an assassin for hire is only slightly higher than dying of old age. The next time someone mentions the word "noir" in terms of crime novels, you can ask them, "And what is your view on how the Most Wanted Hit Men list for 2013 fits into the definition of 'noir'?" To answer that question would require the writing of a multi-volume series of books, and even then I'd be just sweeping away the sand on the path leading to the base of the pyramid, only to watch it blow back the next day.

Part III

Crimes without Borders

Gun Homicides and the Honor Culture

In Asia the idea of face is not unlike the concept in the West of dignity or respect or honor. Add guns to the torque of argument, honor and liquor, and the probability of shots fired rises dramatically. Steven Pinker concludes in *The Better Angels of Our Nature* (page 99) that, "The essence of a culture of honor is that it does not sanction predatory or instrumental violence, but only retaliation after an insult or other mistreatment." The issue of fitting the culture of guns with the culture of honor raises a number of issues, such as how available guns should be, the kind of weapons that should be allowed in civilian hands and the role of the government in regulating guns in places where an insult to honor is avenged with violence.

In Thailand on December 27, 2011, a policeman in the southern province of Phatthalung pulled his gun and killed six other police officers. The gunman and his fellow officers had been engaged in a drinking session in the border patrol police camp canteen. Someone must have said something that didn't go down well. The gunman then walked 200 meters outside the canteen and turned his assault rifle on himself. The investigators' theory is that a "personal conflict" led to the shootings. That is a Thai code phrase for an insult to honor.

Police are trained (in theory) in the psychology of diffusing personal conflicts and convincing someone with a gun to drop it. Using lethal force is restricted in Thailand, as in most places.

The point is that Thai cops are products of their culture, and a face culture is an honor culture. Is this true for other cops around the world? Police reactions to guns, threats, violence, insults and honor differ according to tradition, history and attitude. When the cork flies out of the bottle in an honor culture, it is best the man this happens to does not have a weapon. When cops are involved in an insult to honor, supposedly their training kicks in and they exercise more self-control. That training has its limits. Cops inside an honor culture have the same human emotions that flare up during drinking sessions. An insult, a slight, a roll of the eyes may be all that is needed to trigger the lethal response. Without the presence of guns, it is highly doubtful anyone in that canteen would have died.

No one suggests after such a massacre that the police should be disarmed. Notably, though, in England most of the police are not armed, and the murder rate is significantly lower than in places like Thailand where they are. Yet a fairly significant number of the general population in England do carry guns.

More difficult to deal with is the private citizen in an honor culture who is allowed by law to carry a handgun. The Americans are undergoing a debate about expanding the right to carry concealed weapons and to allow someone with a gun permit to carry that weapon anywhere in the United States. More than 3.5 million Americans in 40 US states have permits to carry concealed firearms. Keep in mind there are approximately 100 million guns owned by Americans. Remember that on your next visit to the States only a small percentage of them have anywhere near the experience of my fellow blogger Jim Thompson with handling guns. The overwhelming number of gun owners are like pilots who've logged a couple of hours in a small plane seated next to an experienced instructor and think that experience makes them ace fighter pilots.

Some states are more lax than others regarding gun permit regulations and rules for revoking a gun permit if the owner has committed a crime. The *New York Times* has reported on a cyclist in Asheville, North Carolina, who had an argument with a motorist. Words were exchanged, and Diez, the gun holder, pulled his licensed handgun and shot at the cyclist. The bullet slammed through the cyclist's helmet. Diez later pleaded guilty to a felony count of assault with a deadly weapon with intent to kill. Pinker also notes that the Southern states have had a long tradition of an honor culture and self-help justice.

The proponents who argue for expanding the right for civilians to arm themselves with concealed weapons say it will allow ordinary law-abiding citizens to protect themselves. The idea is that the bad guys are armed and the innocent are not; that, when the bad guys know that the innocent person might have a concealed weapon, they'll think twice about committing a crime against that person. Also, they point out, an armed citizenry is the first line of defense against tyranny in government.

That is the deterrence argument, which propels many to support legislation authorizing widespread gun ownership. There are a couple of problems with this position.

First, America is one of the few places where there is no historical consensus that the monopoly of violent force should be exclusively reserved to officers of the state. Unlike Europe, the United States never succeeded in disarming its citizens before the citizens took over the government. Most of other countries in the West (they are democracies, too) do not sanction widespread gun ownership among the civilian population. They have a different traditions of gun ownership. And, in European countries fewer people die of gunshot wounds than in America.

Second, the position conflates democracy with gun ownership, positing that armed citizens are the best defense against a state turning rogue against its citizens. Americans have a culture of distrust of government that is closer to the attitudes found in Third World countries run by dictators. The reality is that guns are artifacts from the analog past. Modern governments have multiple digital tools to oppress and repress their citizens, and these weapons of intimidation are more widespread and potent than guns. CCTV cameras; Predator drones (soon to appear in your neighborhood); data mining of your email, blogs, Facebook, Twitter and other social media; and acquisition of your health, financial and education records. A population armed with handguns is no match for the arsenal that the world of *1984* brings.

Third, the idea of "protection" against the bad guys is always one that has everyone nodding their heads in agreement. However, the statistics show that the self-defense theory is not a solid argument, especially in an honor culture. The reality is that human beings are emotional creatures who are quick to anger. Alcohol and other drugs make them unstable. Diez, the fireman from North Carolina who almost killed the cyclist, is not uncommon. The cyclist wasn't a bad guy. He didn't threaten Diez. He had an argument. Diez felt insulted, his ego was bruised, and he tried to kill a man over "honor."

I'd be willing to bet that if you graphed the percentage of people who have used a handgun to protect themselves against a criminal (the self-defense claim), it would be a much smaller percentage than the percentage of people who used a gun because they felt a slight to their honor. By increasing gun ownership, I would anticipate a rise in the number of homicides where the underlying motive was to avenge a loss of face, a slur, a personal argument or an insult. People kill each other over honor. Give them licenses to carry handguns and Diez-type cases will increase. Diez lacked self-control in this situation. This is not abnormal. Expand gun ownership and that will be a good test of exactly how normal the Diez case will prove to be.

Thailand has more than double the United States' annual rate of death by firearms. Anyone who has looked at the debate on gun ownership understands that statistics are often unreliable and often used inappropriately, through such errors as the failure to compare like with like conditions, traditions and histories and the omission of crucial variables that make for complexity. Scholars have cautioned against concluding that widespread gun ownership causes higher murder rates. Russia, for example, has stringent gun control laws, yet between 1998 and 2004 its gun-related murder rate was four times that of the United States. Could an entrenched honor culture in Russia offer insight into the higher murder rate by firearms? The same scholars insist there is no correlation between the strength of gun laws, availability of guns and the homicide rate. Let's admit that evidence of such correlation isn't available. What is left unaddressed is the role of the honor culture.

Another killing in Thailand this week bears an emotionally twisted thread that links it to the Diez type of case. An arrest warrant was issued for a member of parliament, Khanchit Thapsuwan, who allegedly followed a rival politician into the toilet of a petrol station and shot him in the head eight times. He left ten .40 caliber casings scattered on the floor of the restroom where the shooting took place. There also were witnesses. Given this is Thailand, the police issued a statement that would be unusual in some countries: "If we knew his hideout, we would arrest him without heeding his social status."

In Thailand the gunman's social status is a significant factor that in some cases trumps the evidence of murder. But in Khanchit's case, with the social status of shooter and victim being approximately equal, the gunman is in deep trouble. What is the theory of why Khanchit shot the victim? They were political rivals and according to the *Bangkok Post*, "Whenever the two met, they were often heard making sarcastic remarks against each other."

Two days after the killing, MP Khanchit showed up for a session in the Thai parliament. A decision has yet to be made on the question of whether parliamentary immunity will be waived.

The final consideration in the argument to expand gun ownership is the costs. Gunshot victims place a significant burden on the health-care resources of a country. One scholar, Phillip J. Cook, estimated that gun violence costs Americans alone $100 billion annually. That would fund a lot of schools, clinics, bridges, roads and student loan programs. With that kind of money, a decent health care system could be universally available to all citizens.

Honor. Face. Dignity. Governments would do well to closely study the correlation of these cultural factors and how they factor into gun-related homicides before they go about authorizing the carrying of guns in the larger civilian population. Dismantling the culture of honor might, in the long run, be the best way to reduce gun-related murder rates. But that approach wouldn't sell to voters. Arming voters does sell for those standing for election. Politics is a clash over "honor" and sometimes, as with the aforementioned recent murder in Thailand allegedly by an MP, the end result is the delivery of eight rounds to the head.

The Rates of Murder

You've decided to write that crime novel. The single book that, once released into the world, will liberate you from your day job, put you on *Charlie Rose* and the *New York Times* bestseller list, see you interviewed by the *Wall Street Journal* and the *Financial Times*, and bring you stacks of invitations to the best parties in New York, London and Paris. You've heard that international settings are in vogue for crime fiction. But you're not quite certain, looking at the world map, which country might be the best place for your noir caper. Besides, you can write off the expense of research in finding out.

Let me give you some unsolicited advice. Look for a place with danger—not too much, but enough to create tension and risk. Political instability is good—again so long as there aren't bombs going off in the streets, and an exotic culture with interesting taboos, customs, language, history, rituals and artifacts, though not so weird that they can't be understood without long, drawn-out descriptions.

A convention of the crime fiction genre is that the story begins with a murder. A killing is central to the novel. When researching your crime novel, you might have a look at murder statistics. The homicide statistics indicate the the prime crime fiction locations are the mini-states of the Caribbean and Central America. In these places there are lots and lots of murders as a percentage of 100,000 of population.

Homicide victims accumulate in these countries at an alarming rate. You can add Colombia and Venezuela to the high rate of homicide list, too. Frankly, you can write off Europe with the possible exception of Russia and Albania. The Europeans simply have stopped murdering each other at statistically significant rates. Germans seem to have stopped murdering each other in significant numbers a long time ago. Fantasy and romance novelists would do much better in Europe than crime fiction authors.

The ten countries with the highest murder are included in this chart:

Top Ten Countries with Highest Murder Rates

Country	Murder Rates (per 100,000)	Year
Honduras	82.1	2010
El Salvador	66.0	2010
Côte d'Ivoire	56.9	2008
Jamaica	52.1	2010
Venezuela (Bolivarian Republic of)	49.0	2009
Belize	41.7	2010
Guatemala	41.4	2010
Saint Kitts and Nevis	38.2	2010
Zambia	38	2008
Uganda	36.3	2008

(Source: www.mapsofworld.com/world-top-ten/ countries-with-highest-murder-rates.html)

If you want to write a noir crime fiction novel, then Honduras or El Salvador might be a place to go.

Places to avoid as a noir crime fiction writer are on this list:

Countries With Lowest Murder Rates in World

Country	Region	Murder Rate
Monaco	Europe	0
Palau	Oceania	0
Hong Kong	Asia	0.2
Singapore	Asia	0.3
Iceland	Europe	0.3
Japan	Asia	0.4
French Polynesia	Oceania	0.4
Brunei	Asia	0.5
Bahrain	Asia	0.6
Norway	Europe	0.6

(Source: www.mapsofworld.com/world-top-ten/ countries-with-lowest-murder-rates.html)

To judge from these homicide rates, there isn't enough raw material in these countries even for a short crime story— though fellow blogger Quentin Bates, who bases his crime fiction in Iceland, suggests that noir isn't always reflected in the numbers.

The numbers don't tell you everything. Swedish crime fiction is a huge success internationally, but the Swedish murder rate is among the lowest in the world. Yet we have a feeling reading Nordic crime fiction that murder is common in Sweden, that Sweden is a dangerous place. None of that is true. Sweden has a very low homicide rate. Those facts didn't stop Stieg Larsson from hitting the jackpot (though he had died of a heart attack before the big money came in).

The definitive chart on the international murder is done on a country-by-country basis annually by the United Nations Office on Drugs and Crime. Looking at the most recent figures from UNODC (2002 to 2011) on Bangkok, the murder rate has been in decline lately. If this trend continues, it seems that soon I may be out of the crime fiction business in Thailand.

In 2003 the Thai murder rate was 9.8 per 100,000, and in 2011 it had dropped to 4.8 per 100,000. Do Thais feel 50 percent safer from being murdered now, given this corresponding drop in actual homicides? I don't have hard evidence to answer this question, but there's plenty of antidotal evidence to suggest no decline in the fear of being a murder victim.

Why the disconnect between the declining murder rate and our sense of fear about murder? Our feelings are subjective, irrational and difficult to predict or control. And fear of death and injury is one of the most compelling emotions, not to be assuaged by a UNODC Excel file that presents cold, hard numbers.

I take the position that Thais are no less concerned, fearful and watchful about murder in 2013 than they were in 2003. There is little political opportunity and advantage in reducing this unreasonable feeling of fear. In political life, money and fear correlate. More resources can be demanded by and allocated to the police and other state officials charged with protecting an overly fearful public. If our perception of the risk of murder is updated, then state officials stand to lose budgets, training, new employees and better equipment. Actually, you can spend a lot of that money in ways that have little impact beyond public relations. Because the level of homicide is already declining, you can pocket some of that money and still be seen as doing a great job.

Bottom line: our emotional reaction to homicide hasn't been updated with the latest statistics, which show a substantial lowering of the probability of murder. The state has no incentive to focus on the lower risk of homicide. The press will always have enough murders (even at statistically low rates people are still murdered just as people still win a lottery) to keep the flame high enough to keep fear at the boil.

When it comes to murder, we react out of fear, and that closes the door to a more rational and deliberate assessment based on the actual risk as shown through the UNODC statistics on the rate of murder. Murders of foreigners make for dramatic news that reinforces the sense of fear. This happens in Thailand as in many other countries.

The media manufactures a false sense of risk with emotionally charged photographs, statements of witnesses, family and friends in mourning, angry letters to the authorities and so on. If the murder victim is someone you love, care about or know, then UNODC statistics aren't going to mean much to you. But if you are reading about people you don't know, there remains a high possibility of identifying with them, and you will be fearful. Emotions distort your ability to assess the actual risk.

When it comes down to writing that crime novel, it may not matter whether you live in a country with a high or low murder rate. The rate of homicide appears to have little connection to the perception of risk as it is assessed through fear. As long as your novel creates a personal setting between the killer and the victim and does a credible job in following the police or private investigator through the evidence, your reader won't likely write you an angry letter saying that statistically the murder you've written about is as rare as a rose in winter.

But as people love roses, if you can convince them to overlook the improbability of a rose growing in the wild in winter weather, they will follow you down the corpse-laden garden trail and believe this exceptional act could happen in the world. Indeed it could happen to them. Yet you can be assured there will in the fullness of time an Amazon reviewer who will give you a one-star review that goes along the lines that everyone knows that only white roses grow in winter and this author had the color wrong. He said the roses were red. And that, my friends, is more likely than the mountain of cash your book will earn to liberate you from your desk job.

Illegal Spirit Migrants

Spirit houses are a common sight in Thailand. They appear in front of factories, rice fields, houses, condominiums, restaurants, bars, schools, government offices and high-rises. Just about anywhere you venture, the likelihood is you'll find a spirit house. Like the tuk-tuk and *muay Thai*, it is part of Thai identity to believe there are spirits who reside on the land who require appeasement with offerings and the gesture of a wai.

A problem arises, however, when a spirit house is erected on land outside Thailand. In Burma, Violet Cho authored a piece for *The Voice* (Yangon) disclosing a conflict between the Italian-Thai Development Company, one of Thailand's leaders in the construction business, and local people in Burma.

The Burmese have their own set of spirits that they pay homage to; they are called "nats" which have been described as supernatural Burmese elves. There are 37 n*ats* in the Burmese belief system. Among them are Thon Ban Hla, Lady of Three Times Beauty; Maung Po Tu, Shan Tea Merchant; Mahagiri, Lord of the Great Mountain; and Yun Bayin, King of Chiengmai. It appears some of the Nats have jobs. Others are royalty, and I am not certain if the Thais are generally aware that one of the Burmese nats rules over Chiang Mai.

In my novel *Missing in Rangoon* I explore the supernatural world. Each time I've been to Burma, some new and different aspect of spirituality emerges for examination. Indeed it would be difficult to write a novel about Burma without touching upon this belief system as it is and remains central to the identity of the Burmese.

The clash between the Thais and the Burmese over Thai spirit houses is a collision between different supernatural belief systems that lie at the core of the two national identities. The world news offers up a constant, daily stream of the aftermath of such conflicts. Often it leads to violence, the full program—pogroms, burnings, looting, maiming and murdering.

According to Violet Cho's account, the problem arose over a villager in Nabule who claimed a holy Buddha footprint had a sacred claim on the mountain, and that erecting a Thai spirit house was an affront to this object as well as to various ancient pagodas on the mountain, named Mayingyi Paya.

The Nabule villagers claimed the Thai company had not consulted them before installing more than one spirit house on the mountain. There are spirit houses in front of the company office, and other spirit houses at various project sites. The article makes it sound a bit like a spirit house invasion and occupation. The locals noticed the appearance of these structures devoted to "foreign" spirits. And foreigners, in spiritual form or otherwise, aren't always that welcome, especially if it looks like they have moved into the neighborhood and plan to stay and drive out the local nats.

It is unclear whether the local villagers mounted protests, demonstrations, letters sent or other means—perhaps spiritual—of expressing discontent, before locals destroyed one of the spirit houses. As Nabule is scheduled for development in a project involving the Thai and Myanmar governments, it is difficult to know whether the motives might be more than bruised feelings over the local spirits being occupied and displaced by Thai spirits. In this part of the world, when something murky happens, the question usually asked is who might be the "third hand"—who is really behind the incitement, and what does that person(s) want. And usually it is money, says that little cynic that perches on the shoulder of people who've lived in Southeast Asia for too long.

Violet Cho quotes a senior leader at Ba Wah Village justifying the spirit house destruction by the locals. "We can accept it if the project does not destroy our environment but if it is threatening our people, culture and religion then we will surely have to be against it," said U Hla Shain.

This being Southeast Asia, it is no surprise that U Hla Win, the vice chairperson of NLD for Dawei district, would call for negotiations. U Hla Win pointed out that the conflict was spiritual. What he didn't point out is that the rest of the world since recorded history has been trying to figure out how people with different supernatural beliefs can live in peace and harmony in line of site of other believers who erect their own shrines and perform their own set of rituals that pay respect to alien supernatural beings.

On both sides of the border, both the Burmese and Thais suffer their fair share of cognitive dissonance between animist and Buddhist beliefs. The incongruity is never quite resolved as both sides claim they are Buddhist and animist. The Burmese won't negotiate away their rituals involving the nats anymore than the Thais will cease to erect spirit houses containing a wide range of deities from various spiritual and religious origins, from local and ancestral ghosts to assortments of Hindu gods.

As an example of the straddling of the spiritual balance beam, this analysis pretty much sums up why negotiations between locals who support their local team of nats and the visiting team with their imported team of spirits—or even more alarming, the spirit houses—are awakening the local spirits who have been oppressed by the nats.

"We do believe and worship the village's nat but now seeing Thai spirit houses in the area, it is like a guest is taking forced residence in our house. We do not want spirit houses in a religious Buddhist area like this. There is a possibility for cultural mixing and I am concerned about our culture being threatened by another culture," said U Aung Ba, member of the Nabule Spiritual Group.

We will keep an eye on the 2,000 households and 10,000 Buddhists of Nabule as they learn that the opening up of globalization has a cost. Consumers are given new choices. Foreign businesses bring in their own cultures and belief systems. What locals are never told until it is too late is that the idea of choice means locals are given an expanded menu of spirits to worship, and the new businesses bringing in their expertise and technology are not leaving their local gods at home.

Local gods need accommodations. Spirit houses, like drones, are a metaphor for what it means to have invisible forces watching you; the locals lose their historical isolation and the remoteness of the mountain life vanishes. Village life begins to change as new ways, ideas and beliefs appear with people from neighboring lands.

This is only the beginning for the villagers of Nabule. Starbucks, McDonald's and 7-Eleven will not be far behind the spirit house invasion. The nats will have new immigrants from the spirit world as neighbors. The locals will resist these intruders. Yet what can they do? Globalization, like the Borg, has one motto that fits all: Resistance is futile. Development means the bargain you make is to yield up your old belief system. The deal with the devil of development is the new spiritual dimension that brings prosperity and happiness. The true enemy of the local supernatural belief in nats isn't the Thai spirit houses; it is the shift toward a reinvention of identity.

Nabule has had its welcome to the big game played out in thousands of villages before it. The Thai company with its installation of spirit houses has merely softened them up for the final assault on their mountain. It is only a matter of time before the big artillery open up, blasting them into the modern, secular age, which has no place for local gods. Only then will the villagers of Nabule feel nostalgic for the time when all they had to worry about was the conflict over their belief in nats against the Thai spirit houses. The dignity of local deities is in for a rough ride.

Fighting Crime across International Borders

In the Vincent Calvino series the novels are divided between crimes that are set in Thailand—though an expat might be involved—and those novels with a cross-border connection. The distinction between international crime and domestic crime often blurs once cash enters the picture. Mountains of cash from illegal activity make for strange bedfellows inside the world of crime.

In a globalized economy, crime has been at the vanguard of moving money, people, and products around the world. Criminals have an incentive. They don't want to get caught and sent to prison. So they put money, thought and time into avoiding risks. In the shadowy world of illegality, the basic business skills are largely the same. But there is an important difference.

First, the criminal is relying on gaps, flaws or holes in the system, and similar gaps and flaws in the moral and ethical values of those who run the system. They exploit both. Second, criminals use threats, guns and violence if things go pear-shaped. Rather than having recourse to the police or courts to redress breaches, criminals have their own methods of settling disputes. It's called intimidation and violence. Legal businessmen delegate the intimidation and violence to entities of the state. They have less need to get blood on their hands.

Law enforcement has traditionally been a local affair in most countries because most crimes have been local in nature. The criminal and victim were from the same city, province, county and/or country. A case can be made that organized crime kickstarted globalization. The British Opium Wars in the early 19th century form a good example of a legitimate business becoming a crime syndicate (looting and pillaging by merchants/warriors/politicians has a longer history).

As part of its empire and trade-expansion imperial policies, Britain lent military assistance to the East India Company (which became drug dealers, but they weren't called that), who used guns and canon to force open the domestic market in China to sell massive quantities of opium to the Chinese. The British were able (because of the opium business) to cut their trade deficit. Fiscal and monetary policy had different moral dimensions in the 19th century.

Organized drug gangs continue to operate, but they no longer have the overt support of a government to supply them military muscle, confer tax benefits and place their officers on the annual Honors List. There will be readers who will cite examples of contemporary thugs who have received a gong before eventually finding their way to a prison. All of that is true but beside the point. I am speaking about a change in the general arc of history. There has been a shift—led by technological innovations—that continues to weaken the link between organized illegal activities and government officers.

Not all the forces inside governments are working to change the analog cash system. You would expect eliminating corruption to be a priority, but that lofty goal also means the breaking of many rice bowls that have been inside the system for generations. Giving up easy money is harder than kicking a drug habit. Reformers are put on committees to write reports and show the way. But nothing much happens at the grassroots level, at the end of the money pipeline where the rural school teacher, hospital worker, prison guard, cop and migrant worker are waiting for payday. That is money raked off inside the government system by officials skimming money from the low-level beneficiaries.

The other unofficial source of revenue for government officials is generated from illegal activities such as drug trafficking, logging, prostitution, gambling and smuggling. Let's have a look at opium. A big, profitable market that despite law enforcement efforts shows no sign of slowing down in Southeast Asia.

The current opium production in Southeast Asia is on schedule to record a bumper crop year. That means a couple of things: (1) moving the product across borders and (2) laundering mountains of cash.

When the opium finds its way into the international market, how do governments in the region enforce the law? The poppies are grown in one place. The processing of the poppies into opium paste happens in another place. The storage and transportation are likely in other locations. And the money flows across multiple borders, passing through numerous bank accounts. Some of that money is paid as bribes to politicians, cops, military personnel, customs inspectors and others in the chain of security, protection and enforcement. Organized crime is highly profitable because it has the ability to patch together a makeshift set of mutually beneficial relationships that thrives on secrecy, non-traceability and the sanctity of borders.

Cooperation between various levels of law enforcement and security officials complicates the risk factor for organized crime. Cooperation across borders and the sharing of technology and information increase the cost to organized crime bosses dramatically. It's like insurance premiums. If that huge, devastating flood only occurs once every hundred years, the cost of insurance is relatively low. But if the hundred-year flood level happens every six months, the cost of insurance skyrockets to the point no one can afford to buy insurance. Successful cooperation is a real threat to transnational crime.

Everyone sees the part of the elephant standing in their district but not the overall dimensions of the beast. According to the *Bangkok Post*, recently 43 Thai cops traveled to Hong Kong to meet their police counterparts. The idea was to establish cooperation between the two police forces and exchange of information, for example, about finances and training. Hong Kong and Thai authorities have promised to enter a memorandum of understanding on the nature and scope of their cooperation. For which crimes and in what circumstances cooperation will occur remains to be hammered out. Whether anything tangible will arise from this arrangement is impossible to know at this stage. It is hard enough to get people within the same department to cooperate. Extending cooperation across borders with different traditions, languages and customs is what is called a "challenge."

In this part of the world the problem is often not lack of cooperation but that there is too much cooperation between law enforcement, civil servants and politicians and the organized big league crime ventures. A glimpse of that organized crime world of powerful insiders using thuggish methods to drive out competition was revealed recently in China. In this "business" model the local government ran the organized crime business through their friends and associates, and those who tried to compete found themselves beaten and tortured and driven out of the country.

The Chinese government recently released information about Bo Xilai, the Chonguing party chief who recently lost his job in a power struggle. The *New York Times* reported:

"Once hailed as a pioneering effort to wipe out corruption, critics now say [Bo's anti-gang campaign] depicts a security apparatus run amok: framing victims, extracting confessions through torture, extorting business empires and visiting retribution on the political rivals of Mr. Bo and his friends while protecting those with better connections."

How best to approach the problem of corruption and organized crime in league with government officials? Follow the money. The pain the criminals feel the most is when their traditional money routes are closed down. Big, organized crime is a headache because it is largely a cash business. How does the criminal with bags of bank notes work the cash through the financial system? Brokers arise whenever there is a market. Cash is a market, and brokers create an informal banking system to launder the illegal funds.

Money laundering legislation has slowed down but not stopped the Amazon River flow of cash. This is particularly true in less developed countries where there are few banks and almost no one has a bank account. Cash-in-hand systems are vulnerable to corruption. Every time money stops at someone's desk on the journey from the person who sent it to the person who will eventually receive it, someone is taking a piece of the action. This rent seeking happens not just in underground economies; in legal economies we call these cuts banking fees. In the underground world, we call this corruption if the person exacting a fee is a government official.

In Afghanistan payrolls for the ordinary cop and low-level officers used to be distributed through higher-level officers, who took their cut before passing the cash down the line. A Vodafone program, first created for payments in microfinance operations in Kenya, was adapted to pay the Afghan police directly through their cell phones. That computer program caused mixed feelings. The high command hated the innovation. But low-level police thought they'd receive a raise. It was the first time they'd received a payroll without someone above skimming off the top. They loved the new system. In a country where very few people have bank accounts and there are only a handful of ATMs, banking through a cell phone is a mini-revolution. It is also an effective way to reduce corruption—or, to use a lovely term, "money leakage." One frustrated commander demanded that his officers turn over their phones and PINs and attempted to collect their salaries from an M-Paisa agent.

India is examining the new technology to increase the reach of electronic transfers as a way to reduce government corruption. Argentina used electronic voucher cards as part of a successful campaign to beat corruption.

Money as a physical object is so much a part of our experience that it is difficult to believe there were long stretches of history when our ancestors didn't use coins or paper money. We are now headed toward a financial system that is digital. The knock-on effect means that electronic money transfers will continue to reduce the role of physical money passing through many sticky fingers.

Organized crime works at the municipal, county, provincial and national levels in many countries because corruption is difficult to root out. The technology is available to largely eliminate corruption. But those who benefit the most from the current cash and carry and skim system are not likely to step forward as willing first adopters. One would expect those with vested interest to subvert attempts to bypass the original channels in which cash flows.

Meanwhile, cooperation between police forces across borders makes for a good study trip to another country, with the hotel buffets, the sightseeing and the making of new friends. But let's be honest. The problem isn't lack of cooperation, as the officials often cooperate a bit too much. The problem is finding a direct way to make payments that avoids pushing bags of cash down the old traditional ramps in a world where the most powerful porters drive Benzes and live in mansions.

Corporations Carrying out Crime inside Alice's Wonderland

There is a passage in *Alice in Wonderland* that might shed some light on whether a corporation is a person. It is unclear whether the United States Supreme Court might be taking a page out the Mad Hatter's book of logic when it comes to corporate "personhood."

"Why is a raven like a writing-desk?" asks the Mad Hatter. Eventually the answer emerges:

"Have you guessed the riddle yet?" the Hatter said, turning to Alice again.

"No, I give it up," Alice replied: "What's the answer?"

"I haven't the slightest idea," said the Hatter.

Corporations are legal constructs, abstractions that arise because a law allows people to create them, run them, profit from them and defend them. No one will ever walk into a bar and find Microsoft or Apple sipping a glass of beer. People who work to advance the interests of the company are the ones at the bar drinking.

Corporations also have a long historical reputation for being a popular vehicle for colonial expansion. You may read that as meaning raising armies, launching wars of conquest, killing and enslaving indigenous populations, looting treasure, plundering natural resources and corrupting the local legal system.

The United States Supreme Court not long ago (*Citizens United*) decided that corporations were to be treated as a "person" for purposes of political expression. It must have seemed like a good idea at the time. Now that decision has come back like a bad penny. Can the corporation be a "person" for political expression and not a "person" when it comes to paying compensation when it is implicated in Third World countries that engage in human rights violations such as murder and extracting natural resources without caring too much about the environment?

Anyone with a passing knowledge of the East India Company (not to forget the Dutch West India Company) will know that not too long ago corporations had vast monopolies, controlled vast estates, wielded immense political power, and you never had to look too far to find a lot of blood dripping from the hands of the flesh–and–blood people who ran them. Did I mention that they also did a lively business running the slave trade? That's unlikely the image they wish to be viewed taking into account their current corporate TV ads or corporate brochures.

Corporations from the 17th through the 19th century were the vanguard of organized crime, raising armies, selling weapons and drugs, and beating, torturing, imprisoning or murdering the locals who raised their voices in protest. Perhaps you've read along this far, and you're saying, yes, that is all true, but didn't all of those terrible things happen a very long time ago? There are no more colonies. Independent states run their own affairs. The United Nations has mandates about human rights and the environment. And that means that corporations are no longer evil polluters, looters, pillagers and murderers, right? When a dog gets the taste of raw eggs it's hard to keep him out of the henhouse, even though the house looks different from the old days.

The Royal Dutch Petroleum Company has found itself a

defendant in an American case that has reached the United States Supreme Court. So you thought all of that nasty business of colonial plunder and murder was behind us? Let's take a brief look at the *Kiobel v. Royal Dutch Petroleum* case. To do that, put your mind back to Joseph Conrad's *Heart of Darkness*, to the space and time that reappears as officials of Royal Dutch Shell worked alongside officials of the Nigerian government to arrest, torture and murder environmental activists and members of the Ogoni of the Niger Delta, protesting the adverse health and environmental fallout that resulted from unregulated drilling and extraction of oil from that region.

No one is apparently arguing whether the corporation through its officers and employees was complicit in the human rights violations that occurred in the 1990s. The argument instead is whether the victims who otherwise have no connection with the United States can pursue legal remedies against Royal Dutch Petroleum in the American judicial system. To do so, the victims need to convince the high court that the Royal Dutch Petroleum Company is a "person" under the 1789 *Alien Tort Statute*. If they are a "person," then the victims of the faraway crime can sue them in an American federal court. In an earlier case the Court established that an individual who was a foreigner but who did business or had assets in the United States could be successfully sued for wrongful acts such as torture and murder carried out against another foreigner abroad.

It comes as no surprise who has filed briefs in support of the Royal Dutch Shell claim that the case should be thrown out. Britain, the Netherlands and Germany—the countries with a rich colonial past, which means they know a thing or two about using corporations to teach a lesson to the restless natives while enslaving the rest to extract natural resources from their lands, and limiting the outflow of funds to payoffs for the elites and profits for the shareholders. That pretty much sums up how the old corporate system operated and, despite the TV commercials about their responsibility to the environment and to communities, how it continues to operate in many "foreign" countries.

The United States filed a brief in support of the victims' right to bring the lawsuit. Who are the judges going to support? The Europeans, with their corporations harvesting profits that come from valuable resources extracted from the mines, wells, pits and forests of the Third World? The American government may have decided that exposing foreign corporations to the full radiation of the American justice system might cause such corporations to make a correction in their activities that have in the past led to the most ghastly abuses. Paying out large amounts for damages in lawsuits erodes the competitive edge gained through unrestrained exploitation. The Americans have in effect installed an international civil compensation system to penalize Third World murder carried out by corporations to enhance their profit margins.

Assessing American-style civil damages against a foreign corporation operating in foreign lands against foreigners is a revolutionary and clever way of reckoning the true cost of running the international resource business. That's a scary enough idea to get three ex-colonial European governments to come down to rescue Royal Dutch Shell. Come to think of it, I also wonder why China and Russia haven't filed briefs in support of Royal Dutch Shell. The potential countries involved are a cozy club of mutually self-interested resource extractors. Perhaps no one has explained to them what is potentially at stake in this case should Royal Dutch Shell be conferred with "personhood." Knighthoods for the CEOs, but no personhood for the company, thank you very much. They know where to draw the line in the sand.

The Supreme Court justices at oral argument on the case have revealed their thinking about allowing these foreigners to use the American court system to chase down the wrongdoers and bring them to account.

John Bellinger in the Lawfare blog (www.lawfareblog. com) reported on this exchange during the oral arguments:

Justice Kennedy: "But, counsel, for me, the case turns in large part on this: page 17 of the red brief. It says, 'International law does not recognize corporate responsibility for the alleged offenses here.' And the—one of the—the amicus brief for Chevron [written by Jack Goldsmith, a former Kennedy clerk] says, 'No other nation in the world permits its court to exercise universal civil jurisdiction over alleged extraterritorial human rights abuses to which the nation has no connection.' And in reading through your briefs, I was trying to find the best authority you have to refute that proposition, or are you going to say it is irrelevant?"

Justices Roberts and Alito piled on:

Justice Alito: "Well there's no particular connection between the events here and the United States. So, I think the question is whether there's any other country in the world where these plaintiffs could have brought these claims against the Respondents."

Chief Justice Roberts: "If—if there is no other country where this suit could have been brought, regardless of what American domestic law provides, isn't it a legitimate concern that allowing the suit itself contravenes international law?"

Human rights and environment rights are detailed in standards by the United Nations. That's wonderful. But corporations understand that the United Nations doesn't operate a judicial system that can hold them to account. They know that the place of the crime is on their side, and that no effective legal remedy is available to the victims. The question before the Supreme Court is whether to open

American courts as a venue to reign in corporate terror.

A majority of the Supreme Court justices decided in an earlier case, *Citizens United v. Federal Election Commission* (2010), that corporations were persons with the same right to freedom of expression as individuals—meaning a corporation could fund political campaign ads that advanced its political agenda just as an individual could. Having put themselves in the business of bringing individual rights to corporations, the question is, will it take the next step, to apply civil remedies to a foreign corporation implicated in murder and torture? Or someone might whisper in the court's collective ear that the case isn't really about the murder and abuse of victims' human rights; it's about the unfair competition that violence assisted in allowing certain corporations a large cost-cutting advantage not shared by their more ethical competitors. And we can teach those foreigners a thing or two about punitive damages to claw back some of that advantage.

On chasing that rabbit down the hole, the court enters Alice's Wonderland, where nothing is quite as it seems. In that world the successors of the East India Company and the Dutch West India Company are filing their briefs to carry on their business in the traditions of the 17th century. Big-time crime syndicates called corporations, and the big-time criminals who work for them, artfully dodge and dart like virtual particles in physics between separate states: being an individual when it suits their political agenda and being an abstract legal entity when it engages in plunder, looting and murder.

But the Supreme Court can't put Royal Dutch Shell into the Large Hadron Collider and settle the question once and for all. The physics of justice isn't scientific. The justices aren't searching for the judicial equivalent of the Higgs boson. Court decisions are hardnosed, practical, messy, contradictory and never, ever above the politics and economic interest that make the world a duplicate copy of what it has always been. In the future Royal Dutch Shell and other "foreign" companies like them may find themselves entangled in the spider web of defending damage claims in an American civil action.

We will be left wondering if advancing the economic interest of Americans was the real reason behind the decision. Making a corporation a person is a good cover story and it also comes with the added bonus of making the court look consistent with its earlier ruling in *Citizens United v. Federal Election Commission*.

As Alice explained in the film version of *Through the Looking Glass*: "If I had a world of my own, everything would be nonsense. Nothing would be what it is, because everything would be what it isn't. And contrariwise, what it is, it wouldn't be. And what it wouldn't be, it would. You see?"

Organized Crime Building a Supply Chain

You never see a "company" handcuffed and paraded before the press. But in this part of the world, pictures of flesh and blood criminals often appear in the newspaper or on TV. Mostly, they are low-level criminals who were caught holding the illegal goods. Holding the bag, so to speak.

They are presented at press conferences with rows of uniformed officers looking on as the accused sits in front of a desk loaded with parcels containing contraband. Most of the time the parcels contain drugs.

Next time you look at a drug suspect sitting handcuffed as kilos of drugs are displayed, remember that this deliveryman was paid to deliver a product.

Now and again a missing piece of the story pops up in the press.

The accused at the table is the tip of the iceberg, but what sank the *Titanic* lay beneath the water's surface and it was huge. Organized crime is the entity that builds this force of criminal nature. It creates, operates, manages and controls chains of supply and of distribution, and it has operational chiefs, people of influence and status, as well as significant financial and legal talent. In many ways it resembles many other businesses. All of this activity of sourcing, processing and distribution is meant to take place without undue risk to the principals, who earn windfall products from a product that is illegal. Meth possession will likely land the end user in prison, not the one making the money.

The end user is at the same level as the delivery guy, the poor mule, who sits alone before the press. Those are the two faces you see over and over. What about the others? Isn't it time for at least a show of looking inside the organization part of organized crime?

The recent case of 30 Thai hospitals and clinics supposedly implicated in buying and selling pills with the active ingredient called pseudoephedrine, an essential chemical compound needed to make meth—one extremely nasty, ugly drug—is a rare look at a hidden part of the chain. Let's get out of the way a couple of things that you should know about meth and crystal meth before we get to the hospitals and clinics. These drugs put people in the hospital or the grave. Here are some of the short-term and long-term effects: panic and psychosis, convulsions, seizures, permanent damage to blood vessels of the heart and brain, and liver, kidney and lung damage. That's enough. You don't have to examine every last body to know when you are in the presence of a massacre.

Last year the *Guardian* reported, "The number of methamphetamine users in Thailand will reach 1.1 million this year, the head of the country's anti-drug police told the Guardian—equivalent to one in every 60 citizens."

That's a big, profitable market.

According to the *Bangkok Post*, police found that a senior pharmacist at Udon Thani Hospital had a role in diverting some 65,000 cold and allergy pills out of the hospital. Another pharmacist at a hospital in Uttaradit is implicated in using his hospital to launder 975,000 pseudoephedrine-based pills. The upcountry hospitals are under investigation. The reported number of pills from various hospitals and clinics, no matter how many times you read them, simply don't add up in the story. They rarely do in such cases as it seems math and journalistic skills rarely come together in one person in Thailand. The upshot is that a huge quantity of the pills with the essential ingredient to make meth was being sold out of the back doors of hospitals and clinics.

There was no report of any arrest being made of anyone from a hospital or clinic.

The story about how a vast hospital and clinic chain pumped millions of pills into the meth chain of production wasn't discussed. As a classic case of how the free market model of capitalism really runs when left without adult supervision, this aspect of the story is itself illuminating. As this was a story about hospitals and clinics, you suppose they'd run a photograph of such a building. That didn't happen.

Would you like to guess what picture the newspaper ran with this story instead? ... Give up? Three delivery people at a table surrounded by a platoon of cops, and on the table in front of them, 2.5 million speed pills and 50 kilos of crystal meth.

We get the message anyway. The story is about the role of hospitals and clinics in meth production in Thailand. But none of those people wanted their picture in the newspaper. The pool of photography subjects is pretty obvious from the arrested mules. These are the human livestock of the drug business. The same class of people who were hunted down, and some 2,500 killed, some years ago during the last "War on Drugs" in Thailand.

Not that we really need a lesson in the obvious. Yet we have come to not question the lesson anymore. We assume those in the picture are those in the story. Even though we'd likely never find a factory worker's picture in a story about the CEO of Ford or Nokia. In the illegal drug business, it's the employees, the working class—those who drive the trucks—who become the face of the problem, who get all the press coverage.

It is unlikely to happen during the lifetime of anyone now alive that we will ever open an electronic screen and look at faces of high-level officials from the private and public sector sitting at a table handcuffed for their role in the drug trade. Things don't work like that at the present time in most places.

Life is good when you're rich. And it's unfortunate for a few mules who get lost along the way. But as Darwin taught us, we inhabit a world of where survival of the fittest is the reigning principle. And a degree in pharmacology also helps.

We Need to Have a Talk About Greed

The impulse motivating a lot of crime is greed. The outlier wants money for drugs, hot cars or motorcycles, beautiful women, expensive restaurants, foreign holidays—what are perceived as the good things that rich people, or at least well-off people, use to identify themselves as successful, desirable and admirable. Not to mention more sexually attractive. The determinist would argue that our biology compels us to compete for mates and nature has no morality, and that the only meaningful part of the report card is the column marked reproductive success. Things like cheating don't matter. In love and war there are no rules. Anything goes.

Many articles and books have hammered home the lesson that most acts of greed aren't criminalized. In many cases, not only are such acts legal, the greedy are rewarded with large bonus and awards, put on the cover of magazines and appear on panels at Davos. When a huge company or firm threatens to blow up from an excess of greed, they turn to the government to save them.

That's why we need to talk about greed. We live in a time of vast inequality, a state that is defended by a sizeable portion of the population who happen to be the victims of such inequality. How did this happen? Have we been sleepwalking for the last thirty years since President Ronald

Reagan and Prime Minister Margaret Thatcher fired their starter's pistol that allowed the greedy to spring ahead of us at the speed of light? All of this has happened in our lifetime.

How bad is it? What can we do about it? And how did the hive create a unified mindset that tells us greed is good? I don't begin to have the answers to such complex questions.

What I have are a couple of pathways to explore, and one or two signposts that suggest a direction to move ahead.

Our perception of greed, including the qualities that fuel greed—selfish and narcissistic attitudes and an absence of empathy—begins to take shape in childhood

Most of us remember when, as a child, a brother or sister, friend or neighbor, hogged a greater share of the popcorn or Mom's apple pie or the bicycle, or never passed the basketball, always taking the shot from the corner. That was our childhood introduction to the idea of greed—actions that were tiny lessons in the art of selfishness. From an early age we calculate how other people divide and share time, opportunity, attention and of course money. And one shouldn't forget toys and invitations. My parents lectured me that being greedy was morally wrong and people wouldn't like me if I were greedy. Of course you can be disliked for a lot of other reasons even if you're not greedy. But that is another essay.

One would think that with a lifelong series of lessons in the workings of greed in the back of our minds, we'd quietly resolve that once we grew up and ran things, we'd put a fence around greed, herd the greedy inside and watch them roam around being greedy among their own kind. An appropriate punishment for the greedy is isolation.

The problem is, after we grew up, the people who were greedy all around the edges of our lives proved to have the kind of talent and ability most valued by the world of commerce. And there was no need to isolate the greedy, as they were perfectly capable to isolating themselves. Who else lived in gated communities?

As far as I can see, greed is a vast mall where pundits are gathering to talk about fair shares of this and that on a daily basis. Two recent stories made me understand that the lessons of greed learnt during childhood never fully prepared us for the way forces much larger than ourselves have scaled greed to unimaginable levels.

The first story I want to relate is about loan sharks or what the *Bangkok Post* calls "predatory lending cartels." There are about 40 to 50 of these backdoor banking operations in Thailand. Apparently, two of the "businesses" have the resources and what the *Bangkok Post* calls "backing to counter the authorities." You get the picture—no one can do much about the "backed up" greedy. They have juice.

The way it works in Thailand is the borrower can opt for a 24-day repayment period or a "two percent interest" payment plan. Under the first plan, the borrower repays an equal amount every day for 24 days. The average interest on the 24-day repayment plan is 50 percent. Under the Usury Law, the maximum allowable is 28 percent, but as we have established, if you have juice, you can squeeze out another 22 percent over the legal limit without too much of a problem. But the 24-day plan is a walk in the park compared with the two percent interest plan. Under that plan, the borrower is paying only the interest, and that continues until the day the borrower comes up with the principal to repay. If the borrower can't come up with the principal, he or she continues to pay for life.

Greedy lenders couldn't exist without an element of greed in a large pool of borrowers, especially ones who won't ever receive a bank loan because they have no steady income or resources to put up as collateral. But they also want to buy gold, cell phones, iPads and motorcycles. This class of upcountry lenders has an army of "black helmet" debt collectors who do nasty things to borrowers who miss payments. The handmaiden of greed has always been violence. When borrowers take the money from one of these lenders, they forfeit their protection against intimidation and violence.

The upcountry Thai loan sharks show how greed can be organized and scaled on a regional and national basis, and how at least some players in that network are given a free hand to violate the Usury Law and the criminal statues on threats, intimidation and assault. The middle class tend to write off the poor rural borrower as someone reaping their bad karma.

The second story I want to share shows that Thailand's loan shark operation is small-change, backwater, out-of-date, out-of-touch money-making. When someone has a close look at the assets of the global super-rich, we start to see the upper limits to which pure greed, when left unregulated by government and unbundled from any sense of ethics or morality, can take us. The *Guardian* reports that 92,000 people, or 0.001% of the world's population, has hidden out of tax view approximately $21 trillion dollars. That's a lot of ice cream cones, basketball court time and popcorn.

How much money is that? Three percent interest on that sum is equal, according to the *Guardian*, to the combined aid given by rich countries to the developing countries each year.

At one time it was said that money from the rich trickled down and everyone benefited. This hunk of an iceberg sits out of sight and, despite global warming, shows not only no sign of melting but no evidence even of the amount of dripping you'd get from a leaky kitchen tap.

A number of recent studies in psychology have shown that people have a burning sense of fairness. If "A" holds $100 dollars and the rule is she can keep the money provided "B" agrees, and before B agrees, A must make an offer to divide the money. What the researchers found is that if A offered B $20 and wanted B to accept that offer so she could keep the $80, most of the time B would reject the offer even though B would be $20 worse off. The point is A loses the $80, too, and that makes for an incentive for a fairer offer, say a 60/40 split.

Our psychology drives us on a person-to-person basis to reject such an offer, meaning the would-be will get nothing but at the same time knows the other person who made the unjust offer also gets nothing. Once we scale away from the personal level (the level we know from childhood), we discover at the global level of big business and finance that capitalism inevitably, without safeguards and restraints, will always produce an unjust allocation. There are several ways to change things for those who feel that the allocation between the 92,000 and the rest of us is unjust and unfair.

Here are a few ideas. First, find the money; we have the necessary tools. Second, enact tax laws to compel the 92,000 to pay taxes on their extraordinary wealth. Third, enact an "unusually rich" law (there is such a law in Thailand, but that is another essay) that would allow the government to claw back money someone can't account for.

Saying you won a couple of billion in a poker game or a lottery has been tried (and mostly doesn't work). It might be better to cut to the chase and admit that anyone with wealth over $100 million is unusually wealthy. The excess money goes back to the state. The environment, climate change, education, medical care and scientific research would benefit overnight from this cash injection. Though, with the cunning of international banksters combined with this treasure scattered like rice thrown at a wedding, enacting such laws would be almost as difficult as enforcing them if enacted.

The anger over the unfairness of how income and wealth are distributed is coming to a head. Precisely because you can poke large holes in the possible three solutions above, the political solution seems impossible. When that happens, expect to see self-help fill the void.

It won't be long before technology will allow determined Internet Robin Hoods to ferret out the super rich, their bank accounts and their hiding places inside the global Nottingham Forest. Once there is a consensus that the sheriffs have been bought off, the risk increases that self-help will fill the void. The task is a huge one. The construction of a secure fence to encircle greed might be technically possible, but with the amount of wealth involved, the super-rich will have their own army of "geeks" to subvert the Robin Hood assault.

Only a true romantic would believe that our childhood promise to install a means to control greed can succeed. No matter where on the planet the money is stashed, it can be shifted, converted and hidden, with more accumulated in the meantime. Will there be an accounting of the super rich? That's already been done. But accounting and accountability are two separate issues.

The digital auditors need backing. They can run the sums. They've identified the world's elite class of the greediest. It is now over to those who have their hands on the levers of power to adjust the rules and tax laws. The way it looks, though, they are holding hands with the super rich. The levers of power are part of their hidden ownership.

It would be too depressing to leave the matter like a crime that everyone witnessed but where no one can arrest the killer. In the off chance the Internet Robin Hoods need some analogue help in chasing down the super rich, or some technical advice on what do to with them when they're found and confronted, they might consider a consultancy contract with the black helmet debt collectors in Thailand. The men in black helmets know how to produce results. The 92,000 might try to bargain, bribe or come up with excuses. These guys, according to press accounts, are good; they know how to cause pain without leaving marks. The bribing potential is a bit of a problem, it's true, but giving them a percentage of the take should take care of that.

For anyone on the 92,000 greed list, you better start running about now, looking over your shoulder, because I see a crew of 53 kilo black helmet debt collectors recruited as freelance taxmen, and they have your name, address and bank account details, and the message from Thailand is that these guys just don't accept no for an answer.

Part IV

Culture and Justice

The Shadow of Freedom

L ast light as night falls in Rangoon. Shwedagon Pagoda framed against the twilight. It is like watching a great diva, knowing that in less than a generation she will be reduced to a walk-on role. But that is the future. At this moment such a command performance can only leave you in awe. Our world has lost something. And I am witnessing what is front of me and remembering what we've left behind with a sense of joy and regret.

From my balcony the Shwedagon Pagoda is on a hill enveloped in a forest of trees. One way to understand a place is to move beyond the iconic view and into the region of folk tales, proverbs and legends. Buried in these narratives are the treasures that define a people, their morality, ethics and worldview. As you will have gathered from the news headlines over the past couple of weeks, Burma is a society undergoing important political changes.

The people of Burma are like travelers who have been on a dusty road for a long time and are able to enjoy a simple meal.

There is a Burmese folktale★ about a weary traveler who stops along the road to eat his lunch. The traveler is poor and his meal is a meager helping of rice and vegetables. Nearby a food vendor is selling fried fish and fish cakes. The stall owner watches the traveler eating his own meal as the smell of the fish she is frying drifts toward the traveler, who squats alone, lost in thought.

As the traveler finishes his meal and is about to depart, the woman from the food stalls shouts at him, stopping him in his tracks: "You owe me a silver quarter for the price of one fried fish."

"But, madam, I did not eat one of your fried fish."

"You are a cheater," she replies, "a person who takes without paying for what he takes."

"But, madam, I've taken nothing from you. I have not come within five feet from your stall."

"Ah-ha! And you're a liar to boot. I have many witnesses who will testify that they saw you enjoying the smell of my fried fish as you ate your meal. You would not have been able to eat that disgusting mush of rice and vegetables without taking in the sweet aroma of my fish frying. So pay me the silver quarter and don't make any more trouble for yourself."

The confrontation soon draws a crowd. The fried fish seller plays to the crowd, who have to agree that indeed the traveler has availed himself of the smell of the fish frying. Even the traveler cannot deny he has smelled the fish frying. But he insists that he has no duty to pay for that privilege.

The matter is taken to a royal judge, who hears the evidence. The judge deliberates on the matter in a courthouse nestled under the shade of a coconut tree, chickens pecking for grain along the road. Several minutes pass before he announces his verdict to the parties and the crowd who have accompanied them.

The judge finds that the basic facts aren't in dispute. The traveler has indeed enhanced the enjoyment of his meal because of the pleasant smell of the fish frying. He has received a benefit. But what is the value of that benefit? The fish seller said the price for a plate of fish was a silver quarter.

The judge orders the parties to leave the courthouse and to walk out into the sun. The traveler is then to hold out a silver quarter and allow the fish vendor to grasp the shadow made by the silver quarter. The judge reasons that if a plate of fish costs one silver quarter, then the exchange value for the smell of the fish is the shadow of one silver quarter.

As the gold rush of investors are jumping headlong into the newly opened Burma, they might be reminded that so far the Burmese, like the traveler, have only had a whiff of the frying fish called freedom and democracy. Whether they will be left only with a scent or will be allowed to enjoy the full plate remains to be seen. The future will tell whether the price of freedom for 60 million travelers will be judged to be payable in silver or a mere shadow of silver.

*Story adapted from Maung Htin Aung's *Folk Tales of Burma*.

Jailing False Prophets: A Prediction for 2012

It is claimed the Mayans left behind a prophecy that the world is doomed to end in 2012. But as with many prophecies, hundreds if not thousands of years separate the prophet from his prediction. When the prophet is long dead, we shrug it off when the event doesn't come to pass.

Most of us are surrounded by prophets of one sort or another, predicting that stock markets or the euro will collapse, or that you will meet that bright, attractive, hot counterpart if you show up at high noon at Little Harry's Bar and sit on the third seat from the door. What prophets have in common is that they claim to have a direct mystical pipeline from the future. In other words, it ain't science.

I had a look at my horoscope in the *Bangkok Post* for January 4, 2012, and was told: "Indulge in industriousness. Put the finishing touches on projects, but don't initiate anything new. A small delay with a check or a contract could cause worry, but everything will turn out fine."

A long-time journalist friend once told me that, when he worked for one of the wires, he was given the task of writing the horoscopes. He made them up. He produced all kinds of positive, upbeat and uplifting predictions, while handing out dire predictions of life in the gutter, pus-filled boils and inoperative hernias under the zodiac signs of his enemies.

Religious texts including the Bible are riddled with stories of prophets who predicted all matter of things. Believers take those predictions to heart, particularly the ones about the afterlife. Prophets prove that you can't have even a half-baked religion unless you have a good recipe that blends the supernatural, superstition and woo-woo in general.

The problem starts when a prophet starts spouting off predictions about specific events involving specific public structures. He then has crossed an invisible line—at least, it seems, in Thailand where there is a high ratio of fortunetellers to population. A partial list of clients would include office workers, politicians, military personel, police officers, housewives, husbands, boyfriends, maids, CEOs, tuk-tuk and taxi drivers, school teachers and street vendors. Some Thai fortune tellers have legendary followings.

Recently, in Tak province, a 73-year-old fortune teller got himself in hot water over a failed prediction about a dam bursting. Thongbai Khamsi predicted that a large provincial dam in Tak would crumple on New Year's Eve. After dawn arose on New Year's Day in Tak, it didn't take long for the locals to figure out that the dam, despite Thongbai's prophecy, was still working just like a dam should, by holding back the water and generating electricity.

That apparently upset some of the local authorities. A number of people complained that they had sold their land at fire sale prices to get what they could before the dam burst. And even more damaging, tourism to Tak dropped by ninety percent, leaving a 400-million-baht hole in the local economy. If you made a bad real estate decision and your tourist numbers are down, all of this bad luck has to be laid off on someone. Why not Thongbai, the false prophet? The authorities, seeing which way the local wind was blowing, decided that Thongbai got the nomination as a false prophet, the man who had caused substantial public damage.

It would be unfair to say this kind of magical thinking followed by an angry populace howling for blood only happens in Thailand. Deuteronomy 13:1–5 counsels: "Prophets and dreamers are to be executed if they say or dream the wrong things." I've never heard of anything comparable said in Buddhism. In this case, it seems the Thai local authorities are acting quite Christian-like in their zeal.

Thongbai has his own explanation of how he came about this prophecy. It came from his son, Pla Bu, before his son died. That son had quite a track record in the prophecy game, having predicted his own death 15 days before he died, along with having predicted both 9/11 before it happened in 2001 and the Indian Ocean tsunami prior to December 26, 2004. Thongbai was channeling his dead son, and that could be part of the problem. It is better to stick with talking to God—like Pat Robertson, who says God has already told him who the next President of the United States will be. If it all goes wrong, the comeback is, "God is testing our faith."

There is a hint that the charges by the authorities resulted as much from a loss of face as anything. They held a big New Year's Countdown Party at the dam.

There is no word on whether Thongbai has predicted whether he will be convicted, and, if convicted, sent to the big house to serve time with murderers, rapists, arsonists and armed robbers. He might teach a course in astrology to inmates or tell the guards' and wardens' fortunes in order to get time off for good behavior. Just a piece of advice: he should avoid predictions about the durability of prison walls and stay on the more vague, abstract side, following the example of the newspaper astrologers.

Alternatively, he might switch to doomsday predictions because there is far less risk as long as sufficiently projected in the future, and, as predictions go, these ones are much more fun. No one ever thinks of charging a doomsday prophet with a crime. Perhaps what makes their false prophesies more acceptable to authorities is that, unlike the dam, if the whole world is going to disappear, then there's no possible buyer for all of that real estate anyway, and what's the point of going on holiday? No one really loses, and when the all-clear signal is given to celebrate and everyone who was terrified can turn around and laugh at what a fool the prophet was, he, if history is any guide, simply kicks the ball into the future again.

What worries authorities and has them reaching for the handcuffs are dire predictions of doom that cause large public panic. In 1669, a group of Russians called the "Old Believers" convinced themselves the world would end that year. Rather than hanging around to see if that happened, about twenty thousand of these believers set themselves on fire to protect themselves against the Antichrist. I've not found a record of any prophet taking the rap for that failed prophesy. He might have gone up in smoke.

I have a few prophecies of my own to make in this first essay of the year. In the short term, the charges against Thongbai (who has yet to turn himself in to the police) will chill the prophecy business in Thailand well into February 2012; afterwards, these events will be totally forgotten. If using criminal law is found effective against this false prophet, I predict it will be vastly expanded to round up many more of this ilk. In that case, I recommend you buy into companies that maintain a connection to the jail-building business in Thailand, as these companies will enter boom times. Look for promotion of government officials who meet their quotas in identifying and exposing gurus, prophets, seers, fortunetellers and pundits. The era of hunting terrorists has run its course.

As we enter the new dawn of finding, charging, trying and punishing the false prophets, all of us can take pride is working together to weed them out before their false predictions overrun the garden of our common humanity (and make us sell our houses at stupid prices).

Let this be the year of visiting Thailand, where no bad prophet goes unpunished. And to be on the safe side, leave your predictions about the future at home.

The Sacredness of Justice

You're in a foreign country. Thailand. The police stop you. They don't speak much English, but they demand to search you. Now. They want your passport. But it's in your hotel room. You're caught off guard, even though you've done nothing wrong, but the police insist you give them your bag. They take your bag and search it. They search your person. They go through your cell phone messages. They tell you that messages in violation of a law in Thailand known by the number 112 (reference to an article in the Criminal Code) have been sent from your cell phone and you're in serious trouble. You've violated something called lèse-majesté, and you've never heard that term before. But you remember letting someone use your phone. You tell that to the cops. But you don't remember her name. You are told that the SMS came from your SIM card and your cell phone, and that you must prove that you are innocent.

How do you prove that you didn't do something? It's like proving there isn't an invisible elephant in the room.

What do you do? Who do you turn to? There are parts of the world where these are real and pressing questions.

When we think of criminal justice systems restraining criminal conduct, most of the time we are thinking of the system that is near, the one we grew up with, the system that we see on TV, in the newspapers or online. The muggers, killers, car hijackers and white collar criminals all have one thing in common in this system: they are presumed innocent. The cops must have probable cause to search them, and they must warn suspects that anything they say can be used against them.

That's home base (and even there, it can run into the ditch). It's not abroad. There, in a number of legal systems, acts that you take to be a universal right are deemed criminal. In other words, when abroad, the print in the ways the locals write it matters. Try selling a Valentine's card in Saudi Arabia. Time for the religious police to throw your sentimental ass in the slammer. Try doodling cartoons about sacred figures and see how far your claims of artistic license and freedom get you in the 100 meter shackled leg race in the prison courtyard.

In Thailand there has been in recent years a dramatic increase of charges (conviction is almost always guaranteed) under lèse-majesté and computer crime laws. Warnings have been given by the authorities that this Thai law applies to everyone around the world. Press the "like" button on a Facebook page deemed to be in violation of Article 112 and the computer crime law, and you've committed an offense punishable by up to 15 years in prison. In other words, you'd be in serious trouble, and it is no defense that you did this outside Thailand or didn't know that it was an offense. You still go to jail.

Such attitudes are more obvious (and better reported) in Middle Eastern countries. But you'd be wrong to think that is the only place where fundamental freedoms are absent. Thailand is an example where normative values about sacredness are backed by stiff penalties against those who seek to question them. This is in contrast to the Western Enlightenment idea of criticism as a positive and progressive value. We are taught the importance of give and take in political discussions. In the West, our normative values cast a spotlight on justice, equity and fairness. But don't make the mistake of thinking this judgment is universally accepted. It's not. In a system of sacredness no one is ever forced to resign, no matter how zealous the enforcement. Such a legal system encourages the true believer to step forward and undertake communal action. Those who are less committed soon fall under a cloud of suspicion.

Ever since Oliver Stone's *Midnight Express* hit the silver screen in 1978, we've become familiar with chronicles of Westerners caught up in the nightmarish gulags of foreign criminal systems, where most people recoil at the idea of justice being meted out in ways that are transparent, fair, honest and unbiased. In short, there is a perception that if you find yourself caught in the vice of a foreign law enforcement investigation, you will likely suffer an injustice. The recent case of the young Seattle university student who spent four years behind bars in Italy only to be acquitted of the charge of murder reinforces the idea that a brush with the law in a foreign country can go sideways quickly.

The problem experienced by many Westerners is compounded by complacency and ignorance. First, let's deal with complacency. You are on holiday and want to relax. You buy drugs from a stranger who turns out to be an undercover cop. Your holiday ends along with your freedom. Most people are aware of that risk. But sometimes they forget that the local rules in an exotic place don't have holiday exemption clauses for foreigners. In those circumstances, no one blames the locals for enforcing their laws, which in many ways aren't much different from their own laws at home.

Second on the list is ignorance. Let me be clear: most of us are ignorant on a vast number of subjects. It's not a stigma not to know something. But if you are going on holiday to a foreign destination, you can equip yourself with basic knowledge about the laws and customs and act accordingly. You don't need to be a lawyer or legal scholar in the criminal justice system of a place, but it is wise to learn if this travel destination has some laws quite unlike those you are familiar with at home.

Aside from the Article 112 cases, the ordinary run-of-the-mill run-in with the law in Thailand can become an ordeal. A couple of recent cases in Thailand raise issues about how the justice system works and how it is perceived to work. Often there is a wide gap between reality and rumor. The first involved a case in Pattaya where a young Englishman (25 years old) with a Thai girlfriend (22) was questioned about what appeared to be a failed suicide attempt by the girlfriend. She fell or jumped or stumbled—we don't really know what verb to insert based on the press reports—from the seventh floor and managed to survive. There has been no follow-up report on her condition and what she told the authorities had happened. The point is that the Englishman was hauled in for questioning as a possible suspect. A number of foreigners complained that when a foreigner falls off his condo or hotel room balcony, it is assumed to be suicide, and his Thai girlfriend is given sympathy rather than the third degree.

There is a video series titled BigTrouble in Thailand. In the first one, jet-ski operators seek to shake down a customer for supposed damage to the rented equipment. Scams like this often surface like a bubble from a deep sea diver to the surface before disappearing.

These two cases are classic examples of the perception by foreigners that they are at a disadvantage. The larger fear is that the local thugs are presumed to have the police on their side in any dispute. Also there is a widespread perception that a foreigner will be at the receiving end of unfair, unequal treatment by the police in circumstances where locals would not be questioned. There are many examples where foreigners are presumed to be in the wrong and locals in the right, and the foreigner is presumed to owe compensation for damage based on the local's version of events. The fear, in other words, is that there will be no even-handed justice. That the deck of cards is stacked in favor of the locals.

In Thailand that fear is also projected by the Thais when a request is made for extradition for a crime they're accused of committing when abroad.

An example is the recent case involving two mid-twenties Bangkok men who are alleged to have been involved in a murder in Australia. A Thai court has ordered their extradition to Australia to stand trial. This raises questions that are the opposite of the Pattaya attempted suicide case. Here the locals are doing everything in their power to resist justice in Australia. The Australian authorities introduced evidence sufficient to authorize an extradition. There is no indication the Thais wouldn't be given a fair trial. Young men from wealthy families in Thailand have been known to walk away free from murder cases. The Australian case raises the issue not about whether the men will receive justice but the underlying processes that accompany a criminal case in Thailand, where the relative rank and status of the perpetrator and victim may outweigh other considerations.

Criminal justice isn't some universal set of abstract principles, procedures and institutions that everyone agrees upon. It is built on local practice and custom, and embedded with relics of tribal traditions, kinship, and lineage. In the West societies are more pluralistic, and that is reflected in how the criminal justice system is administered. Members of the elite are sentenced to prison in the West. Sure, there are those who escape conviction. But it isn't a given they will convince a cop, a prosecutor, a court and a jury that their status is their right to immunity. That Get-Out-of-Jail-Free card is a reality in other countries. People living in these countries have, in the past, accepted this state of affairs though this may be changing—as we see with the Arab Spring.

If the prevailing consensus of the general population inside a country is that they belong to one single racial, religious and/or ethnic group, expect that this will influence their notion of justice. Such a country has its own way of dealing with local crime and criminals. An outsider should understand that justice as applied to locals and as applied to him will not likely match up. In such places, it is right for the foreigner to experience anxiety over his or her fate, fearing law enforcement agents will resolve the conflict or confrontation in favor of the locals. Or in the absence of such conflict, apply such laws against foreigners while turning a blind eye when a local breaks the same law. The racial purity argument pulses through many different nationalities and ethnic groups around the world. Mixing purity and justice is like mixing oil and water.

The danger is being caught out by the uniquely criminalized norms that you'd consider to be neutral if not actually virtues in your home country. Some countries have religious police. Saudi Arabia, Iran and Malaysia are three countries that come to mind. But other countries like China and Thailand have secular equivalents (computer-literate volunteers) monitoring the Internet, Facebook pages, blogs and Twitter looking for insults to their notions of the sacred. Prosecutors stand ready to arrest and imprison anyone (insider or outsider) who violates laws. This category of law is carefully patrolled and guarded, ensuring that local norms and taboos attached to the sacred are strictly enforced. You should recognize that when you travel abroad, the sensitive nature of local beliefs and faith are backed up by stringent laws with lengthy prison sentences imposed on violators. You may be unaware of the norms as they lack a direct counterpart in your culture. But ignorance won't be a defense.

There are eyes and ears in the street that hear casual remarks that violate a taboo, and the incident may be deemed not just offensive but illegal. This is a category of crime that lately is appearing more often because of the free-ranging discussions that social media and the Internet encourage. In the West a lively exchange of opinion, criticism and argument is considered normal. But in other places thought crimes, once they are given expression, can land you in prison for periods as long as a first-degree murder sentence.

The best piece of advice you will ever receive is this: when you travel outside the cone of the Enlightenment, steer clear of all discussions of politics and religion, and refrain from making any negative comments on local customs and culture. Stick to discussions about fashion, food, shopping and the weather, and you'll be safe. Smile and ask for another one of those tall drinks with a happy little umbrella, sit back in your beach chair, and look at the sea. Tell yourself this is the good life. You have earned this piece of paradise. But remember, too, paradise has its prisons ready for those who stray from that beach chair and mingle with the locals under the delusion that the free-ranging intellectual tradition of open discussion of the European coffee houses is welcome. It is not. You will be talking your way through a field of thought landmines, and if you trip over one, say goodbye to your freedom. And there will be absolutely nothing your embassy, your lawyer, your mother or your best friend can do to help. You will be another casualty of the war to protect the sacred.

Above the Law

I studied law. I taught law. I acted as a lawyer. Still, even with that legal background, I find it difficult to wrap my mind around systems where people are "above the law." In practical terms that means if they commit an offense, they are not processed through the legal justice system. They receive a free pass. This is the real world. Not one you find in law textbooks except in footnotes.

In Thailand there are multiple examples of someone with political and social influence getting away with murder. There were witnesses. The act was caught on CCTV cameras. But the evidence gets lost along the way. Nothing comes of the case. After a few months it disappears from the newspapers, from the public mind, until it has vanished from collective memory. Time erases the crime. In the real world our memories can only have so much overload before they no longer function.

The victim's family in such a case is lost in the void. There is no public accountability, no explanation, no reconciliation of the rules of the system. In the real world none of that matters a great deal. Power accumulates. Power is the gravity that shapes, bends the rules to fit the interests of the powerful.

A few days ago in Cambodia an environmentalist was shot dead as he sought to lead a couple of reporters into a forest where illegal logging was apparently going on. He was shot dead by a soldier guarding against troublemakers like Chut Wutty, who led a Natural Resources Protection Group. He sought truth and justice. In the real world people on the side of truth and justice get into conflicts with powerful people. Push turns to shove, and a shove takes the conflict to the gun stage. "Above the law" means that a death of this kind is unlikely to lead to the arrest of the shooter—who, it turns out, was a soldier, later said to have shot himself (twice) in the chest with his own AK-47.

Chut Wutty is an example of someone who confronted a powerful interest. In this part of the world that confrontation is more likely than not going to end badly, and when the gun smoke clears, the body of the man seeking truth and justice will be revealed. In the real world there will be an "investigation" and no evidence will be found linking anyone powerful to the crime. There will be no trial. Only a dead gunman who killed himself.

China is in the spotlight for the impunity of Bo Xilai, ex-political heavyweight who by press accounts waged a reign of terror against "enemies" in his city of Chongqing, which has a population of 30 million people. Bo Xilai's wife is charged with murdering by poison British national Neil Heywood. She showed up shortly afterwards dressed in a Chinese Army general's uniform.

In the real world the most powerful people in Asia have political power. This is the Get-Out-of-Jail-Free card for them and their family, friends and associates. But what the downfall of Bo Xilai—a huge political event in China— illustrates is that a man may be powerful, but there may be more powerful men above him. It appears that Bo Xilai wiretapped the phone of President Hu Jintao when he was in Chongqing. No doubt he only wanted to know what good things the president was saying about him. Unlike American banks Bo Xilai wasn't too big to fail. The Communist Party pulled the plug and Bo Xilai, a feared, ever-powerful force who ruled with an iron fist, is now on the sidelines. In the real world the powerful fall only when they double-cross someone more powerful than they are.

High-tech surveillance on the Chinese scale doesn't come cheap. This year the Chinese government will spend around $110 billion on domestic security. Regional leaders like Bo Xilai have access to such systems. That allows these powerful regional leaders to keep watch on the Chinese counterparts to Chut Wutty. In the real world people who seek to remedy injustice need to be watched. And as we can see in the case of China, some significant cash is put into systems to scan the citizenry for such troublemakers.

When a 40-year-old blind Chinese lawyer named Chen Guangcheng escaped from house arrest, he found a way into the American embassy in Beijing. His fate is still unresolved. One thing is clear. Once such matters are thrust into the international spotlight, the authorities scramble for cover, citing the usual reason: it is a matter of internal interest and outsiders shouldn't poke their nose in domestic affairs. The powerful don't like other powerful people looking down at them. That causes loss of face.

Chen's "crime" was making noises about forced abortions and other repercussions of China's one-child policy, and the powerful wanted to turn down the volume by putting him and his family under house arrest—after he had already served over four years in jail for "damaging property and organising a mob to disturb traffic." His other crimes included organizing a petition to eliminate taxes on disabled farmers, signatures on a petition to close down a polluting paper factory and a successful law suit to force Beijing's subway operator to allow the blind to use the subway for free.

Clearly Chen was a world-class troublemaker for the powerful. They did what powerful people who are above the law do; they took him out of circulation. No more official charges for him? No problem, just put him and his family under house arrest. Have a squad of armed men circle the house and beat up the man, his wife and kid because, in the real world, you can.

Chen complained of mistreatment at the hands of authorities, and that included abuse of his wife and six-year-old daughter.

What has Chen asked for? Basically he's asked that government officials not be above the law. The *Toronto Star* quotes Chen as saying, "I also ask that the Chinese government safeguard the dignity of law and the interests of the people, as well as guarantee the safety of my family members."

The breaking news is Chen has checked out of the American embassy in Beijing and into a hospital—of his own volition, or so the American officials say. The American embassy is gaining the reputation of a halfway house for everyone from embattled police chiefs to blind activist lawyers. They get shelter, food and some counseling before being sent back to the street. The Americans apparently received an assurance from Chinese authorities that Chen would be treated like "an ordinary citizen." That shouldn't be a hard promise to keep because that was exactly how he was treated in the first place. Ordinary citizens are below the law; those in power above it. Those in between sometimes seek a middle ground in the foyer of the American embassy. You just know that ain't going to work the way they think it will.

Here's the executive summary. Chut Wutty is dead in Cambodia. Blind lawyer Chen Guangcheng, who was hiding out in the American embassy in Beijing, has decamped to a hospital where he will be treated as an ordinary citizen. And strict criminal libel lawyers in Thailand prevent naming the powerful killers who walk the streets of major cities in Thailand. That's another thing worth mentioning. Speech in the above-the-law jurisdiction is inevitably censored to make certain ordinary citizens don't start asking awkward questions about truth and justice.

Because in the real world, those above the law remain above the law, and those who seek truth and justice will wind up in an early grave or under house arrest or in the Chinese transitional guest room in the American embassy with a map of China and suggestions of where they might want to live next.

If you live in a country where the rule of law applies to the powerful, then you should light a little candle tonight and, despite all of the misfortunes of class, race and inequality, count yourself lucky that as an ordinary citizen you can raise your voice and ask for justice. You can go public with your grievances and your proposals for change, no matter that others disagree with you, and you can go home, turn on the TV and not worry that the government will send men around to beat up your wife and kid. Or to put a bullet through your head.

Because if you lived in the real world that most people occupy, you'd understand just how dangerous truth and justice can be, and you'd know that the costs of seeking them will fall like a ton of bricks on the person making such a noise.

Poison

Quick quiz: What is the first weapon that comes into your head when I ask you to name a murder weapon? Chances are you've chosen a gun, bomb, knife, sword or a blunt instrument. My guess is that you won't have chosen poison.

For young readers this murder weapon might bring to mind the band named Poison. They have shiny chrome skulls on their website.

From 331 BC onward the Romans used poison to lace their enemies' food and drink. The fad of resorting to fatal substances over a personal, business or political conflict ran through all classes of Romans. By medieval times the Arabs had developed arsenic, an odorless and clear substance, to kill a rival or enemy. There were no CSI teams in those days, so proving that someone was poisoned as opposed to dead from natural causes was more difficult. Asia joined the ranks of cultures where poison became a tool to eliminate competitors.

It is easy for anyone to buy poison from a local shop. Either pesticide or disinfectant, in sufficient doses, will kill a horse. And either product will snuff out the life of a man, woman or child.

William Shakespeare captured the essence of our fear in a line from *Henry VI, Part II*, Act III, Scene 2: "Hide not thy poison with such sugar'd words." In a word, poison works by deception. When a person pretends to offer friendship and hospitality, the recipient's guard is down. If someone pulls a gun or knife, we have no difficulty understanding the threat. But poison in our tea—that hits us in a fear region that lives way below the belt line.

Pick your poison: arsenic, antimony, mercury, lead and thallium. All have been used to murder.

Women historically had a number of motives to commit murder. Their civil, property, inheritance and marital rights were restricted in most places until the last hundred years. What better way to end a marriage or ensure the reception of a father's inheritance or cover up an indiscretion than to use a little *poudre de succession* or "inheritance powder"—the name the French gave to arsenic.

Poison and women are back in the news in Asia. And the case comes with all of the intrigue, deception, back-door financial dealings and corruption that would have left William Shakespeare struggling to catch his breath.

A young British businessman, Neil Heywood, died suddenly last November in China. The official cause was alcohol poisoning and heart attack. Only Neil Heywood, the father of two, didn't drink. Forty-one-year-olds don't normally die of heart attacks. One would have thought the British authorities might have made some inquiries. But at the time the British authorities accepted the Chinese verdict. Big mistake. The ground has shifted. The allegation made in China is that Gu Kailai, the lawyer and wife of the former Chongqing Communist Party secretary, poisoned Heywood.

That's a big deal. The theory being developed, now that Bo Xilai has been sidelined from his powerful position, is that the couple had used Heywood to transfer money abroad. The allegations are hundreds of millions of dollars. That's not the official salary for a Communist Party secretary, but it is a good indication of the economic opportunities that go with that position if the office holder is so inclined. The case is building that Heywood and Gu Kailai had a falling out over the commission that was to be paid to Heywood.

Soap operas, tabloid newspapers, talk shows all embrace such sordid cases and they can also join the ranks of the *New York Times* and the *Guardian* in allowing readers to follow what is bound to be one of the most interesting international murder cases in 2012. A murder case with potentially profound political implications for the Chinese Communist Party in the way it selects, monitors and disciplines members who cross the line where greed and murder override ideological purity. The CPC Central Committee has ordered a thorough investigation of the case. That doesn't happen often. In fact, old China hands would have to be consulted the last time the Central Committee investigated the possibility of a murder carried out by the wife of a high-ranking party official.

Now for the noir part. The murder case became so toxic in Chongqing that the police chief tried to defect to the US consulate. I'd like to have been a fly at the gate to the consulate as the police chief rolled up and explained to the 19-year-old marine on guard there that he was the chief of police and wanted to defect to America.

"A powerful woman will have me killed," I imagine he said—but I am a novelist. I am certain he said something more along the lines of, "I want to see the consul."

Wang Lijun, the police chief, must have looked like an emotional mess, glancing over his shoulder, chain-smoking, his uniform rumpled from being on the run for a few days and nights. "Yeah, right," the marine must have thought. "I let this guy inside and they'll be checking my urine for drugs until I'm 100 years old."

The American consulate, true to their creed of offering asylum to the oppressed and those about to be murdered by their own officials, did what you would expect. They turned Wang Lijun over to the authorities in Beijing. Maybe the rendition planes scheduled for Iraq were all booked up. We'll never know.

Now that Heywood's death has hit the tabloids, the British government has done what you'd pretty much expect them to do: ask the Chinese to investigate the circumstances of Heywood's death. Questions are being raised in the UK parliament and no doubt in whatever room the Central Committee sips its tea. What does the foreign secretary, William Hague, have to say according to the *Guardian*? "We now wish to see the conclusion of a full investigation that observes due process, is free from political interference, exposes the truth behind this tragic case and ensures that justice is done."

Free from political interference? Justice? Truth? Excuse me, exactly what alternate reality does Hague live in? The man should have his urine checked for drugs. There must be some substance that explains how tragedy has been converted into farce without anyone laughing. Or noticing that farce is more likely our existential finality.

Politics, jealousy and greed share a long history with poison as a partner in crime. This case is no exception. What makes Heywood's case one that may go down in the annals as a significant crime is the classic setting of court intrigue, betrayal, greed and power. Much as in *Game of Thrones*, a power struggle is afoot. In that whirlwind, Gu Kailai's guilt is what appears on the official stage.

But what happens backstage is likely far more interesting as the downfall of Bo comes at a time when a secretive generational shift is happening in China, and new, younger faces (men with less hair dye) are taking their places at the seats of power. No doubt taking a new oath to swear they will endeavor to instruct their wives not to resort to *poudre de succession* to eliminate foreigners. And also the wives must promise never to scare local police chiefs into defecting to America. That leaves such a bad black eye for the rest of the world to see.

Proportionality and Crime Suppression

"**P**unishment" is the term often used by lawyers, judges, prosecutors and the police to describe a sentence ordered by the State on someone found guilty of committing a crime. The idea of proportionality is that the amount of punishment inflicted should be measured against the damage or injury caused by the wrongdoer. The gravity of the punishment should fit the gravity of the crime. We don't sanction the death penalty for shoplifters, even though such a penalty might have the support of retailers, shopping mall owners, and the rest. Even though it might indeed be an effective deterrent to shoplifting, no Western country would enact such a law.

We shouldn't think that modern sensibilities and normative values have always defined what punishment is proportional to a crime. Our ancestors had much more capacity for the State spilling the blood of its citizens. For long periods of history, a high level of state violence was normal.

In 18th-century England there were 220 designated crimes for which the convicted felon would be hanged. Robbery, burglary as well as murder invited the hangman's rope. Britain no longer has a death penalty. The gradual shortening of the list of capital crimes from 220 to zero is a political and social development that indicates the majority of the population accepts the idea that capital punishment is disproportionate to any crime. Today, ninety-five countries have abolished capital punishment.

In places like China, North Korean, Yemen, Iran and the United States, capital punishment remains a penalty imposed by the State against its citizens convicted of certain crimes.

The BBC recently carried a story from Saudi Arabia of the beheading of a "witch." Fortune tellers and faith healers once risked the death penalty in the West. In Europe and elsewhere, heretics and blasphemers were burnt at the stake, nailed to crosses, torn apart on wheels or drowned, and no one—at least no one who had any real voice—thought these methods were cruel or unusual. Capital punishment often came after the person was tortured. We shudder when thinking about such public demonstrations of cruelty. But we'd be wrong to think that human nature has largely overcome its capacity to inflict horrific violence if the stakes are deemed high enough.

What you need to have done to be burnt at the stake is one issue; the other is burning people at the stake for any crime. What we find is that how a State carries out capital punishment also has changed over time. The electric chair and hanging have given way to lethal injection, giving a quasi-medical appearance to the procedure. Our modern sensibilities no longer accept state sanctioned death by beheading, hanging, shooting and stoning. In 2010 there were ten women and four men who remained under sentence of death by stoning in Nigeria, Pakistan and Iran. And along with the more graphic, cruel means of death, the idea of using torture on citizens has moved from commonly accepted to the category of a taboo. That is why in the Bush Administration convoluted arguments were made that "water-boarding" was an enhanced interrogation technique rather than torture. Much the same could have been said about the medieval rack.

Notions of universal fairness and equality also define proportionality. A punishment that is disproportionate to the crime raises issues of legitimacy of the State. In other words, the State in maintaining law and order is considered to be under constraint in how it inflicts punishment on its citizens. People in the West would be shocked if a faith healer were convicted witch and then beheaded in a public square in London or New York because the sentiment about what conduct is criminalized changed long ago. Similarly the State is required to control the rage and anger a vast majority of people may have toward an ethnic group or a class of people.

In 2003 the Thai government policy to invoke a war against drugs led to the extrajudicial killing of at least 2,500 "suspected" drug dealers. The campaign had overwhelming public support. Even though there was evidence a large number of these people were not drug dealers, the campaign was deemed a success. Given the nature of the crime and the extrajudicial punishment inflicted, the concept of proportionality was violated.

The idea of severity in terms of matching punishment to a crime shifts from one culture to another. Iran hangs children. The nature of what is a crime is fluid as well. And of course, there are the "victimless" crimes such as gambling, prostitution and drug use where the State seeks to regulate and control a range of behaviors they believe are adverse to the public interest, are immoral or violate a social norm.

So far I've looked at individuals who have committed acts that have harmed other individuals. Part of the function of a State is to stop revenge and feuds arising to settle scores. The Goldilocks Principle of not too hot and not too cold is a measured way to satisfy the victim and his/her family and to deter others from committing the same crime. But proportionality also applies, as a principle, to actions by the State against foreigners in the case of war and against its own citizens in the case of suppression of certain kinds of conduct.

In the case of war, the armed combatants are under a duty to tailor their military actions to cause minimal damage to civilian populations. There is a vast literature detailing what amounts to the transgression of proportionality rule in the time of war. The main message is that States waging war can't ignore the damage caused to civilian populations in their quest for military victory. Currently a United Nations war crime trial is under way in Phnom Penh, in which three members of the Khmer Rouge leadership are in the dock for crimes against humanity, a crime that enshrines the notion of disproportionate violence against a civilian population.

Historically the institutions of the State have reacted with disproportionate violence against citizens who have challenged the State's legitimacy, authority, sanctity or rulers. Threats, real or perceived by the State as being against its own interests, can easily descend into repression. Imprisoning people for political or religious opinions contrary to the myths, legends or official positions has a long history. Often the punishment in these cases is swift and severe, meant to serve as a warning to others to fall into line with the official position.

When people fail to fall into line or refuse to do so, we see the State intervene to preserve its authority, to suppress those challenging authority. Recent examples include police actions against OWS (Occupy Wall Street) demonstrators in the United States, the use of the military to repress demonstrators in what is called the Arab Spring in the Middle East and the use of harsh penalties in Thailand to restrict political expression.

The reaction to the security services in these countries has highlighted that when the elites of a State feel an existential threat, the first casualty is proportionality in striking back. The modern State has been credited with civilizing the general population, reducing dramatically citizen-on-citizen acts of violence. The UN has sought to play the role as the civilizing influence on States themselves when they use violence against their own citizens.

The reality is the UN can use war crime trials such as the one going on in Cambodia as warnings about the limits on state violence. But does it actually deter the actions of the State? Judging from the action of many state players in modern times, the leaders have concluded that a lot of violence can be employed against citizens before they are hauled off to a UN war crime tribunal. These players don't think of themselves as criminals, and that is part of the problem. Institutions that believe in the legitimacy of their actions under law are carrying out the excess of violence.

We live in a time when officials who are responsible for violence believe that proportionality doesn't apply to them or their actions. The next great awakening in criminal justice will be that state actors can't be trusted to use measured responses when they feel threatened. Who will civilize the State? And who will punish the State? We are still in the 18th century when it comes to addressing these questions. It may take another 200 years before the answers appear. The way forward will be to establish the proportionality principle as a line that will define more clearly how to monitor what justifies a State in using its armories to inflict violence against its own people.

Part V

Government, Crime and Technology

He Said, She Said

Technology is the major driver of change in our world. Creative destruction is often used to describe the train-wreck-like effect that new technology has as it destroys jobs, industries (think of publishing and newspapers), institutions and markets. The bodies left in the path of creative destruction can be charted by examining the technological history as battle axes and arrows were replaced by muskets and cannon, only to be replaced by machine guns and then onto atomic bombs. Now drones deliver lethal ordnance by remote control.

What hasn't kept pace with the rate of technological change is the way our brains process the Big Data that washes over our lives. It is likely that our cognitive biases and the narratives we invent from the patterns of information that stream through our lives daily are little changed over thousands of years. The fundamental neural wiring is 100,000 years old.

There is evidence of a disconnect between the new methods, structures and networks that we have invented and how we continue to perceive and behave in the world. Most people's behavior and mindset appear immune to technological change. The world inside their head is largely untouched by innovation. If you want to witness cognitive limitation, spend a little time in a courtroom, a police station or a legislative assembly.

One of the reasons that crime stories, mysteries and courtroom dramas remain highly popular as novels, TV programs and movies is that people can relate to the conflicts in perception, the stories, the mistakes, the lies and the biases. I suspect it has always been so. We aren't robots. We are cognitively flawed human beings who have the simplistic idea that since we innovate, we too have benefited from this technology in the way we behave and think.

That notion is plain wrong.

Lawyers, judges, prosecutors and police spend lifetimes listening to conflicting versions of events from those directly involved and bystanders. I call this the magic realm of "He said, she said." As in a tennis match, each player hits the ball across the net to win a point, only to find the ball somehow comes back. In the courtroom game people bring their points of view, emotions, hindsight and biases and assume their memory is the complete record of the experience, and any other version is wrong, biased and based on lies and fraud.

While technological changes designed to update our cognitive abilities may reduce biases and flaws in the distant future, there is an intermediate period of change that is happening now to redefine the "He said, she said" world of diverse, confused and biased memory recall. In the real world, who "he" is and who "she" is, at least in my part of the world, is a significant factor in determining what happened.

One such technology is the car camera. Real-time video cameras with high-resolution lenses that are fixed to your dashboard or rearview mirror can record everything within a 150-degree view of the road as you drive. In Thailand, where I drive on the highway a couple of times a week,

I witness something approaching low-level warfare on wheels. That is likely my bias talking. But in the event of an accident, having the video footage leading up to the event should in theory eliminate the relative social status of the drivers as a factor in determining what happened. Having a car camera that also records your speed should also be an advantage when the police stop and say that you were speeding.

I can see a couple of flaws in this technology, however. It is possible the video recording could be confiscated and "lost" (this has happened not with car cameras but with CCTV cameras in Thailand on occasion). Some places in the United States have made it illegal to photograph or video the police. Shaking off our long history of cognitive biases will be much more difficult than landing a man on the moon.

From judges to cops, to school teachers, prison guards, welfare officers, bankers and government officials, certain people's status has given them an edge when the stories they tell conflict with the stories told by those beneath their level of power and authority. As more and more ways of monitoring come on the market, we hear the cry of loss of freedom and free will. That is mainly an illusion. We have enjoyed only a limited amount of freedom since we became domesticated about 9,000 years ago, and free will was one of those "just so" stories we accepted on faith.

The yoke of our flawed cognitive abilities and authority structures based on power rather than facts or truth won't be overturned anytime soon as that is the nature of who we are. Revising our cognitive abilities won't be easy.

Just as the modern GPS on iPads, cell phones and other devices reduces the chances of us getting lost when we travel to a new destination, the car camera promises to resolve the

"He said, she said" stalemate by producing a neutral way to establish the facts of what happened.

Those in power and authority will hate being challenged with the Third Eye. The technological eye that lacks bias is not obedient to authority and has no past or reputation to defend.

Forcing People to Shut Up or Throw Up

You're not the only one looking to high-tech to solve all of your problems. Repressive and not (to date) so repressive governments alike are taking notice of new weapons technology.

If you are a protester or demonstrator, your future will likely include being made mute or stuttering uncontrollably and throwing up. These weapons are currently in development and in some cases are operationally ready. Welcome to the Brave New World of high-tech equipped security forces.

Controlling people is something governments have traditionally sought to achieve. There is a long history of political demonstrations and most of it is violent, repressive and bloody. Power instinctively seeks to stamp out challengers. Thumbs screws, the rack, beheadings, the chopping off of hands, arms or legs and burning at the stake often drew large crowds who found that sort of thing highly entertaining.

Except for a few places, we don't live in that world any more. Our world is one of modern technology that has rapidly added new weapons to the arsenal of governments. CCTV surveillance cameras and the high-tech monitoring of phone calls and online activities are already in place. The newest technology pushes the life of demonstrators from difficult to miserable.

We've entered an age of mass demonstrations brought to us in news reports from many countries around the world. The powerful would like a neat way to cause the speakers in such crowds to find themselves either unable to speak or dizzy to the point of vomiting. Speech may be free, but those who insist on exercising their right can still be made to pay a high fee.

Police forces in America and many other countries have become militarized. Crime fighting is more warlike than ever before. The new weapons on the ground and those patrolling the skies such as Predator drones give the cop/soldier hybrids better information, firepower and protection against return fire. It is better to think of the cops and soldiers as one unified security force with shared weapons, intelligence and tactics to marginalize common enemies. That includes demonstrators.

A number of the new high-tech toys fall in the category of shock-and-awe firepower, stealth capability and protective gear for the cops/soldiers. That means that bank robbers, car thieves and muggers will find it increasingly more dangerous to carry out their self-employment. They won't be missed.

What governments wish us to believe is that dangerous, violent criminals—when they aren't robbing banks or stealing cars or handbags—are attending political rallies and demonstrations. However, the cops/soldiers (the security forces) are finding the general public is disinclined to support their decision to order their security forces to shoot demonstrators in the streets. Even repressive governments have come to understand that slaughtering demonstrators is bad public relations. And such behavior invites charges of crimes against humanity and genocide and a public trial in Geneva.

The Chinese government labels demonstrators in Tibet as "outcasts, criminals and mentally ill" people. This description, with a few local variations, pops up on the lips of politicians in many countries once activists and protesters accumulate in crowds to challenge the central authority. How best to stop demonstrators has been the work of some creative scientific minds. The first goal is to disperse a crowd. Second, weapons are needed to discourage, demoralize or disable people who demonstrate against the government. These are government goals in many places.

In the bad old days the security forces used rubber bullets, tear gas and water canons. These low-tech responses to demonstrations only partially worked. In a large political demonstration of 50,000 people or more, a high-tech response is needed. What's the latest way for the political class to mess with the rest of us?

One answer is the LRAD (long-range acoustic device). This little baby will blast 95-plus decibels of sound—heavy metal music or a cat in heat—at the crowd. That's loud, and later models will likely burst eardrums. Though at this stage of development, I am not certain a crowd in Thailand would notice 95 decibels of sound as anything other than normal. But that is another matter.

Scientists are working to increase the range of the LRAD and combine it with other features, such as scents. These good scientists have done research on what smells induce uncontrolled vomiting, inability to maintain balance and reduced sensory capability. The political demonstration starts to look like an alliance of binge eaters, acidheads and disabled lap dancers with everyone bumping into each other on their rubbery legs. Some of the Bangkok *klong* water will at last find a market, as it could be bottled and sold to the manufacturers of the new LRAD for ammo. The slogan will be along the lines of, "KlongBomb: Smells worse than shit" and "Knocks out a skunk." Politicians will claim that Bangkok is an LRAD ammo "hub."

But the remaining problem for security forces is leaders who manage to hold their ground, demonstrators for whom the smell of shit is only incitement to get more fired up. For these people the scientists have come up with the Speech Jammer. The Japanese came up with this wonderful idea. Who wouldn't want their own jammer for use against the loud, rude talkers who always manage to get a table next to yours at a restaurant or a seat beside you on the subway or at the cinema or a lecture?

But do you want your government using them on you when you beg to disagree?

Here's how the Speech Jammer works. It delays a speaker's words for a couple hundred milliseconds and blast the words back at the speaker. The technical term is "auditory feedback." What this means is the device messes with out brain's cognitive processes. In non-technical terms it makes you stutter. Apparently these jammers were originally developed to help people who stutter to overcome this disability. Of course the security forces of the world often see a golden lining in such developments and wondered whether, since it cures stuttering, it might be tweaked to make people stutter. The answer is, "Yes, General, you can turn this baby on the speaker on the stage and turn him or her into an incoherent, jabbering fool." And when you label the leader of the demonstration an incoherent, jabbering fool, you can replay the words from his or her latest speech as Exhibit A.

Shut up or I'll jam you into a stuttering retard. That is an improvement on stop or I'll shoot you. But this is only the beta model. Ten, twenty years down the road, the implant versions will be ready, and demonstration leaders will have sentences handed down that include insertion of such devices.

We have eight more years left in this decade. By the time 2020 rolls around, the security forces will have effectively curtailed public demonstrations as they will have their squares and streets ringed with high-tech weapons that make such protest impossible. We are just at the start of the civilian repression that lies ahead. It's not just a pre-Enlightenment dark age that threatens all of us; it is that cone of silence in which we are left alone with our thoughts. And those too are on the high-tech drawing board for the post-2020 world.

Data Mining in the Age of Terrorism

hai police arrested two terrorist suspects and were searching for a third man after three reported bombings in Bangkok on February 14, 2012. The *Bangkok Post* reported that the bombings took place on Sukhumvit Road (Soi 71) in a crowded residential area of Bangkok. It appears one of the blast happened in the alleged terrorists' living quarters.

One suspected terrorist was arrested at Suvarnbhumi Airport, Bangkok's main airport, as he was about to board a flight to Kuala Lumpur. Another suspect, who had apparently sustained injuries during the bomb blast in the house, was further injured when a grenade he reportedly threw at police bounced back, blowing off both of his legs. The house occupied by the three men was searched by police, who discovered C-4 plastic explosives along with detonating devices. Based upon their travel documents, the three men are believed to be Iranians.

The target of their attack at this stage of the police investigation remains unclear, as does the possibility of whether a suicide mission was planned by the trio. From the initial reported evidence, it is difficult to conclude they were trained professionals.

For the last month or so, American authorities have issued travel advisories to their citizens, warning them of possible terrorist attacks in Bangkok. Thai authorities had sought to have the United States (and a number of other countries that followed the American lead by issuing similar travel advisories of their own) withdraw their advisories as the warnings were thought to have a potentially negative impact on tourism.

The Bangkok bombing illustrates the tension between warnings of possible terrorist attacks and the damage such warnings have on local economies. Protecting one's own citizens can and does conflict with the interests of other countries that rely on the tourism dollar. International crime prevention is difficult as law enforcement is local and cooperation can be uneven. That means the best other countries can hope to achieve is to alert their citizens who travel abroad about the possible risks of criminal activity, including terrorism. No country likes to be on the receiving end of such an official warning, as not only does it have adverse economic impact, but it also reflects on the competence, capability and intelligence gathering and assessment of local law enforcement agencies in charges of security.

In the past the target country and the country giving the warning have found themselves in public relations wars over which set of officials has superior intelligence, information and risk assessment capability. In the immediate future the data divide between nations will be larger than the wealth divide. It is likely that the Americans and the Chinese will lead on the front of cutting-edge technology, which will exponentially accelerate the scope, nature and quantity of data collected and the ability to analyze, assess and evaluate it. The distinction will lie between the data-haves and the data-have-nots. An information arms race has already started. Suspicion and doubt will follow in the wake of database monopolies that have the potential power to ruin local economic fortunes. Like control over sea lanes, control over data lanes will be crucial for development and political power. Information will be the predominate resource, the value of which will outstrip all other resources.

We are at the beginning of a phase transition in data collection and mining. For a glimpse of the future, have a look at Recorded Future Inc. (at http://en.wikipedia.org/wiki/Recorded_Future), funded by Google and the CIA, which is in the business of web intelligence and predictive analytics for the prediction future events. Astrologers, politicians and priests have traditionally been at the forefront of the business of predicting the future. Recorded Future Inc., a private company, is poised at the threshold of a new sort of future. This future is a place where the most valuable of all resources will be privatized. And that raises a number of questions about the continuing role and importance of government in data collecting and mining, privacy, intellectual property law and shifts of power arrangements in business, finance, medicine, universities, investing and banking. There is a good argument that governments will not win this race. Corporations already have a head start.

My big idea is that certain elements of the criminal justice system will soon have the capacity to acquire and store an exponential amount of information, including psychological profiles, medical histories, iris scans, childhood illnesses and school absence records, test scores, teacher evaluations, immunizations, family backgrounds, DNA, detailed neurological data and sequencing, work records, employer evaluations, emails and the data of Facebook accounts, Twitter and other social network media. These "wells" of information will be linked into vast reservoirs that will be larger than their individual parts. Those who control that network of information will know the future before it happens.

We are some distance from that day.

But it is only a matter of time before the old barriers used to screen off that data will be dismantled or overrun. Over time, as more and more people voluntarily disclose their personal histories and private information on the social networks, the space for privacy will shrink and the value of privacy will unlikely survive the quest to predict the future.

Law enforcement agencies will rely on data feeds and analysis programs to evaluate large amounts of information in order to deploy resources to monitor the most vulnerable neighborhoods. Schools, parks, public centers will all have profiles on those who use those facilities, and the information will be updated constantly. Future cops will start their shifts by analyzing the latest day and time markers, such as holidays, sporting events, concerts, as well as unusual signs within networks of individuals, looking for data matches that correlate with past criminal activity, and use software that will efficiently assign security resources to prevent the crime through targeted, scaled-up police presence. Surveillance, detection and intervention will be digitally determined, coordinating events detached from "gut feelings." Crime is largely possible because criminals exploit the lack of information in the hands of authorities. Inefficiencies in deployment of policing resources are also a criminal's friend.

But that is about to change.

Massive information is difficult to manage. We would likely, at the current state of development, run out of our capacity to manage it as the storage of information outstrips our ability to process, analyze and assess for patterns and correlations. That is where data mining comes in. Mathematics will gradually tame and control the torrent of information. You will hear a lot more about Power Laws in the future—that is, a mathematical connection existing between the frequency and factors constituting an event. This is the networked world of correlations. For example, correlations between the sale of beer and pizza, the issuances of traffic citations, the number of drug arrests, divorce and abortion rates, deportation of illegal aliens and reruns of *The Wire* may indicate police resources should be reallocated from homicide to domestic violence within a sector of the city.

In the future the most important qualification for a politician may be his or her science background, as the job will require interpreting a complex world of new technologies for a general population. The risk is that, at some point, no human being will be able to fully grasp such a system without the aid of artificial intelligence.

That day may be a long way off, as Professor Paulos recently wrote in an article titled "Why Don't Americans Elect Scientists?" for the *New York Times* (February 13, 2012). In future, political leaders will need a new set of skills to understand the implications of probability distribution theory and the risks, benefits, costs and dangers inherent in applying it. We will live in a world of probabilities calculated by artificial intelligence systems. That world will include corporations, individuals and government agencies that will know far more about each of us that we can know about it or others around us.

Future Bangkok bombers will have more difficulty carrying out their operations. That is the theory. Governments such as that of Thailand will need to adjust to the reality where warnings are issued based on large pools of information pointing to the probability of a terrorist attack. Of course, probability is not certainty. But the political space to ignore probability distribution assessment will be vastly diminished in the future.

We are in the midst of a huge transition in how we acquire, store, access, analyze and use information. Technological breakthroughs will accelerate the creation of information filters that aren't tainted by the usual fear and loathing that human intelligence brings. The hard, cold, objective assessment will drive authorities to take precautions because the cost of ignoring such an assessment will become too high.

There will be resistance to the kind of changes the new, technologically wired information system will bring to the customary ways of doing things in society and the way we think about ourselves.

There is a close correlation between conservative political associations and religion or sacred quasi-religious beliefs. A recent article for *The Atlantic* by Richard Florida titled "*This Is Why America Keeps Getting More Conservative*" illustrates why America has become vastly more conservative over time. The least educated, lowest-income earners and the most religious are also likely to be the most hostile to science. Perhaps this answers Professor Paulos's question as to why scientists aren't elected in America while those with fundamentalist religious beliefs at odds with science are routinely elected.

Over the next decade or two, as science advances, as those who embrace religious dogma, myth, fable and literal interpretations of ancient religious texts and those who have mastered the digital world of infinite information computing collide, a battle will be waged between faith and science. It will be a battle for hearts and minds as to which side is better able to predict the future of disturbances, riots, revolutions or market crashes. The probability is that the neurological reason for religion will have been decoded and an abundantly more efficient way of coping with fear, uncertainty, survival, authority, threat and hostility will appear. Once the mystery of the ancient amygdala's role in overriding reason is revealed, religion will lose its traction.

Finally, beyond religion is another widely-accepted core concept: free will. As sacred cows go, free will is the prize heifer. It, too, will come under close examination. It is likely that we will learn that our ideas about free will were shorthand expressions for insufficient, error-prone or unreliable information in complex systems that, because they made outcomes uncertain, meant we had choice, though in fact the inefficient information system only made it appear that we had choice.

With infinite information, artificial intelligence, unlimited broadband, neurological enhancements and nanotechnology, our sense of free will, like religion, will erode and vanish as a personal operating system.

Science, which gave us evolution, is undergoing a revolution. Political science, religion, our sense of self, individuality, crime and criminals will all be overhauled and re-evaluated in the process. How we catch criminals and what we do with them once they're caught may one day fall to scientists to determine rather than a cop, prosecutor and judge. But that is in the future. As for today, science works quietly in the background, while the usual voices urge us to be fearful and to seek protection under the big umbrella of agencies and officials who tell us when to worry and what to worry about, and remind us to honor our communal sense of sacredness as our best defense against an uncertain and unsafe world. This will change in the lifetime of our children and grandchildren, who will look back on the day of the three bombers in Bangkok and wonder how we ever lived inside such a primitive information network.

Big Data Noir

No noir story will match the ones told by Big Data. In the future, noir stories will emerge from Big Data, only they won't be fiction. Authors of crime fiction—noir, hardboiled or otherwise—are like monks writing manuscripts before the printing press. Our end will be as noir as their end. Here's the story of how that will come about.

I've thought of writing as a way to discover and explore vanishing points, light fading to the void of total darkness. That is the point where we can no longer predict what will happen next. It is a brick wall. A blank. We stop at the door to the future and are resigned it will never open.

In *Big Data: A Revolution.*, authors Viktor Mayer-Schönberger and Kenneth Cukier have opened that door a crack. But don't buy this book. You don't really want to know what is inside our near future in the data-time-space spectrum.

Toward the end of this provocative book, the authors sum up their message: "The ground beneath our feet is shifting. Old certainties are being questioned. Big data requires a fresh discussion of the nature of decision-making, destiny, justice."

That is only the beginning of the transformation that will happen within our lifetime. It is already happening, and it's started to come into the open—the huge weight and force of Big Data and the hunger of power to own it, share it, distribute it and exploit it. We are in the middle of that Big Data war. Government officials and big business owners are in their bunkers figuring out what to do next. No one has explained clearly what is at stake, the options or the current state of play. *Big Data: A Revolution* attempts to provide context and meaning in an era where data is no longer scarce or expensive but readily available and infinitely valuable in making predictions about future outcomes.

Our preferences, attitudes and mental states will be predicted with advanced probability software and hundreds of millions of equations—and that raises a number of questions.

It is happening now as you read this essay. You are the composite of your data. Your choices, likes, purchases, friends, emotional connections and routines have been data-fied. This data of your past can't be erased, deleted or changed; it will follow you wherever you go into the future. The days of starting over are finished. You can never go missing or disappear completely as you pull behind yourself a history that is your digital DNA.

Your mental thumbprint is permanently registered in the metadata system and one of the whorls identifying your interest is this book. It doesn't stop there. Others who read this book are linked to you as an associate. That affiliation data is stored in the system. Websites, blogs and online book portals are hoovered for information, and this is how Big Data continues to grow four times faster than America's GNP. There is a probability that you share certain habits or buying traits, or be connected to some free-thinking troublemakers who enjoy reading outlier essays.

You can no longer control, handle, supervise or understand the scale and scope of your data or Big Data.

But we have seen nothing yet. Big Data is set to grow exponentially. Some of it will be extremely useful in understanding and dealing with important problems like climate change and diseases, or advancing entire domains such as physics, chemistry and mathematics. The assumption is that our understanding of the world, our ability to describe it and predict it, is limited by our current quantification of data.

To fully exploit the potential of Big Data, we need to appreciate the scale and scope of the power that comes from collecting, storing, distributing, selling and analyzing the range of correlations that emerge when N = All. We will also pay a substantial price. Big Data will not be ours without some changes wrought on our long-standing beliefs, habits, attitudes and customs. The next stage of development is data. It is being built from masses of data as you read this essay. Real economic, social and political power will reside inside them.

Since the 13th century we have searched for answers about the world and our behavior that are precise and exact, and sought to establish causation between events, people and things. Our quest is to know if what we believe about the world is true or false, right or wrong, good or bad. But when we address the implications of Big Data, we bring our moral and emotional sense of being in the world in the crosshairs.

Big Data doesn't predict with exactness; it premises that reality is messy and data can provide a probability of what will emerge in the future. Big Data promises a set of predicted outcomes according to a scale of probability based on what will likely happen. In turn, we give up the mission to understand why something has happened or may happen. The "why" question is one that asks about causes to explain what is the nature of the world. Big Data leaves causation to the side because it is not helpful. The messiness of reality renders inquiries about causation and precision less reliable. These ideas spring from the old way of thinking wherein sense had to be made of limited information and data. Causation and precision are relics of data scarcity and can be largely ignored as correlation is sufficient in the world of Big Data. Limited or Little Data required us to formulate a theory about what we'd expect the Little Data to prove, and then we used the Limited Data to test whether it supported or failed to support the theory. Think of climate change and the theory of CO_2 concentration as the cause. That's the old way of using Limited Data modeling.

The very randomness of Big Data yields a probability analysis that is more useful and predictive than a targeted, sample size of data. Sampling of data, the default measurement of the world, has become or will very soon become obsolete. Those conducting the data gathering in the past lacked the tools (processing speed, storage facilities, etc.) to collect Big Data and the tools (software and algorithms) to analyze such vast quantities of it. They opted for precision, sampling and theory testing. This old paradigm goes out the window with Big Data in many cases. With the full dataset available, researchers can explore many more angles and perspectives, whether it is predicting the next bird flu outbreak or the outcome of sumo wrestling matches in Japan.

Big Data has the capacity to scale entire populations of a city, region or country. Now when all telephone calls, emails, Internet searches, Twitter mentions and retweets, and Facebook "likes" are captured and stored, this isn't a *sampling*; it is the whole enchilada. "[W]e can accept some messiness in return for scale. 'Sometimes two plus two can equal 3.9, and that is good enough.'"

We already have an example of the limits of our capacity when tested against advanced algorithms. There are chess algorithms that are used once the computer has six or fewer pieces left on the board that allow the computer to process the probability for *every* possible move (N = all). The *Big Data* authors conclude, "No human will ever be able to outplay the system."

We have created a Big Data system that is much better at making predictions about outcomes than we can manage with our native brain power. We humans have dropped down in the league ranking of the best, fastest brain processing capacity in the world. In coming up with a translation program, Google didn't test a billion words, they used a trillion. Its services cover 60 languages and are more accurate than other systems. It won't be long until online translators, like chess-playing computers, will perform vastly better than any human being.

Big Data also demonstrates the transition in thinking between viewing the reality of the world as not only a messy place but one in which predictions of what will happen rest on correlations that emerge from data. Amazon has recommendations for you. Each time you visit Amazon they remember your digital history and present you with the kind of books that from your prior purchases indicate you are a "reader of interest." One-third of Amazon's business is from buyers like you who click on and buy the recommended purchase. For Netflix online rentals that come from the company's recommendations account for seventy-five percent of all business.

Amazon and Netflix offer two good examples of how using probability tools can increase the revenue of a company. There is no certainty that you will buy the recommended book on Amazon or rent the recommended film online from Netflix, but you can see how probability makes the effort pay off in rich rewards for both companies.

Big Data can't tell Amazon *why* you buy a particular title. Indeed it is not interested in the why question; it is focused on what you are likely to buy given your past purchases and searches through their catalogue of books. The data opens up links that are also useful. A secondary use of the same data may show that California international crime fiction readers are more likely to book a ticket to Beijing, Tokyo, Hong Kong or Bangkok, and targeting them with discounted fares may increase sales. The big deal about Big Data is that it has the potential for so many uses, and many of those uses will only become apparent much later. That's one reason why storing data for long periods is in the interest of business and governments, and they will fight to keep this option; they want indefinite storage as they can't predict what future technical and social dynamics might arise, and they want all of the cards, old and new, on the table.

We were born into a world that was very poor in information. Our beliefs, our political and social structures, our science and education were created from a small sampling of the information. We've spent our lives making decisions, forming opinions and making judgments based on limited data that could not yield precise answers about the state of the world and each other. We are wired to look for causation. In the Big Data world we are told this is delusion. There is no math that can easily show causal links, but correlations are easily translated into mathematical equations.

Big Data, the book, also looks at the "risk [of] falling victim to a dictatorship of data." While Amazon uses algorithms to recommend books, lawn mowers, watches and clothes to you, there is the potential for repression if the gathering, storage, use and distribution are carried out in secret. We don't know the limits that push back against the collection and use of Big Data. In a generation people will look back and see our time as the tipping point when we lost privacy. The Big Data world will continue to strip away the possibility of privacy. Privacy existed because of the messiness of information, it's limited nature and the expense and difficulty of collecting information about the world. You once had the power to divulge personal information. In the average day, you willingly and largely unknowingly disclose pieces of data about yourself—your likes, dislikes, activities, friends, purchases, health, schooling, and plans. We've uploaded our life onto the common Big Data network, a small fragment at a time, and by doing so we are forfeiting our own privacy. Privacy as we know it will vanish.

Crime and punishment will change as will opinions about proof beyond a reasonable doubt and the presumption of innocence. If Big Data can show a correlation between a person's Big Data/information file that he has, say, a 79 percent chance of committing rape or murder within the next three years, will the state make a decision that this "probable perpetrator" should be removed from society in order to protect society? The state would hold this person not because he's committed a crime but because it predicts he will offend in the future. Many people may feel that in such cases the state should intervene and prevent the harm from happening.

The *Big Data* authors find that "the very idea of penalizing based on propensities is nauseating." The future causes a sense of vertigo. It doesn't share our values or our thinking, or account for the difference between potential actions and the real thing. The authors fall back on the premise that the problem isn't intrinsic to Big Data but lies in the way we will use the predictions. The irony is the book is a call to loosen our fixation on causation and theories, and to learn to embrace messiness and predictability. When push comes to shove on preventive detentions, the authors retreat back into the world of causation and find decisions based on predictions "nauseating." My view is that once we jettison causation in the Big Data world, the use of predictions won't be easily caged inside Amazon and Netflix's world of recommendations. The data will get bigger, the predictions more accurate, and once that happens, "assigning" guilt based on a person's actions will look like another example of medieval thinking.

An important takeaway from *Big Data* is that in a world of Big Data, "when much of data's value is in secondary uses that may have been unimagined when the data was collected, such a mechanism to ensure privacy is no longer suitable." The debate we will soon have is what is the continuing role of human agency in deciding individual responsibility for actions. Another part of that debate will be whether the decisions of Big Data will ultimately be made by machines. Humans will likely never fully understand or control their moves any more than an international grand master of chess can do so in a game against Big Blue. Time moves on as does the debate, and the tools continue to improve with faster processors, larger memory capacity and better algorithms. We will wake up one day to find that "rational thought" and "free choice" are no longer part of the world that we control.

The data story doesn't end with Big Data. There is no endgame, as has always been the case with new technologies. Each innovation seems so incredible that we can't imagine an improvement. Remember the Beta videocassettes? Our current technologies for Big Data will look like Beta cassettes in five to ten years—probably much sooner—as the period of change has accelerated from centuries to decades to years and looks ready to upend existing technologies in months. This period is a prelude to a much bigger transition in humanity's quest to understand the world and our place in it. We have gone "from compass and sextant to telescope and radar to today's GPS." Compared to the promise of what lies in our immediate future, our existing technologies to harness Big Data will be judged by future generations as akin to finger-painting a horse on a cave wall.

Buy *Big Data* and give it to someone on whom you want to drop a freight load of sleepless nights. My predictions about the scale and scope of Big Data, what will replace it and how we will change our values and attitudes as a result are beyond what we now know. It seems that all bets are off as to whether this transition will be easy or smooth. Adjust to the fact that others will have infinitely greater information about you than you can ever imagine. You have become datafied. You can't shake free, you can't hide, you can't go missing, and you can't even hold your own ground.

The founder of Amazon has bought the *Washington Post*. Will the owner use the newspaper to suggest to politicians and others which policies, regulations and laws they should adopt? Will somewhere between one-third and seventy-five percent of the *Post*'s readers click on and download those recommendations into their memory? The sale of the *Post* is not just another sale of a newspaper to someone who is very rich; it is the sale of the newspaper to one of the founders of the new paradigm of gathering and distributing information. It is as if the owner of printing press bought a failing monastery and scribes writing manuscripts. You know that change is coming.

You'd be a fool to bet against the odds that one morning you will wake up to the fact that you live inside a data *panopticon* and there is no way out. Not heard of panopticon? Get used to seeing more references to that word. It is the prevailing metaphor of our time.

Inside Galileo's Fear Chamber

alileo has much to teach us about the nature of fear. He learned all about the suppression and intimidation that having an alternative worldview can bring. Belief systems rest on a unified, consistent and cohesive set of ideas. Galileo, the Wikileaks front man of his age, championed the theory that the earth isn't the center of the universe. The idea had originated with Copernicus twenty years earlier and was revoluntionary in its time—the sun was at the center of the universe and the earth and other planets revolved around the sun.

In 1633 Galileo was charged with heresy. No doubt that beyond his scientific knowledge, Galileo knew a thing or two about the kind of torture that his heresy might unleash if he failed to repudiate his view. He had a choice—continue to advocate the Copernicus heresy or face torture. Love of knowledge and the emotion of fear of pain and suffering must have dueled inside Galileo's mind as they have inside the minds of countless men and women ever since.

He endured the Inquisition and was found guilty of having been "*vehemently suspect of heresy*" for his support of the Copernicus view of the universe. The verdict required Galileo to "abjure, curse and detest" Copernicus view. After he recanted, his sentence of imprisonment was commuted to lifelong house arrest. His book *Dialogue* was banned, and he was forbidden to write anything in the future. That ban wasn't lifted until 1718.

More than 300 years after his persecution Pope Pius XII said of Galileo that he was among the "*most audacious heroes of research … not afraid of the stumbling blocks and the risks on the way, nor fearful of the funereal monuments.*" As a testimony to an example of revisionist's history, Galileo's case is tough to beat.

Despite Copernicus's heliocentric view of the universe, the Christian belief system and the institution of the Church had not been destroyed. The fear of the alternative theory of the cosmos had been irrational. But that is the nature of fear.

Recently I wrote about the campaign in Melbourne, Australia, by government authorities to use the image of a rhino to provoke a sense of fear of people driving and walking near the tram system. What does Galileo have to do with the rhino campaign in Melbourne?

What could link the fear instilled by authorities such as the medieval church in defense of its belief system and the modern manufacture of a fear when none naturally exists?

The answer is existential. In the case of Galileo the church feared that if an alternative to its worldview were allowed to go unchallenged, its authority, status and role might be not just undermined but destroyed. Suppression and intimidation by authorities to preserve a worldview is their way of signaling that no alternative worldview will be allowed. Belief in the absolute view is the only legitimate way of understanding, explaining and accepting the universe, political, social and economic life. As Galileo discovered, when the study of objective facts led to a conclusion that the worldview required revision, which crossed an official line and demolished a central tenet of the belief system, something had to give. And it wasn't going to be the true believers.

Galileo's support of the Copernican universe caused church authorities to experience an existential crisis. To the mind of the official church Galileo's view was intolerable. There were a couple of reasons for this fear. The first was the loss of control over the understanding of the nature of the cosmos. That had been a Church monopoly and cartels don't easily open up to competition to outsiders. The second reason was that the possible acceptance of this alternative view of the universe made them fearful their beliefs and church would be destroyed. Allowing Galileo to proceed with his Copernican logic caused the fear of something like the meteorite that struck the Yucatan Peninsula 65 million years ago, causing mass extinction. In the face of the potential oblivion of their belief system, its institutions, the rituals, the priesthood and the community founded upon belief and ritual, the Inquisition turned to repression. When faced with loss of control of the message, turning the screws on the thumbs of the messenger is a time-honoured tradition.

The threat, the fear lies in the alternatives to any belief or institutions resting on a set of assumptions. There might be a better explanation in the alternatives to an existing belief system. Established institutions found their legitimacy on beliefs that are static, eternal and absolute. That is a dangerous game. It means someone, somewhere, whether Galileo or someone like him, may ultimately succeed in presenting compelling evidence contrary to the established explanation.

The conflict between old beliefs and new evidence exposing flaws or overturning the old beliefs entirely is a mortal battle. In this struggle the existing authorities have the advantage of power, which is used to defend to the death the old beliefs and institutions.

When institutions and their infrastructure of beliefs are under attack, their back to the wall, and with a sense that the survival of an entire system at stake, it is no surprise that brute force and threats are in the short run effective in silencing the Galileos and their information, data and evidence.

Galileo must repent. Or Galileo will be imprisoned, tortured, exiled, murdered, disappeared or sent to Room 101 and strapped into George Winston's chair.

Officials who patrol the borders of a belief system based on absolutist principles looking for the next Galileo aren't pluralists or open-minded. Such qualities of thought are not suited to finding and eliminating all ideas that represent existential threats to the belief system. They scan the Internet like astronomers scanning the horizon for the killer meteorite on a collision course with Earth.

True power rests with those who have the authority to absolutely reject an idea and label the messenger an apostate. Once the patrols appeal to the necessity of protecting their beliefs, and most people go along, it is only a matter of time before it becomes apparent that those on patrol are difficult to control or restrain—as any hint of criticism, dissent, questioning or challenge brings the Galileo solution.

Fear us. Fear our ability to make you change your mind about the alternatives you have proclaimed to our beliefs. It is up to you. After all, it is your big, new idea or the water board (which by medieval torture methods would have been viewed as benign). History has been hard on Galileo for his submission to authority, his official recanting. Would you have gone to the torture chamber for an alternative vision of the universe? Would your reservoir of courage have drained as your saw what waited for you there?

The larger question is why fear triggers the terrifyingly strong and powerful emotional reaction against those who present these existential threats. My theory is that evolution has equipped us with a basic, if not primitive (just good enough) response system to deal with what in our early environment were indeed existential threats. Predators saw us as part of their food chain. Mistakes in dealing with predators and strangers often proved fatal. Outsiders, strangeness, unusualness, all triggered a fear response. We inherited this alarm system. Unfortunately it hasn't been upgraded from its original purpose and imported into the world of ideas and institutions.

In modern times governments employ an assortment of laws to monitor, identify and suppress modern Galileos—including censorship, proscriptions of blasphemy, computer crime laws and *lèse-majesté* edicts or their equivalent. The common thread is the existential fear that the unrestricted exchange of information or data will undermine and fatally wound the belief system, which may have remained unaltered for centuries. The longer the duration between updates of beliefs to match the current state of knowledge and information, the more repressive the laws and the response of authorities enforcing the laws.

Technology has brought more information, more channels to disseminate and access information, and more people connected, rendering geographical location largely irrelevant. Innovation and technology is disruptive. It threatens to replace existing institutions. People inside and outside these institutions are fearful. Their lives have never been less certain. Control over new information used to create alternative theories and principles remains unresolved. One side promises answers from their belief system to all questions; the other side makes no promises and demands an acceptance of uncertainty and ambiguity as the natural order of reality.

We are in the midst of a new Inquisition in many cultures. Like the medieval European elites who processed Galileo, their successors are playing out their hand in a last-ditch effort to suppress alternative information messengers from challenging the official belief system. There is fear on both sides of the knowledge equation as each side seeks to draw supporters to its reality-based bias. Those with a vested interest in absolutes butt heads with the modern probabilistic thinkers. In this tango along the edge of the event horizon of fear, it is unclear who will blink first.

Controlling who can gather, assemble and disseminate information and knowledge is crucial in a belief system seeking to preserve itself. The more out of date the worldview becomes, the more likely that more and more resources will be devoted to suppression and intimidation. At some stage the main preoccupation is reduced to internal fear management.

As an example of resource allocation to patrol the digital borders where belief systems are challenged by access to vast quantities of information, Chinese authorities have mobilized a large workforce:

"At yesterday's municipal propaganda department meeting in Beijing," reported the *China Digital Times*, "Vice Mayor Lu Wei implored 60,000 propaganda workers 'in the system' and over two million 'outside the system' to 'use Weibo.' According to official records, Beijing has a population of more than 20 million—from Lu's statement, one out of every ten Beijingers is a 'propaganda work.' "

With new advances in software, it is much easier for regimes to track the modern Galileos, shut down their websites, charge them and imprison them. The essence of fear, which began as an individual response to survival in a hostile environment has morphed into an institutionalized fear monitoring system to preserve existing societal arrangements, beliefs and customs against possible alternatives others might find more equitable, transparent and fair. Most governments wish to avoid that discussion. Room 101 will likely not be closed any time soon. Nor has the last Galileo been forced to recant his alternative worldview.

It is said that fear is our friend. But when fear is scaled to institutional size, it has every tendency to the same emotional, intuitive, gut feeling that all alternatives are existential threats. As George W. Bush famously said, "Either you are with us, or you are with the terrorists." Think fast—are you with us or with our enemies? Those are your only two choices. And here lies a key point. Old belief systems lasted because of their commitment to absolutist worldviews. We have moved into an era where probability analysis rejects absolute outcomes as automatically flowing from existing beliefs.

That idea is as dangerous as Galileo's heliocentric universe. It leads others to hold all beliefs as tentative possibilities open to revision through better questions and better information. It assumes we are likely to find that we change our minds about all kinds of arrangements and relationships as we sift through information, finding new and novel patterns and explanations in information and altering patterns of existing beliefs along the way.

For now we are at a stage not much different from the one of Galileo's day. New information is the cause of fear. We experience certain events, activities and signals as outward signs of existential threats. Scaled to the institutional dimension, fearmongers will likely continue down the time-honored path that worked on Galileo.

I have a feeling Galileo would recognize much of the repression that routinely occurs in various countries today in the name of national security or preservation of the faith as variations on the age-old theme of keeping Earth at the center of the universe. We are some ways from the day when Room 101 is converted into a computer room with an Internet connection to anyone with a sense of wonder and curiosity about the nature of the cosmos and our place in it.

Falling into The Trap

Falling into The Trap

Isometimes stumble upon artifacts, small information packets from the past, and wonder why I haven't seen this or thought of this myself, or whether everyone else except me reached that milestone years ago. A case in point is the BBC series titled *The Trap*. The series aired in 2007. I didn't see it in 2007. Six years later a good friend (thank you, John) said *The Trap* was something that I had to see. He was right.

The Trap is also something you should see. You owe it to yourself to watch all three parts. Unless, of course, you saw it six years ago, and have a six-year head start on assimilating what it means.

I am just starting out on that journey. Forgive me if I am taking you down paths that are old and familiar.

Our emotions and the range in which those emotions are allowed to express themselves are cultural. The past couple of months I've been investigating "fear" and "anger," the evil twins that kidnap us, forcing us to do and say things we later regret. What *The Trap* brilliantly does is elucidate the ideological framework erected during the Cold War. Once the Cold War ended in a victory for the Americans, the battle turned inward.

What emerged from that struggle was the notion of game theory. Developed by Nobel Prize winner John Nash, game theory assumed that all people were by nature selfish, self-centered, self-interested and highly suspicious of other people and acted rationally to maximize their advantages against others. This is the amoral landscape where each person tries to outwit the other and will betray the other to obtain an advantage. It is a bleak, paranoid vision of humanity. John Nash was treated for mental illness and later pulled back from the nature of humanity assumed in the game theory he had created. His struggle with paranoid schizophrenia was dramatized in the Hollywood movie *A Beautiful Mind*.

Never mind that the theoretical framework of game theory was woven by a mentally unbalanced mind, the dose of insanity did not prevent others from embracing this noir vision of humanity.

This vision spread like a virus from the geo-political contest between the Cold War superpowers, infecting psychology and economics. The role of the State was to get out of the way. There was no belief in "public interest" as a guide. This position was taken up by Reagan, Blair and Thatcher in the '80s and '90s as the rationale for downsizing the State and outsourcing to private company functions traditionally performed by state officials.

In the the first program of the series, titled "F★★k You Buddy" (March 11, 2007), we find ourselves thirty years into the Neo-Noir Era. *The Trap* illustrates how our political, economic, cultural and social institutions have fallen like dominos under the weight of game theory. The second in the series, "The Lonely Robot" (March 18, 2007), takes us still farther down that road.

Last week I wrote about Ben Goldacre's *Bad Pharma* and how the $600 billion pharmaceutical industry has been able to establish the new norm or new standard for acceptable behavior, attitudes and conduct. Game theory was a natural ally with its bleak view of the human condition.

Pharma promised to bring medical relief to those who were "abnormal," and who better but Pharma to redefine normality? If game theory sees humans as highly rational and deliberate in their actions, drugs like Prozac could take the edge off irrational feelings or emotions that get in the way of the robot-like approach to life.

In the Neo-Noir Era populations are seen as anxious or depressed. Big Pharma has made a hugely profitable industry in exploiting the game theory exponents' desire to "improve" the rational mind and to neutralize thoughts considered irrational. Doctors have redefined mental health in such a way as to narrow the margins of where emotions are allowed a role. Beyond the narrow bands drugs are prescribed for people whose emotions fall outside the diagnostic register that has been put in place in the last 30 years. This isn't about medical necessity; it is about the political necessity to control the emotional lives of people.

The elite of the rationalists sit on a mountain where the people below are feared for their emotions. Big Pharma could not have re-engineered our notion of mental health and brought in a new vision of normal without the consent of the ruling class that saw major benefits in a sedated population.

In the Neo-Noir Era Big Pharma has prescribed Soma. It is being swallowed around the world to cure the anxiety of living inside the Walmartization of both the local and international political, cultural and economic systems. It is the remedy for discontent, frustration and anger as the master game theory players pick the flesh from the bones of society.

Aldous Huxley's *Brave New World* predicted a world in which a drug called Soma is administered to the general population. The Soma of fiction and the real-life new Soma-like drugs expand mental health intervention, producing citizen patients who are docile, malleable and useful tools. In Huxley's 1932 novel he foresaw an American in the early twenty-first century where the State provided drug-induced comfort to self-medicating citizens.

The other visionary in literature who saw decades ahead was Stanisław Lem. In *The Futurological Congress,* which was published in 1971 (forty years after *Brave New World*), our hero finds that mind-altering drugs have been put into the hotel tap water. He drinks it without knowing he's being drugged. In this future utopia money and lending lose all meaning. Banks lend whatever amount you request and no one bothers to seek repayment.

The State uses multiple kinds of psychological drugs to create all kinds of mental states. Some bring transcendence, others pride and high status, and others bliss. Everyone in the resulting delusionary condition can win a Nobel Prize, own a Renoir or two, drive a Rolls Royce, win millions in Las Vegas at blackjack and play the piano like Mozart. The fact that it is all illusion doesn't matter because the mind reads it as real. Life inside Lem's Psych-Chemical State is all in the mind controlled by drugs. A movie based on Lem's classic novel is in the works for 2013.

The last segment of *The Trap*, "We Will Force You to Be Free," explores the meaning of freedom, and how forcing people to be "free" became the new mantra of the neocons. Their Orwellian notion is that freedom can only exist as a by product of a cleansing, a tyranny of "freedom fighters" who wipe the slate of those with incompatible ideas of freedom. Freedom requires a certain mental state. Big Pharma has eased people into this space, and the government assures them that now they are free. Freedom is an abstract state of mind that is imposed by force or chemical substance, and the newly freed people are happy with their condition and place in life. Having achieved freedom, they want for nothing else.

Only it hasn't quite worked out that way.

In *The Trap* we confront directly the idea that the State has been quietly dismantled. A better metaphor: dismembered and reassembled as a private-enterprise tool in the interest of the ruling elites.

In the Neo-Noir Era governments have given way to private interests. Before that transition can be successful, there needs to be a pacification program as citizens—deprived of their safety nets, trapped within falling down infrastructure and living with dysfunctional health, safety and educational systems—rely on the assistance of Big Pharma to keep them pacified. The BBC series *The Trap* visits a landscape made popular by a number of novelists. As usual, fiction has been our early warning system, the canary in the mine.

Lem and Huxley left slipped their notes into bottles, so to speak, and threw them into the river of time. Today, in the Neo-Noir Era, their messages are finally drifting to shore. Go back and read *Brave New World* and *The Futurologists Congress*. Both of these two novels could have been written today.

In our time science fiction has a new ally in this attempt to call attention to the realization of prophecies—it's called noir crime fiction. The main difference is that we are gradually entering the world foretold by Lem and Huxley.

In *Missing in Rangoon* I take a look inside the brave new world of Burma, a place of magic, illusions and cascading greed, as private corporate interests have found a virgin market in which to apply game theory and to bring their version of freedom. It takes loads of Soma, widely distributed, before there can be transition from one political/economic system to another. Freedom is on the lips of people. A word they once knew and thought they understood. It has gone mustard color, opaque, and is tattered. The last of the free men and women exist here and there, isolated, dwindling in numbers, knowing they have reached an intellectual and cultural dead end. In time the memory of them will be extinguished as people who lived inside a dream before Big Pharma acquired the exclusive monopoly. Be mindful of the hotel drinking water in Rangoon. Like the good professor in *The Futurological Congress*, you may find that you wake up in a different time and age.

Part VI

Anger and Fear

Angrier Thais

Anger and fear are the pick and shovel used to bury the truth in a shallow grave. I am trying to make sense of an impression that Thais are becoming angrier, and with more violent results than a quarter of a century ago. News reports, impressions based on firsthand observations and stories from friends can distort reality. What I have confidence in is the idea that levels of anger correlate with crime. Anger rarely brings out the best in us; quite the opposite, it is likely to lead to a rash, irrational response against the object or person responsible for triggering this emotional state. Laws are part of the security shield the state provides to protect us against the violence ignited by anger.

The union of anger with crime makes for an unhappy marriage right around the world. Every week there are reported cases where someone has become angry and punched, slashed, shot, kicked or shoved another person. Parker, the criminal in Richard Stark's series, has drawn an audience in part because the character has no discernible sense of fear. Had Parker been fearful but lacked a sense of anger, we would have had a quite different criminal personality. It is likely that a Parker emotionally wired in this way would never throw a punch. Such a character would be more like

Mr. Bean than Parker—an object of amusement. We laugh with our heroes, not at them.

A lot of crime novels are built on characters who are angry, and that emotion feeds and motivates their actions. When reading such a novel it is an interesting exercise to ask how the author handles emotions such as anger, whether it has explanatory power and whether the anger satisfies the reader's sense of fairness, justice and equality.

Anger is the opposite of fear.

Anger is the subjective experience of mind. It is pure emotion and cuts off access to rational thinking. It's physiological and neural. Insults, threats as well as physical violence are common reactions anticipated from an angry person. Frustration, resentment, cheating are three examples of events that trigger anger.

Looking at the building blocks of anger, one that stands out is scarcity. Most of life is a competition for mates, examination marks, jobs, promotions, honors, reputation and status. Such resources are scarce and unevenly distributed among a community. Excluding or denying someone what they believe is their entitlement or removing something they already have can lead to anger. And anger leads to revenge and reprisal.

I started this essay with an assertion that I thought Thais are angrier today than they were in the late 1980s. It is not based on good statistics, so the observation is subject to being modified if not rejected with solid statistical evidence. That caveat stated, my impression is with the vast increase in cars, trucks and motorcycles traffic and the relatively slow building of alternative modes of transportation, road space has become more scarce. Drivers are no better trained or skilled than before, but there are more of them, and they compete for the same lanes on jammed roads. *Nam jai* or "water heart" is a Thai expression used when someone gives way as a courtesy to another, a small act such as waiting and allowing someone else caught in a blocked lane of traffic to enter the moving lane in front of you. I still find acts that qualify as *nam jai* when driving, but like a disappearing form of wildlife it is becoming rarer and seems to be headed for extinction.

A few cases from December 2012 to February 2013 illustrate circumstances where anger leads to physical confrontation.

In one incident, reported under the headline "Man killed for jumping queue," a Shan-Burmese man and his wife went to a temple in Chiang Mai for free food for his child. The Burmese man saw a queue. Rather than join the queue, he cut in front, causing two teenagers to blow up with anger. One of the pair used a broken beer bottle to slash the man's throat. The man died at hospital. The police are gathering more evidence before seeking arrest warrants, according to the *Bangkok Post*.

Anger flaring into road rage has been more commonly reported in the Thai press of late. A couple of recent cases serve to make the point that the emotion of anger is a dangerous thing that seeks to express itself in violence. This kind of anger leaves the person without self-control and thrusts him into fight mode.

A YouTube video that has currently circulated for days in Thai social media caught a 48-year-old man claiming to be a law lecturer beating up on a small young woman after their cars became stuck in a small soi. Frustration erupted as neither would give way. A The newspaper *Thai Rath* reported graphicically (with pictures and the video which was taken by a bystander) that the young woman had picked up her girlfriend and was driving out of the small soi when a black Mercedes Benz came in.

She could neither pass nor go back. The young woman felt that the Benz driver might have a bit of *nam jai* as she saw he had a bit of room to move, so she asked him to squeeze in the lane and let her pass. He refused and insisted that it was she who had to move. She said she couldn't and he threw the car key at her face and stalked off to his friend's house. The young woman returned to her car and called her relatives for advice on what to do. In the middle of the phone consultation the Benz driver returned in rage, shouting, ordering her to reverse her car, while slapping, pushing and shoving her. The young woman's girlfriend came out to intervene and was shoved. Now fearing escalation, the two women ran back to their car and started driving in a long reverse to let the Benz go to its destination.

Recent reports are the lecturer was fined 1,000 baht for the assault, and he apologized to the woman he assaulted. End of case.

In another incident the *Bangkok Post* reported two women drivers were in a car accident. A Thai man between 30 to 35 years in one car got out and repeatedly struck the 36-year-old woman who appears to have been the driver of the other car. One car hit another. The occupants of each car apparently got out to inspect the damage and became angry at each other. In this case the anger boiled over into physical violence—the Thai man knocked out the other driver. He left her unconscious on the scene. And in the time-honored tradition of people who do bad, he fled the scene.

Anger and rage in crime becomes more interesting when someone in uniform spits the dummy (Australian for blowing one's stack, eruption of Anger with a capital "A").

The *Bangkok Post* reported a story involving a military officer who was unhappy with the driving of the car in front of his, saying later that the car was straddling two lanes so he couldn't pass. He flashed his high beams at the car ahead to move into the slower lane. But the car stubbornly refused to move. Finally the officer seized an opportunity to pass the car and then apparently positioned his car so as to stop the car he'd passed. When he saw three people inside, he took out his gun and fired three shots. Self-defense. He was outnumbered and felt threatened.

The event in this case was also captured on video and later uploaded on the Internet, and that caused the person uploading the video to receive a number of threatening and hateful comments. It seems a video was viewed as twisting the truth. That's the problem with a netizen videos: they capture a moment of anger, snatched from the jaws of reality, and those involved have little room for the usual defense of "misunderstanding" or "it didn't happen that way; they pulled a gun first" or "it was someone else in another car who fired a gun."

A day ago in Phuket, the driver of a mini-bus followed a car driven by a woman. She had made an illegal turn. She had braked suddenly, causing the mini-bus driver to brake as well. He became angry and raced after her in his bus. After he caught up (the traffic was moving slowly) he jumped out of the bus and ran up to her car and pointed a handgun at her. He returned the mini-bus, drove on, phoned his office to say he has other pressing business, and they should send another driver. The driver left the bus and disappeared. The police said, "We have a warrant for his arrest and he faces multiple charges relating to attempted murder, criminal damage, carrying a gun in a public place, and issuing threats. We believe we will catch him soon." The police are continuing to look for him.

Such stories are appearing more frequently in the Thai news. Road rage has been imported into the street and highway system in Thailand. The physical confrontations are pretty much recognizable to anyone from another culture. It seems that anger—while its triggers and reactions have a cultural component—has a common, universal aspect that transcends cultural differences. In Thailand, as elsewhere, the road rage cases are increasing, and if you were to substitute Bangkok, Phuket or other Thai cities for Chicago, Toronto or London in news stories of this kind, little else would need to be changed to localize it.

You can draw your own conclusions on what cultural biases make it permissible for men in the heat of rage to physically attack a woman. Beating up women deserves a closer examination as an extension of dysfunctional behavior in the land of anger. I'd start with the theory that in any political/social system which provides extensive impunity for members of the elite class, those deemed inferior in that society such as women, immigrants, handicapped or the peasant class are the object of violence because their failure to acknowledge another entitlement means the other person must automatically yield.

The insults, threats and violence attributed to the angry person create a universal brotherhood/sisterhood—road rage, domestic violence, pub brawls or that moment when your computer hangs and you lose a week of work that should have been backed up but wasn't. We've all experienced such moments.

There is a correlation between anger and criminal conduct. Acts of violence are outlawed. The criminal and civil laws patrol the emotional borders to deal with angry people whose emotional fuel motivates them to commit such acts.

Anger is the father that begets much violence. Sometimes the flash of anger leads to a squeeze of the trigger. Each culture tries to control that space—to diffuse the anger, to teach self-control and to provide substantial punishments and other disincentives for the angry whose emotion causes them to harm others.

The lack of capacity to control anger is a major reason to carefully restrict gun ownership. Anger, alcohol and guns are a lethal combination. In today's megacities, as resources become scarcer, be prepared for more violence generated by angry people.

Primal emotions like anger provide crime writers with material for several lifetimes. It is one thing to write about anger; it is another to experience anger directly, whether exploding inside your own head or inside the head of a person charging at you with a handgun because you stepped on his foot and caused him to lose face.

If you think that by escaping into the digital world you can avoid anger, think again.

Hate is an offspring of anger. You can find him in many places on the Internet. Online expressions of hatred are the digital equivalent of a handgun waved in your face. Next time you want to know if someone is angry with you online, check out emoticons.

The digital world has emoticons for anger, including **:-||** and **:@** and

Previously published under the title "Anger fueled crime" on March 1, 2013.

Thai Political Super Storms:
Kreng Jai System under Attack

A series of political super storms has hit Thailand in recent years—in 2006, 2008, 2010 and 2013. That's a lot of bad weather. The turmoil and fallout have occurred with the frequency of super typhoons, with each bringing more damage than the last. At the moment a number of commentators in Thailand and abroad, like weathermen, are trying to forecast the political weather in the days, weeks and months to come. Most are finding it difficult to make predictions with any degree of confidence.

Political predictions in Thailand suffer from limitations comparable to those of weather forecasting. The political climate involves complex systems that constantly change, reassemble, merge, expand or shrink in ways that are uncertain until they happen. I'd like to examine one feature of the ongoing turmoil—the cultural world of *kreng jai*—that may partially explain the political instability of Thailand's recent past.

Some years ago I wrote a book titled *Heart Talk*, which reviews the large (seemingly limitless) Thai language vocabulary about the heart. The Thai expression *kreng jai* has the longest entry in the book and was the most difficult to explain in English. I wrote: "The phrase reflects a rich brew of feelings and emotions—a mingling of reverence, respect, deference, homage and fear—which every Thai person feels toward someone who is their senior, boss, teacher, mother and father, or those in powerful positions such as a high-ranking police officer."

What is driving the political turmoil, in my view, is a breakdown of this ancient *kreng jai* system that has until now been the bedrock of the political establishment. The patronage system, the *pii/nong*—older and younger person system and the automatic deference to rank, uniform and position were built from the stone and cement of *kreng jai*. Even voting has been fenced in by the unwritten rules of deference.

There is much talk recently of vote buying, talk that is aimed at undermining the legitimacy of a popularly elected government. The historical record indicates that the exchange of gifts and benefits for votes has long been a feature of Thai politics and is another example of the *kreng jai* tradition. Poor villagers deferred to the educated, well-dressed "betters" with more power and money because that was how the system worked. Gift giving was the oil that lubricated the system.

In the *kreng jai* system it was inappropriate, rude and unforgiveable to question or criticize people in power or who hold positions of authority. From a policeman to a village head man to a schoolteacher or civil servant—the status was sufficient to guarantee compliance without worry of being asked to justify an action or a policy or a belief.

Until recently there was a widely accepted faith that an older person would take care and protect a younger person. That those with power, in return for deference to them, would keep the poorer, "powerless" people from harm's way. What has happened in Thailand is that the faith in this grand bargain promised by *kreng jai* has been broken—with a new political consciousness arising from a fledgling system of electoral politics.

Once the general population of voters understood that they had power in their vote, they started to wonder about the role of *kreng jai* in a world of newly empowered voters. This modern, new power to elect officials promised to secure for them a better life than the one they had traditionally received under a pure *kreng jai* system. What happened next? Pretty much what you'd expect—people's previously unshaken belief in the old faith that had driven the political process was replaced by doubt and skepticism. In response, both anti-government and government officials have attempted to reinforce the *kreng jai* system by taking advantage of the legal tools of criminal defamation as defined by Article 112 of the Criminal Code (*lèse majesté*) and the Computer Crime Act.

A yawning political divide has opened up between those who wish to institutionalize a political system based on the old notion of *kreng jai* and those who wish a substantial modification of automatic deference as the appropriate attitude toward the political elites. To this extent the elites on both sides of the current political impasse share the same interest. It shouldn't be overlooked that a separate *kreng jai* system operates inside the class of elites. In fact, the more one investigates *kreng jai*, the more one starts to see that, like the weather, it quickly becomes very complicated.

Thailand's anti-democratic forces are embracing the idea of *kreng jai* to preserve their world. That means a code of conduct based on deference within the elite class and between the elite class and everyone else. The Bangkok elites rail against Thaksin Shinawatra, who comes from a Chinese political/commercial family in Chiang Mai, with the kind of deep, committed hatred that can be understood as emerging from their existential fear of his growing power. Like the Israelis' hatred for the Iranians, nothing and no one is going to change the emotional voltage.

Thaksin Shinawatra's mistake was to play the popularity card to trump the informal *kreng jai* code among the elites—one that kept a rough parity of power so no one was hugely more influential than the others. The Bangkok elites saw Thaksin's political agenda as a betrayal of the long-standing elite power arrangements. He refused to honor those informal arrangements in a way that made them feel threatened. The Bangkok elites had every reason to support the 2006 coup against this internal *kreng jai* violator and encourager of the upcountry voters' growing inclination to seek political power rather going through the old patronage system.

Of course, it might be said that Thaksin created his own personal *kreng jai* system, perverting the original one for his own personal profit. Another view is that Thaksin saw an opportunity to ride a wave of cultural and social change. He hadn't created that wave that threatened to wash out the old temple walls of *kreng jai*. But he found clever political ways to tap into the power of that wave through health-care programs and other populist policies that *kreng jai* had never delivered.

The start of the current round of turmoil began when the government tried to enact a grand bargain among the elites. The idea was to pass an amnesty bill that would have absolved Thaksin and the opposing Bangkok elite side of all crimes since the 2006 coup.

The opaque nature of power arrangements and agreements on the informal side of Thai politics hints without any solid evidence that a deal was struck and provided cover for the government's push to enact the amnesty bill. Whatever the deal was (assuming there was one), it excluded the possibility for justice for the people who had gone into the street to protest against the regime installed by the 2006 coup, a number of whom had been shot, injured or killed. Those responsible for the camage would be let of the hook. No one would be made responsible for any of the wrongdoings. The stark reality sent a clear message—the "little" people would have to accept their karma. It was a deal by, for and between the elites only.

The political struggle over amnesty ironically ignited the current turmoil. What went wrong? A couple of factors fall into the category of miscalculation. The Bangkok elites have traditionally enjoyed the type of immunity that normally extends to foreign diplomats. The traditional elites had no real fear of criminal prosecution for their activities. Why would they need an amnesty bill when they already enjoyed virtual immunity? Thaksin had, in their view, betrayed them, and he was allowed to go and remain in exile. No one tried to stop him from leaving Thailand. For his betrayal, he's hated at a distance. So for Thaksin, living in exile to use Skype and other high technological means, to go over their heads with an amnesty bill was intolerable. They perceived, from a distance, he'd found yet another way to overrule the traditional elites. His continued influence was an insult, another thumb in the eye and a display of power to force them to acknowledge his right to run the show.

What is interesting was the uproar the legislation caused. The hatred among the elites and their supporters for Thaksin's betrayal intensified as they saw the amnesty bill as another attempt by Thaksin to pull the strings to overrule the verdict of exile and asset confiscation by the unofficial power structure. To add insult to their injury, he pointed to his legitimate right to have his way as he had gained the popular vote from what are, in their view, the "uneducated," "stupid" and "unwashed masses." The non-Thaksin elites were livid—how could these people who historically owed *kreng jai* to them ally with Thaksin to undermine their position and power?

Those same unwashed masses who delivered Thaksin his power also felt betrayed. They turned on him. For a brief moment the shared hatred of the traditional elites and the upcountry masses gave them a rare glimpse of solidarity. That didn't last long. The elites might have funneled that joined hatred into meaningful political reform. But no, they seized the opportunity to go in for the kill by scotching a constitutional amendment to allow for a wholly elected Senate. While the little people felt let down by the amnesty bill, the proposed amendment would empower them to extend their political voice to the upper house. The traditional elites saw the extension of the voting franchise to the Senate as another power grab by Thaksin.

With the amnesty bill Thaksin managed to alienate his friends and supporters and bring them in common cause with his old rivals. It would have been his weakest political moment. He was vulnerable. The traditional elites saw an opening to root out what they'd started to call the "Thaksin Regime" and to return Thailand to the pre-Thaksin political era. That was a far bridge to cross. How to get from the present to that ideal past? The big idea was for a government ruled by an unelected "People's Council" which would complete the job of destroying the remaining elements of the "Thaksin Regime."

The government's and Thaksin's miscalculation on the amnesty bill showed that they had not read the hearts and minds of the Thai masses very well either. This mistake gave the traditionalists an opening to attack the government, democracy and elections. The government is only lucky in that, as disappointed and betrayed as its supporters had felt with the bill, they understood a much higher cost would be paid if they were forced to return to the old full-blown *kreng jai* system enforced by edicts of the People's Council, handpicked by the elites.

The yearning for the stability of a strong *kreng jai* underpinned the calls for the government not to dissolve parliament and hold new elections but rather to put democracy on hold. The elites have not quite caught up with the rank and file who have opted to leave their feudalistic deference behind. *Kreng jai* hasn't vanished. It remains a value for many Thais. But the nature of deference is changing.

Globalization, social media, cheap travel and the Internet are forces that have chipped away at the Thai *kreng jai* system. Once exposed to the crosscurrents of ideas, thoughts and images, *kreng jai* begins to have a dated, worn and artificial quality. The ritual *wai* remains. I remember years ago buying a poster at the Weekend Market that showed more than a dozen different wais. This was a poster used in schools to teach students the intricate but meaningful differences in the kinds of *wais* and who was entitled to which kind. The *wai* a tourist receives, for instance, is part of the hospitality industry; it is a commodity, a product, one that makes foreigners feel special. It comes with a warm smile.

These political storms mask a greater change in the cultural atmosphere. The jet streams have shifted in the way most Thais perceive their relationships. It would be premature to say that *kreng jai* is gone. Indeed the *kreng jai* aspect will remain for a very long time. That said, the core faith has evolved from a kind of quasi-religion to a secular position that honoring and respecting people is a good thing—only they should earn that respect. That's a big change. And that those with rank and status should be accountable to the masses is a full frontal assault on an ancient system that continues to resist, protest and posture.

Can a self-governing non-elected "People's Council" of "good" people reinstate, defend and protect this cultural cornerstone of the political establishment? Think how long it has taken for Darwin's *On the Origin of Species* to change minds and hearts, and how incomplete that process is, and you start to have an idea that great shifts in belief systems happen over many generations. We live in a world where change has accelerated. Information is widely available and information is empowerment. So long as the schools and universities, the civil servants, the military and the courts draw ranks to retain the *kreng jai* system, the political turmoil will continue.

There are certain to be more political super storms as the existing elites have put their finger into the air, and they don't like way the wind is blowing. It isn't the government or the constitution that is the problem. It's that Thais are changing a key feature of their hearts. The political climate is complex. There are hidden forces we can only guess at. There are connections and undercurrents that we are only vaguely aware of. No one element, in isolation, is ever the whole story. Shifts inside Thai culture are part of the political instability matrix. But there are other elements, such as technology, social media and the values and ideas flooding in from all directions.

To return Thais to the old system of *kreng jai* would require sealing off the country and imposing re-education camps. There are voices, here and there, that suggest such an alternative, but the reality is that going back to an idealized state of deference would be like speeding backwards on a moonless night on a mountain road without guard rails. It would no doubt end in a terrible accident. The question is, what will the new rules of the road be? That's like asking what the weather will be next month. We can only guess at the most probable outcomes. No one knows.

Anger and the Medical Solution

A s a crime fiction writer, I find that anger is an emotion that figures into the psychology of the characters in a narrative where people are threatened, intimidated, disrespected or frustrated, or where their worldview/belief system is attacked or challenged.

Anger is on the A-list of *negative emotions*. If anger were an actor, he would never be out of work. Drama is basically what authors and film directors use to keep the audience on the edge of their seat. When someone goes postal with anger, people pay attention. It is hard to take your eyes off someone who is truly angry. Volatility in stock markets may cause an unsettling experience, but when personal volatility closes in, the situation becomes tense and fraught with danger.

Years ago, in the 1980s, I rode along as a civilian observer with members of the NYPD. That New York is long gone. My memory of that time is connected with a particular kind of anger. The one job the police hated was a call to investigate a domestic disturbance in some high-rise slum or bad neighborhood in Brooklyn. When they arrived, they would find a couple, a husband and wife fueled by pills and booze and still screaming at each other. The same shrill, loud threats, the sound of glass being broken that caused their neighbors to phone for the police.

By the time the police arrived, everyone would be at an emotional, irrational peak. It is precisely that moment that is most dangerous—for the parties involved and for the cops who arrive to calm things down. I suspect police in most cultures equally fear an out-of-control, angry domestic situation.

The police hate domestic violence calls. And for good reason. When two people living together uncork, they sometimes work themselves into a highly unpredictable negative emotional state inside their own homes. They become temporarily insane. They are literally out of their minds. Just as they reach this state, cops walk into a place where angry people know where the knives and guns are hidden. It is, after all, their home. Couples beating each other up don't like outsiders coming into their lives. They want to inflict pain on each other. Cops get hurt in these domestic situations. That's why they hate these calls.

Emotions come with up or down ratings. Joy, hope, love, generosity and relief are positive emotions. But anger is a bad boy and hangs at the same saloon where you find alarm, panic, fear, sorrow, hate and cruelty. That's a tough crowd. Anger counts as his relatives some nasty first cousins: outrage, wrath, hostility, scorn, spite, vengefulness, resentment—to name a few.

Physical assaults, maimings, beatings and killings, I would speculate, have a heavy anger bias as the emotional state that prevailed at the moment of the crime. Add drugs and liquor and you can explain a fair amount of criminal activity. "Criminologists estimate that alcohol or drug use by the attacker is behind 30 to 50 percent of violent crime, such as murder, sexual assault, and robbery."

In the past, anger and angry people were mainly contained by the police. One of the reasons that the violent death rate is historically (looking at large periods of time) low is the State has become gradually much better at devising institutions that deter, contain or punish violent anger. For a detailed analysis see Steven Pinker's *The Better Angels of Our Nature*.

In England the statistics indicate that young males, especially those visiting pubs, should be carefully watched. That is to be expected from young men. What is more interesting are the statistics for those who have been either an offender or victim of violence.

The *Home Office* reported in 2009:

• The 2002/03 BCS shows that over four-fifths of victims were emotionally affected by the incident (83%). This is an increase from the last set of results (2001/02 BCS). Twenty-six percent were 'very much affected', and 24 per cent 'quite a lot', a further third were affected 'just a little.'

• Victims of domestic violence and mugging were most likely to be emotionally affected, as shown in all recent survey years. Latest data show that victims were very much affected in 40 per cent of domestic violence incidents, compared to only 17 percent of stranger violence incidents. In around one-fifth of incidents of acquaintance and stranger violence the victim was not emotionally affected.

• **The most common reaction to violence was anger** (51% for the 2002/03 BCS). This is also a recurring finding from the survey. Shock, annoyance, fear, loss of confidence or feeling vulnerable are also fairly common experiences.

No one is arguing that all emotions—positive and negative—are the filters we automatically use to process a lot of daily life. Anger, like fear, is a natural state. Living in close proximity to each other only works if anger can be contained. The size of Bangkok—estimated to be as high as 12 million people—is a good illustration of a system that keeps down anger-fueled violence. And yes, there are news reports of someone going *jai rawn* and hacking up a relative or friend. It happens. But it is also relatively rare.

What has changed is the arsenal assembled against anger seeking to express itself. Anger has been undergoing a substantial taming process. In this case there is more than one lion tamer under the Big Tent—psychiatrists, scientists, chemists, neurologists and Big Pharma. The old political/criminal justice system that worked together to build more prisons and to hand out much longer sentences has worked to curtail the anger/violence connection.

First, give anger a medical label. Give it over to the white coats, whom everyone admires and respects. Science and Big Pharma will solve the problem. Thus, containing anger becomes the role of medicine in general and psychology specifically. Sending anger into the medical camp has inevitably led to the creation of a medical conditions like "intermittent explosive disorder" (IED), one said to be "characterized by persistent, uncontrollable anger attacks not accounted for by other mental disorders." *Science Daily* reported a study which found that one out of 12 young people (in the USA)—close to six million adolescents—meet the criteria for IED. The normal emotion of anger becomes another form of mental illness.

Second, scientists have split the emotion of anger apart like a particle shot at near the speed of light inside one of those huge accelerators, but this time to discover not the secrets of the universe but the chemistry of an emotion—a mix of underlying hormones including low serotonin, high dopamine and high noradrenalin. With this knowledge, the next step is to test people for their hormone levels and medicate to adjust them. In another part of the laboratory, research on the genetic elements that form patterns that shape the boundaries of temperament and personality are leading closer to a DNA explanation.

Third, there is a large and profitable anger pill industry. Google "anger control medication" and you'll get more than 18 million pages. We live in a medical era of pharmaceutically designed emotional restructuring. The rush has been on to create a new class of drugs to modify or subdue the behavior caused by effects of negative emotions like anger. The search for the perfect emotional state through drugs has opened up big opportunities for the pharmaceutical industry. It has large political implications, too. Treated with a drug, the teenager becomes docile. Nothing bothers him or her. The drug takes away the emotional equipment to respond. Here are some of the antipsychotic medications circulating in the marketplace: Risperdal, Haldol, Depakote.

The net cast for angry people continues to expand. That *Science Daily* report also said, "Nearly two-thirds of U.S. adolescents have experienced an anger attack that involved threatening violence, destroying property or engaging in violence toward others at some point in their lives." Big Pharma product developers aren't overlooking the size of this market.

There are significant problems arising out of the first three points outlined. *Bad Pharma* by Ben Goldacre is a detailed examination of the crooked game played by all of the players in the medical establishment.—from the industry-paid researchers, scientists and journals that use cherry-picked data to show effectiveness to the culture of burying negative news. Most of the negative trials that show drugs don't work, cause harm or are no more effective than a placebo or any other drug currently on the market are deep-sixed. That's right, negative studies go missing. The basic truth is there is no easy way to get good information about which medicines work or which psychological categories are accurate. Whether the source is a drug company, a government regulator or a professional body, the outcomes are distorted, misleading and often wrong; the missing data on negative trials are more difficult to document than war crimes.

Fourth, with a largely non-angry and medicated population, it becomes much easier for economic and political manipulation to pass without angry people to take into account. We are, at least in theory, safer from some categories of physical violence because of the medicalization of anger. The political class gains part of its power by acting out the anger of a medicated voting population. Politicians are surrogates for anger. Political campaigns in many places—Thailand is no exception—are a kind of theatre, and political consultants act as generals fighting in the trenches of fear and anger. This spectacle, along with the medication, keeps people from noticing how they've given over anger to the medical and political establishment, and big business has now found a way to make a profit from this transfer.

Lastly, it pleases the powers that be to make anger into a Hollywood comedy, as in the Adam Sandler, Jack Nicholson film *Anger Management*.

We are, in other words, in the safest, most secure period of human existence. But we pay the price for this safety. We've corralled anger—this negative emotion—as if it were a beast in a cage. Not that many years ago we called people with strong views and feelings eccentric. Some of them were angry people. We often celebrated such people, but now they would be so uninteresting, being medicated, subdued and watching the latest YouTube offering or video game. Anger is defined as IED in such a way as to rope in a lot of young men. If anyone has any right to be angry examining the real state of the world and their place in it, the young unemployed men in Spain, Italy, Egypt and many other countries should be angry. And they don't like the medicine that's been prescribed. They should be angry with a medical/pharma system that distorts evidence and medicates them with dubious pills and psychological analysis. The system based on controlling anger, as it turns out, is a hugely profitable game.

IED reminds me of the acronym for unexploded ordnance. Anything dangerous hidden underground or temporarily caged by drugs is an explosion waiting to happen. Anger will continue to shape and define crime fiction. The medical battle is yet to be assured of an easy victory. The unfolding of the anger management industry may provide fertile ground for a crime novel.

The State of Fear

The first reaction to a threat or a possible threat is one of fear or anger. We are emotional by default, and once our feelings and intuitions are engaged, our so-called rational mind's duty is to justify the hot emotion that has us sweating and short of breath. When the State is the one creating fear, the emotions are heightened. Isn't the State supposedly the one to protect us against those who would induce fear?

That is the story the State wishes us to believe. The dividing line between States isn't so much between democracy and autocracy as between States that do or do not spin a story of protection from feared outside sources that most people believe is true. We are at heart, all of us, security seekers. That plays to the advantage of the State as the officials rely on the reality that there isn't an alternative. A revolution merely changes those who operate the State and, as history shows, the new operators are no different from the ones they replaced—in many cases, they become addicted to terror to cow their rivals into submission.

Criminal laws regulate conduct and are the citizens' first line of defense against the "wrongful" or "bad" conduct of others. In reality, many criminal laws authorize the State to protect itself against those who would challenge its authority. Broad and imprecise wording—as in the phrase "national security"—grants those who enforce the laws broad powers and substantial penalties to charge, convict and imprison a person whose activity is thought to be a threat to those in power. The threat of prosecution chills the exercise of free speech and stops political discussion. The State uses such power in the age of Internet access to censor what is sent and received by users.

The State is an intangible entity. We are accustomed to railing against an oppressive or abusive State. These emotional outbursts are like taking a swing at a cloud. You never quite connect your feelings with the object perceived to cause those feelings.

The functionaries and officials who make up the State are many. They interact with each other. Some are more powerful than others, and there is an institutional bias or culture that prevails across those institutions as well as legacy traditions and customs within individual agencies. This makes assigning responsibility difficult. Who do you point the finger at when the State acts to criminalize political speech? Or criminalizes conduct that serves the interests of a small but powerful elite that benefits from a cone of secrecy and immunity from criticism?

In the new Orwellian world—everyone is guilty, and those charged are selected through the exercise of prosecutorial discretion to send a message to all the other potentially guilty citizens that they, too, are being watched and are vulnerable. And there is nothing they can do and no one to turn to.

Having been placed in the situation of being charged and the realization there was little chance of escape is thought to have led Aaron Swartz to commit suicide in New York. He was a 26-year-old computer genius, co-founder of Reddit, who'd been charged for "freeing" academic data at M.I.T. Since his death there has been a firestorm of protest, questioning, criticism and hand-wringing.

The best explanation of why writers write is George Orwell's essay *On Writing*, written 70 years ago. Orwell said that the subject matter of a book is determined by the age in which the writer lives.

Context is what matters. Look around your space, inside the room where you are reading this essay. When you go out, look around the city. And recall for a moment that it wasn't always like this and won't stay like this either. But for the moment, the present, this is our context that determines how we think about books, each other, information, security, politicians, guns, drugs, pollution, the opposite sex, police and doctors and hospitals. We think of them in the now.

Commentary like this essay, films, books and the comments others make online are collections of our context, where we find the signs of social, cultural, psychological and political reality. We try to make sense of all these signals, picking through the noise. It is hard work. The noise is always far greater than the signal. The distractions and limited attention we can bring to anything directly in front of us should give us pause. It should give us a sense of humility. We are overwhelmed by the emotional words of others, the details pile up, the ambiguity increases. We hate doubt. We love certainty. One we avoid, the other we embrace.

Those employed by the State understand this bias. To avoid randomness and uncertainty gives the State actors an edge. Officials promise that they can and will remove the dread of doubt and once removed, we will feel safe and happy. The State understands that we are first and foremost emotional creatures. That insight is the source of their broad, vague powers and discretion.

We filter the justifications, the defenses and the words of State officials as they weave a pattern that shows their actions are lawful, correct and in the interest of the State and its citizens. Orwell taught that writers have a duty to challenge these state-manufactured patterns, deconstruct them and offer original, alternative patterns. You can read volumes of Internet commentary taking this road about the official actions of the State in pursuing Aaron Swartz.

The best writers communicate an essence of insight, meaning and purpose. They distinguish between intuition and rational, objective evidence. To use Daniel Kahneman's distinction, one is automatic, lazy thinking and the other is slow, deliberate thinking. They are connected. The lattice of biases that we all have ultimately shape and distort the way we think about reality.

The best books embody the way people think and feel. A good novel or short story hits an emotional chord in the reader that seems true.

The best books reflect emotional attitudes as people bump up against the reality found inside the context we live in. The emotions we find floating above us include anger, hostility, envy, jealousy, suspicion and deception.

Crime novels embrace these negative emotions and fine-tune them into stories where characters seek to escape their context, their destiny or their moment in history. No matter how fast you write, the book is much slower than the click of a camera shutter, and even at that speed there is a transformation captured and the reality that follows that moment.

Orwell wrote that authors have four reasons or motives to write:

1. Sheer egoism. The desire to appear clever, talked about, remembered after death. The great mass of people are far less selfish than writers. Serious authors are vain and self-centered.

2. Aesthetic enthusiasm. Perception of beauty in the

patterns found in the exterior world and converted into prose. The firmness of good prose, the rhythm of a good story that carries you along.

3. Historical impulse. To see things as they are outside the filters, biases and prejudices that every context presents as barriers to truth.

4. Political purpose. To use words to push the world in a certain direction—to shape or alter people's idea of the kind of society we live in and whether that society is fundamentally just and fair.

Psychology has advanced a fifth reason, **mindset exploration**, to identify the connection between our emotional, impulsive, intuitive mind and our deliberate, rationale mind. To understand the interplay between the two aspects of our cognitive resources that create our system beliefs, we defend and define the perimeters of our reality.

Our impulses war with one another and change over time, but our beliefs are difficult to shift even when the evidence is clear that what we believe is false or wrong. The Aaron Swartz suicide and background prosecution have ignited debates about core beliefs and the role of prosecutorial discretion, freedom of speech and the nature of information—who owns it, has access to it and can use and exploit it.

The context of Aaron Swartz's death engages at the emotional level when the distrust of state actors and their bona fides are in doubt. His death is used to emotionally confirm our worst fears—the State is patrolling the products of our mind and our actions, seeking to find violations of laws. And the question being asked is whose interests are being served in such prosecutions?

In *The Orwell Brigade*, a dozen authors, including Barbara Nadel, Quentin Bates and Matt Rees, who blog on the same site I do, have joined John Burdett, Colin Cotterill, Ruth

Dudley Edwards, Mike Lawson, Ernesto Mallo and Gary Phillips to reclaim the role of telling truth to authority, to examine abuses of power and to question the false histories and narratives officials use to justify their decisions and policies. The traditional media have retreated to the safety of entertainment and gossip to turn a profit. We have paid a high price for that retreat.

One positive legacy of Aaron Swartz's life is this questioning of the official exercise of power that once was done by journalists, essayists and novelists has spawned thousands, if not millions of questioning voices. It is difficult even for the State to shut down, arrest and lock up all of these people. I suspect they will lie low, wait for the faint breeze of time to blow away the anger. Once that happens, the State, through its officials, will slowly creep back and remind us that without them we will live in a State of Fear.

Creating Fear

Fear is one of the basic emotions that springs auto-matically from a threat. It can be a real threat or a symbolic threat. A lion charging at you is a real threat. A story about a lion charging creates a symbolic threat. Our heart races in both cases. Evolution has equipped us with a fear mechanism that is triggered in circumstances where the risk of our survival is at stake. For a couple of hundred thousand years it served the purpose of focusing our attention on the threat and escaping the threat. The old proverb that says fear is your friend has a large element of truth.

We don't do a very good job of processing modern reality where the threats are new and novel. Fear, like most emotions, makes for an automatic, unthinking reaction. We think fast when threatened. In the case of the charging lion that is a good thing. In modern cities the chances of being attacked by a lion are small. But the chances of being run over by a bus, car or truck are much higher. But we don't fear them. And that is a problem.

Recently I was in Melbourne and used the tram system there. I noticed signs on platforms with a "Banksy-like" image of a rhino on what looks like a skateboard. (Actually Banksy used rats, but his motive wasn't to stop people from being run over by trams in Melbourne.) A larger sign on the side of a tram depot has the rhino ballooned up in size and with the word "rhino" translated into a couple of dozen foreign languages.

The sign informs us that a tram is 30 times the size of a rhino, and you should be careful crossing tram tracks because one of those enormous rhinos in the form of a tram might run you down.

Later I found the "Beware the Rhino" advert made by Yarra Trams and posted on YouTube. It certainly brings the scary 30 rhinos message to life. There's also a "Beware the Rhino" Facebook page which has some 3,000 likes.

I thought about the message. BEWARE THE RHINO. FEAR THE TRAMS. The government in Melbourne has gone into the fear creation business to provide safety to its citizens. I suspected that years ago there must have been a number of accidents involving people being run down by trams, and some bright spark said that people were oblivious to the dangers of the slowly lumbering vehicles. (A quick bit of research revealed that the Beware the Rhino campaign started in May 2011. It was aimed at tackling car to tram accidents.)

How can we get people's attention so they will focus on trams when they cross a street in Melbourne? That thought must have led to the inevitable series of committee meetings and public hearings, and inevitably quite a lot of money paid to an advertising agency. However it happened, finally someone must have asked what are we afraid of, what ignites the fires of fear and alerts us that we might be killed? No doubt the reply was that trams don't eat people. That is the point. Rhinos as far as I know don't eat people either. The room must have been jumping with creatures that cause us to be fearful: rats, cobras, cockroaches, elephants, lions, tigers, water buffalos. No doubt there were divisions and disagreements over the appropriate animal to strike fear into the citizens of Melbourne as well as tourists coming to the city for the first time.

Whatever political dealings went on behind closed doors, we know that ultimately those in support of the rhino prevailed as its image is on every warning sign in the complex and extensive tram system.

Whether the campaign has reduced accidents as intended is not readily clear, but it has certainly achieved a notable degree of recognition as far as advertisement campaigns go. It won the "Postcard of the Year" award for 2011–2012.

The Melbourne tram rhino got me thinking about the role of government in the fear business. Whether we like it or not, governments have two major fear related policy tools. In the case of the Melbourne tram rhino, the government manufactures fear. They take an activity, a situation or an event which they believe may cause harm because citizens have not evolved an appropriate fear reaction. In these circumstances, the government's policy is to artificially create a fear by association. Trams = 30 rhinos. You wouldn't want to ignore a rhino on the streets of Melbourne, would you? Of course not. Then you certainly would want to pay attention to a machine 30 times as powerful as a rhino that is on the streets daily, rushing up and down like a charging wild animal.

How do you feel about having the government manipulate your emotions? To hit your fear button even though it is for your own protection, safety and welfare? The answer is governments, pundits and private corporations do this all the time. We become immune to fear creation. We fear our health will suffer if we don't take vitamins, though the scientific evidence is inconclusive about whether our daily dose of vitamins actually does anything to protect our health and extend our longevity. Pundits in the political election season pump up the fear in their audience: elect Mr. Brown to office and you will lose your right to carry an assault weapon. That means you can no longer protect yourself, your family and friends against the rhino-like crazies who threaten you on the street.

There is a second aspect to the fear business in politics: it is fear containment.

Unlike the first case, where there is no natural fear and one must be manufactured, in the second case fear is irrational and cascades through the population, and citizens demand protection. Fear of bird flu or another contagious disease can quickly spread through an Internet-connected population. Governments react swiftly with vaccines, quarantines, school closings and medical advice. In this mode the government is seeking to contain fear because generalized fear running out of control is as dangerous as the problem that ignited the fear in the first place. Public safety has always been a powerful political tool to gain votes and to cast an opponent in a negative light. No politician wants to be labeled as soft on crime, for instance.

The Shoe Bomber is a classic case of fear containment. One man with homemade explosives in his shoes resulted in fear contagion that governments contained by restricting the civil liberties of citizens. In the name of containing this fear, plane passengers by the millions remove their shoes and belts, empty their pockets, walk through metal detectors or X-ray machines. By containing fear, governments have found a way to increase their authority and power over citizens. As far as I know, no one in government produces an annual report listing the number of shoe bombs discovered in the shoes of millions of airline passengers. One suspects they have found none. If they'd found even a single shoe bomb, that fact would have been revealed to indicate people should remain fearful and the containment policies were working. We are suckers for fear containment because it seems so reasonable to buy into at the time, and so difficult to unwind when most people agree that making and enforcing government policy based on an irrational emotion isn't in the best long-term interests of citizens.

Once people look to the government to contain irrational fears, they create a monster that is more fearful that the original event that generated the initial fear that cascaded through the population. How does anyone unwind a fear containment policy once it has been funded, institutions have been created and people hired and inertia has settled in? If you have the answer to this question, please let me know. This is a modern problem. We end up fearing the wrong things, events and people, and we pay a high price for our irrationality.

Returning to the fear creation side, we can understand the role of government is once again being pitched as falling into the public safety category. Are the rhino signs in Melbourne effective? Has anyone done a comparative study with other tram systems that lack such signs or maybe use a giant spider rather than a rhino to make people fearful? Because citizens don't think much about the sign, perhaps it works on an unconscious level. We process the rhino in a part of our brain that makes us instinctively more alert to the danger of stepping in front of trams.

I've been told the authorities in Melbourne are considering increasing the security on tram platforms at night. Apparently the evidence indicates that a tram rider is at greater risk of an assault during daylight hours than at night. But if we know one thing as crime fiction writers, it is that night is noir, and night is dark, our vision is compromised. There are rhinos in those shadows. So even though the best allocation of resources to protect public safety and welfare would be to increase security during the day, that is too rational. Our irrational mind ignores the actual evidence and falls back on the primitive instinct that the night is always much more dangerous than the day. That's why we invented fire. And that is probably why the authorities in Melbourne will ramp up the security at night even though they know the actual benefit will be less.

Counterfactuals and Fictional Worlds

What is it about a novel that draws us into the story? The standard list would include the characterization, the voice, the setting or the suspense and thrills. I'd like to add an item to this list: the way the story illustrates the psychological state of fear, the choices made under the duress of that emotion and the consequences of the choice made and the choices that weren't made.

Fear elongates as faith in the security and the protection of the authorities erodes. We live in an age of heightened fear. Authorities use fear both to grab votes and to curtail civil liberties. We are pushed in two separate directions: distrust of what the authorities can do to protect us and the willingness to allow the authorities to play to our fears for their own benefit.

We are a product of our times, our age and our culture. The occasional book spans time, the age it was written and the cultural distortions in which the author worked. Would George Orwell have written different kinds of books with a different mindset if instead of being a colonial police official in Burma, he had gone to live in Thailand or Singapore or Saigon and worked as a journalist for twenty-five years? Or what would Graham Greene had written had he stayed in Saigon for years? Or if Nelson Algren had been raised on a farm in Kansas rather than Chicago and his father had been the local mayor and his mother the county judge.

I have lived for 25 years in a political system where officials have fewer restraints on the exercise of their power, fewer inquiries, questions and criticisms to face—a soft police state. I thought of this as once again I was on the back of a motorcycle taxi, which was flagged down and stopped by the police at a two-man ambush T-intersection where Soi 16 and Soi Paisinghtoh meet. The police were interested in the driver. I was the person of interest. I got off the back of the motorcycle, showed a copy of my passport. I was physically searched, made to empty my pockets and submit to a pat-down. Next the cops opened each compartment of backpack, opening the plastic bag containing my freshly used gym clothes. This happened at 1:45 p.m. in the afternoon.

The police questions: "Do you speak Thai?" *Of course not.* "What your name?" *I gave them my name.* "Where you go?" *Home—one hundred meters from your ambush point.* "What you do in Thailand?" *I am a retired lawyer. (Never be a writer.)* "Where you live?" *I point up the road.* "Show me your wallet." *I showed him my wallet.*

Finally one of the cops asked the motorcycle taxi driver if he knew me. The driver gave a reference: "He live in Thailand a long time." I'd never seen this driver before, but he seemed to know who I was. Based on the testimony of the motorcycle driver, I was allowed to leave.

There was a time when I would have found such an arbitrary stop, search and questioning unsettling, upsetting and annoying. But after the third such incident in less in a year, it has become an ordinary feature of life.

"Show me your papers." Right out of an old Bogart movie on the tarmac of some remote airport in North Africa. Police roadblocks are small change in the scheme of things. They are a kind of theatre where the actors know the drama is about fear and money and power.

I've learned a thing or two about all three having survived coups, street fighting and violence, and walked through minefields where villagers had erected bamboo huts. I've seen the aftermath of war in Cambodia and Vietnam not long after the guns had gone silent. I know many others who've seen much, much more than me. But I saw enough to learn a couple of lessons about myself. What I am capable of feeling when fear and power and money rollerblade straight for me. I don't like it. I don't like being afraid. But I put myself in a position where that would inevitably happen.

If I'd stayed a law professor at the University of British Columbia, walking the beaches, skiing at Whistler, buying salmon at Granville Island market, my life and what I wrote about would have gone in a different direction. In the multiverse there is a version of me who never left Vancouver and is still teaching law. That version also writes. But I doubt he writes books set in Southeast Asia, or if he does, they would be very different books from the ones I've written.

The stuff of writing that is worth a second read, I believe, comes from writers who have felt the bone chilling sound of gunfire, seen ordinary people panicked, wounded, suffering, people without jobs or connections, hungry and homeless people. This is where the rubber connects with the road of life. Not in the office towers or exclusive clubs or shopping malls. Those illusions take away the fear that power and money, our natural enemy, should instinctively make us weary. We believe that we can reach out and cuddle the cute lion. The lesson of literature is a warning that anyone who has been in this context never forgets what emotions flood through the mind.

Nelson Algren was a writer I discovered when I was very young, and like Orwell and Koestler had an influence on the kind of books I read (and ultimately wanted to write). Colin Asher has written an insightful essay, "Never a Lovely so Real," about Algren:

"[Algren] pressed that refrain throughout his life, at every opportunity he found. The formulation that best captures his intention and method is: 'The hard necessity of bringing the judge on the bench down into the dock has been the peculiar responsibility of the writer in all ages of man.' After his first book, Algren never traded in the idea that the poor are purely victims. Sometimes the accused were guilty, he believed, sometimes innocent, either way their perspective deserved consideration."

Algren like Orwell never sentimentalized the poor. He never looked down on them. He understood how money and power circled around them, caging them, controlling and fearing them at the same time.

The book I remember reading when I was fifteen was *The Man with the Golden Arm*. Asher nailed that novel in this passage:

"If *Golden Arm* had a purpose, it was to challenge the idea, then congealing into ideology, that an individual's social value is related to his or her wealth. Its message is that lives lived in the twilight hours, after swing shifts, in the shadows of newly erected towers, or beneath the tracks of the El, are as passionate, as meaningful, as funny and pointless, and as much a part of the American story as any."

What was then congealing into ideology has long since dried into hard stone. Where is there a place left where social value isn't calculated in terms of wealth and influence? Those who have no wealth are left out of the story of our time. Algren, Orwell, Koestler and Greene threw a literary lifeline to these people. We live in a time where cutting that lifeline is the business of government, and writing has become an entertainment business. Walking away from a secure university professorship was something a foolish fifteen-year-old boy who'd read *The Man with the Golden Arm* would do, but not a grown man. At any stage things could have gone very wrong.

But if I'd stayed in my university office, something I needed to see and do and think about would have never come alive. The theory of the multiverse says our universe is one among an infinite number of universes, and all possibilities are a reality. That's too much like magical thinking for me to take seriously. False comfort is no comfort. Making a choice in this life means taking a hard look at the cards you hold and then making a bet on yourself. If you are a writer, you shuffle the deck and deal the hand your characters will hold. Every book is a new game of poker.

But before you write that first sentence you must find the interiority of the main characters. I find my characters in the most unlikely places and most of them live off the radar screen for most people. The best characters in novels are the ones society judges as having no value—and that allows us to put society in the dock to judge it. I am drawn to characters who push beyond the rejection society brings to their everyday life, and I like characters who face the high wall behind which an army of money and power pulls up the drawbridge. I like characters who don't feel sorry for themselves because others regard them as worthless, who don't give up, who keep advancing against the forces assembled to destroy them. I like them because they have more natural dignity and grace than any university professor could ever imagine.

Parker's Absence of Fear

ichard Stark, a.k.a. Donald Westlake, started a series only after his editor convinced him to change the ending of the first novel. In the original ending Parker was killed.

Apparently, so the story goes, Westlake's editor changed literary history, and crime fiction hasn't ever been quite the same since that first novel was published. Parker changed the face of crime fiction for many readers and authors who later came down the line.

Parker is a professional thief. Thug. Gangster. A killer. You get a glimpse of each persona as you read the series. Crime is his business; it is how he supports himself. He doesn't have friends. He has associates he works with on a specific job. He lives outside society. And he's forever planning where to leave a stash of money, and finding that his money is running low and it's time to return to plan a job. In the early books Parker lives alone but he doesn't work alone. His women often come to a violent end. He carefully handpicks members of a team for each job.

In each of the 24 novels in the series, Parker goes through a process of selecting the members for his team, matching their skills to the demands of a particular heist. He runs the team like a military commando unit officer. A job sometimes is brought to him by an insider, and this stranger, a non-professional—his head dancing with riches—finds his way to Parker. He or she is usually a small-time non-professional motivated by greed and handicapped by an overweening ego. Most of these heists go sour. Violence follows.

Parker has had conflicts with organized crime members and bosses who have tried to cheat him out of money owed because he is a "little," unconnected guy. Big mistake. They underestimate Parker, his determination—a kind of post-human persistence in a mission—and his lack of fear in pursuing his goal.

I like Parker. Sometimes I'd like to be more like Parker. I suspect that Parker makes lots of people wish also they could live without ever feeling a cold steel blade of fear touching the back of their neck. There is something compelling about his absence of fear in situations where the vast majority of people would be pale, speechless, paralyzed. Not Parker. But I've been asking myself lately whether Parker's lack of fear should cause us to feel revulsion. Here's the case against liking Parker. After you've read a half-dozen of the Parker novels, there is a pattern of reality that fits into the category of pocketbook fascism.

Parker is *never* afraid.

Parker is a deliberate, calculating, logical, analytical planner. He's not snatching gold chains or mugging old ladies on security check days. Parker thinks big. The heists he chooses share a common link—they present large risk of failure but a corresponding large payoff if successful. Parker carefully chooses his team for their experience, competence and trustworthiness. He's often worked with them before on prior heists.

But Parker can't always control new members—often the insider who brings the idea to Parker—and all the planning can come undone when an incompetent, cheating and lying member of the team threatens the operational goal or the dividing up of the loot after a heist.

Parker has no sentimentality. When someone double-crosses him, he has no hesitation in killing them. Not out of hatred or anger, but out of a sense of violation of his conduct for doing business. Never double-cross Parker. It is a line drawn in the sand. His regular team members understand the code. For those who violate it, there is no learning curve for the next job. There is no next job. They are dead.

Killing people is Parker's way of controlling destiny, punishing those who are disloyal. Fascists show no emotion in erecting kill paths and demand absolute, unqualified loyalty. You find a similar mindset in men like Rumsfeld, Cheney and McNamara. Violence and body count is their way of exerting authority and control. Violence shows who is the man, who deserves respect and who must yield. Violence and intimidation flash the signal—you are either for us or against us, and either way we aren't afraid to take the fight to you. There is no neutral ground.

Removing the emotion of fear in a mindset produces a powerful, relentless and brutal force that becomes an object of fear and hatred for others. And where the person who uses deliberate violence lacks fear, such a person unbounded by fear becomes an existential threat. This is doubly troubling—we admire Parker's qualities but find ourselves uneasy that absence of compassion and empathy rob him of his humanity.

Parker is a cold, calculating machine dedicated to planning successful criminal ventures. Instead of blood, he has sequence algorithms running through his veins. Parker is the anti-hero who never suffers from doubt.

Parker's game depends on detailed planning and ruthless execution of plans, and loyal team members define his personality. The emotional side of Parker is held in check—

or it may be non-existent. Parker never has sex when in the planning stage of a heist. Sex, friendship, drinking and fun are all distractions, and they are sidelined until the crime is committed. Then Parker, off screen—as the novel ends—spends the next six months spending the money before finding a new heist.

Parker might easily fit into a CEO position to run a Forbes top 100 company. He could slip into the role of a Wall Street investment banker or a high-level government official—though most such people would be hard pressed to remove sex and fun from their lives to achieve their mission.

Parker sees emotions as an enemy of forward planning. They are a distraction, a nuisance, and can get a man killed. Parker, as a survivor, spends a great deal of time planning the details of the heist, assigns the specific jobs to members of the team gathers the materials and resources, scouts the location and looks for getaway cars, untraceable guns, hideouts and alternative exits. He's thorough, cold, calculated and, when the plans hit the unpredictable forces of reality and fall apart, he is quick to find ways to shore up the broken scaffolding. Parker's steadfastness, his belief in keeping promises and his workarounds when plans come unstuck are all part of his appeal.

Parker is a man who can control and overcome his emotions. Secretly many of us wish we had this ability. As we don't, Parker gives us the vicarious thrill of inhabiting a character that is a sociopath. When we enter Parker's mindset, the feeling evokes a sense of admiration and power, and we can forget that Parker's cognitive abilities are dangerous and deviant.

The heart of the Parker novels is his ability to meet the challenges of the uncertain, unpredictable world of crime at the point where all planners must face the reality that the plan isn't working, the outcome is in doubt, and an inventive alternative plan must be created on the spot. Otherwise Parker gets arrested. Or he is killed.

Like a fascist, Parker employs whatever means necessary, including violence, to achieve his goal. Nothing or no one who signs on can expect mercy if they fall short of Parker's expectations. Parker's heart never does anything other than pump blood. It's never soft. Until he gets his money, nothing short of death will stop Parker from coming after someone who has cheated him. But he doesn't kill out of hate. He kills people without feeling. Killings are simply part of his job. Plans don't call for a murder, but circumstances may make murder necessary for the plan to succeed. This is the way Parker thinks, how he perceives the world. Parker is like a drone, hovering for hours in the air, observing, calculating, seeking his best shot for a direct hit. Collateral damage is unfortunate. Planners have bigger fish to fry. The little ones blown out of the water are just among those things that happen on the way from the kitchen to the dining room table.

Parker is a man of deliberate violence. He has a steel rod for a spine and has never shared a beer with a man named Regret. Parker represents that most human urge for control over others and reality. Like a good poker player, Parker figures the odds of his hand, looks at the cards on the table and the other players seated around him and makes a calculated gamble. If someone is cheating, they're dead. Parker plays for keeps. There is no fun in the winning or losing. Getting the job done, the money, getting out and back to a good hotel, somewhere warm, in his swimming trunks, a drink in hand, he finally looks at a woman and decides it is time. The 24 Parker novels continue to sell, and eight Hollywood films have been made from the books. It seems the original editor had a scent of something special in the idea of a Parker series.

Richard Stark, a.k.a. Don Westlake, had the right instinct when he wrote the first Parker novel. Kill off this guy. Parker's death would be applauded by the reader who'd spent hours inside his head. But Richard Stark's editor saw the opportunity for a series and that required keeping Parker alive. Economically, politically and socially the decision-makers elect, like Richard Stark's editor, decide to hire and keep Parker alive. They think having a Parker running things is useful. Such a planner can be relied on to ensure the desired outcome happens. They also think such a man (or woman) can be kept on a short leash. But a man who knows no fear can never be controlled. He takes control, and when that happens, what comes next?

Read a newspaper, watch the news on TV, walk down your street, look around you, and you will find that you are living in a world where Parker has become the model of success. It's too late to kill Parker off. He's on automatic pilot. And he's in your future for years to come.

Insanity at the Gate

There is a fifty-year publishing anniversary that needs celebration. It has to do with the meaning of "insanity" and related terms. Our use of language in everyday conversation—in novels, movies, newspapers and TV and on the Internet—changes the meaning of terms from the past. Take the trio of "insanity," "craziness" and "madness." These three ideas have been around since we've had language, and one day someone will learn from Big Data on the development of language that one reason we acquired language was to keep tabs on people who the community thought weren't quite right in the head.

It has been fifty years since the Ken Kesey novel *One Flew over the Cuckoo's Nest* was released. That makes it a good time to revisit and ask questions about how insanity, craziness and madness remain powerful and effective tools to protect state power and authority.

The film based on Kesey's book won five Oscars. The book and film struck a chord with the Academy and filmgoers. The character of McMurphy could be any of us who pushes back against authority. McMurphy, a criminal in the prison system with a relatively short sentence to serve, thinks he has gamed the system by getting transferred from a prison to a mental hospital. He challenges the power of the head nurse. What he discovers is that he is now inside a system that can detain him indefinitely, and no law, no institution, no authority can prevent the head nurse or her staff from using the full range of "treatments" (in the name of medical science) to break him (or from their point of view, cure him).

If you are anti-authoritarian, then you run the McMurphy risk of being labeled insane, rebellious and troublesome. You go on a list. Nothing that you can do, as McMurphy finds out, will prevent the authorities from carrying out a lobotomy. At the end of the story the Chief sees what they've done to McMurphy, whose unresponsive face is a testament to the power of the State—the entity whose agents employ the words "insanity," "craziness" and "madness" with the precision of Predator drones.

"Insanity" is both a legal term and a medical one. "Madness" and "craziness" are ordinary, common usage to describe abnormal mental acts of another person. Political correctness has erased insanity, madness and craziness, and discussions that would once have used "insanity" now refer instead to "mental disorders."

Science has dispatched madness and craziness to the old world of magic, herbal cures and shaman trances. Science has replaced the local shaman with doctors, nurses, scientists and psychiatrists. That has been called progress and a victory over superstition and backwardness. In the fifty years since Kesey's novel was published, science hasn't been successful in changing the attitude, nature and emotions of mankind. In 1963 the medical workers, in the name of science, doomed McMurphy. Science acted then, as it does now, as a good cover for those in power to legitimize the repression of people like McMurphy.

It is difficult to say what is more dangerous—the old witchdoctor, non-scientific approach, or the new scientific, medical approach. A person's liberty should not stand on the magical thinking of superstitious people. It is cruel and senseless and barbaric. Has science has put an end to the era of witchdoctors? Many people are doubtful. The history of insanity correlates not as one would wish with the developments in science. The idea is that science brings progress and the ways of a superstitious people are left in the past. What we are discovering is that science is creating better tools to lobotomize critics and opponents. "Insanity," "craziness" and "madness" become mud-slinging words hurled against the rise of new ideas, philosophies and technologies.

Don't forget that, at the end of One Flew over the Cuckoo's Nest, it was Nurse Ratched who won. In 2013 we have a new cast of Nurse Ratcheds and McMurphys and every indication that the outcome will be the same as it was in 1963.

Remember the bottle thrown from the plane in The Gods Must Be Crazy? Whenever a tribe comes in contact with an unknown technology, the existing system of belief and thought starts to list like an oil tanker that's rammed a reef. Soon the peaceful tribe is racked with high emotions such as hatred and envy, and violence follows as the hotheads arm themselves to control, own and monopolize the novel invention. At the end of this 1980 film, the hero, Xi, throws the bottle over a cliff and returns to his village.

But the days when the hero could return the world to its pre-bottle ways are over. What is new is not a bottle thrown from a plane, but the Big Data quietly culled, stored and analyzed into marketing, economic policy and dissent suppression. That bottle won't be thrown over a cliff. It is here in the village to stay. New tools to spot and isolate (or control) the "hostile disruptions" increase the reach to track and watch people who are "mad," "crazy" or "insane"— though you will be less likely to see those terms used.

As insanity has been tainted by the long history of loose standards, terrorism has been copied and pasted in places where insanity, madness and craziness were commonly found.

The mental health issue always has risked being politicized into a campaign to reduce violence and maintain security and order. We don't have to look very far back in history before we stumble upon the inconvenient truths about state authorities using mental health as a method of repression and control.

A list of the Reasons for Admission used by the Trans-Allegheny Lunatic Asylum from 1864 to 1889 (widely available online) gives an idea of the range of thinking and acts that could have landed you in the bunk next to McMurphy back then. These nineteenth-century reasons, describing the mental state or behavior of a person before being admitted to the asylum, included "time of life," "dissolute habits," "self abuse," "egotism," "political excitement," "over taxing mental powers," "immoral life," "novel reading" and about six dozen more. From the 1963 film of *One Flew over the Cuckoo's Nest* a case could be made that many items on the list survived well into the twentieth century. A case could also be made that, dressed up in different terms, the list is still sufficient to catch the 2013 version of McMurphy.

"Business nerves" and "bad company" along with "brain fever," "sexual derangement," "dissolute habits" and "women trouble"—more items on the Trans-Allegheny list—could fit about ninety percent of the writers I have met over the years. The reasons associated with the definition of "crazy" may explain why many people view writers, painters, dancers and others as belonging under the big tent of art as insane. The point is, people who don't wish to fit or are incapable of fitting into the morality and norms of their society are by definition psychologically abnormal, and their alternative ways of living might be further evidence of abnormality. Religious or ideological fanatics see other non-believers as abnormal. Our technology hasn't updated the definition of "craziness," only the power and capability of tracking people who fit one of the categories.

The clear and present danger of the concept of "insanity" that finally caught up with McMurphy in *One Flew over the Cuckoo's Nest* has been summarized on Wikipedia as a term that "may also be used as an attempt to discredit or criticise particular ideas, beliefs, [principles], desires, personal feelings, attitudes, or their proponents, such as in politics and religion."

In 2013 would McMurphy's outcome have been any different? Have the last fifty years, with all of our advanced technology, given us better outcomes? Or are we still back at the gate of the Trans-Allegheny Lunatic Asylum, where McMurphy is put out of his misery and the Chief's only hope is to escape as fast as possible from the clutches of repressive power? There is a big difference. In 1963 escape was an option. In 2013 Nurse Ratched's forces would find the Chief, and he would end up like McMurphy.

Whether you identify with the Chief or McMurphy doesn't matter. It is Nurse Ratched's world. *One Flew over the Cuckoo's Nest* was a warning unheeded. We live in the shadow of the Reasons for Admission to the Trans-Allegheny Lunatic Asylum. As "novel reading" is one of the grounds for admission, you'll forgive me if I put on my track shoes and go looking for where the Chief has gone to ground.

Part VII

The Capacity of Memory

Memory Bottlenecks

What do you remember from this morning? Yesterday, last week, last year? When you were thirty years old? When you were nine years old? What passes through the memory bottleneck and can be recalled with ease? Our memory capacity is finite, limited, unstable and dynamic. Witnesses to a crime inevitably report events that contradict each other. To bear witness to a crime, an accident, the shock of the unexpected is a high memory-value moment. We process such moments into memory with more success than the normal, routine activities that arrange our lives like a dance card where the tunes, faces and activities unfold as if by automatic pilot.

We have a memory carrying capacity. Beyond that point is the well-traveled path of overload and forgetting. How many times do you wish you had a memory stick for your brain? It would make learning a foreign language much easier. We are some time away from expanding our personal memory capacity. The irony is that we are drowning in a huge sea of information, most of which we will forget the next day.

Groundhog Day is the classic movie about the repetition and sameness of life. Bill Murray the TV anchor finds himself stranded in a time loop that endlessly repeats one day's events in the same order. I have that sense reading the daily newspapers in Bangkok. The stories about corruption, murder, incompetence and lying unfold as if I am caught in the Thai equivalent of *Groundhog Day*.

The spider's web of memory stretches across our days. Sometimes we catch a fly. It satisfies a hunger. Memory, controlling it, determining its contents and ensuring that the right things are remembered all fall into the political realm. A great deal of vested interest may be found in the way the political process uses our memories, often against us and for the politicians' own interests.

There are the candlestick makers, and their vision of memory is the warm, soft glow that only lit candles can bring. The rituals of birth, marriage, graduation and death are framed in this candlelight. One day a group of electricians come to the realm. Their technology doesn't depend on candlestick makers; indeed, the electricians have a technology that will remove the candlestick makers from their high position in society and in politics. The new elite will be the electricians. The clash between the candlestick makers and the electricians is life and death. We are reminded of those precious candlelit moments, ones that are shared with our parents, their parents, going back far in time. Candles are our memory cue. How can we turn to electricity, an alien technology, which threatens continuity and ultimately will cause us to forget about the world when our lives were illuminated by candles?

The electricians, if they succeed, will be the new elite. The candlestick makers and their wealth, status and authority will fade into oblivion. No one will remember how powerful and important these candlestick makers were. We will remember the world of electricians, and they will assume their role of the new elite. The history of technology suggests that one day, like the candlestick makers before them, the electricians will be replaced—and not without a struggle. There is always a battle to win before the old memory keepers are lost to history. Except as a footnote, and being demoted to a footnote is not what any candlestick maker wishes for. People rarely read footnotes and almost never remember them if they do.

We pay attention to what we are shown and to what we are told. A great deal of what we pay attention to is preselected for us. We rarely question the selection process or consider what it means for our understanding of priorities in the larger world.

I have been asked what I remember about the 2012 Olympics. What I remember is watching the Olympics at my gym. Perched on a LifeCycle, I watched the end of the women's triathlon. I saw clips of the earlier stages of the competition, devoted to swimming and cycling. The main event was the footrace. On the TV screen I saw athletic women from a number of countries on the last stretch of the race, their arms and legs finely honed with muscle, their faces determined and serious as they found the last reserve of strength to give that final kick of speed as they approached the finish line. One of the women runners glanced behind to see how close her nearest competitor was. A moment later, arms raised, she broke the tape across the finish line. It was a moment to file into memory. The triathlon runner crossed that finish line as her trainers, nation, family and friends, along with the eyes of the world, watched. But the completion of the event isn't what I have in my memory of the 2012 Olympics.

As the Olympic events flashed before me on a TV screen, there were two other TVs mounted on either side of the one with the Olympic programming. The TV sets on the left and right—mounted on the wall—were tuned to a CNN news broadcast. Images of a dusty road winding to a low ridge of hills against the horizon flanked the Olympics. The images were from a road in Syria. There were no runners on that road, but as far as the eye could see, the road was choked with women. Dressed in black traditional dress, heads covered under the hot sun, they carried children and the things they had grabbed as they fled the bombs falling on their homes and as the tanks shelled their men. The black clothing blended in a sea of thousands of women, covered head to toe, creating a solid, moving body. They walked by the thousands along a road without end.

The sound on the TVs was turned off. But the CNN news report needed no soundtrack. The long unbroken line of women needed no explanation. There were no medals waiting, no tape to break, no trainers and fans to hug and congratulate them. They were alone. How does a person travel along such a road for days?

That's my memory of the Olympics. An official triathlon enveloped in celebration, congratulations, medals, pride and accomplishment, and a different kind of triathlon with only endurance and obscurity, hardship and despair, along a Syrian road. That's when you know that *Groundhog Day* is a movie about one kind of triathlon. The cozy one that happens to talented and beautiful winners and brightens our day as we observe excellence. The memory of those refugees will be forgotten, if they were ever remembered to begin with, and tomorrow our personal Groundhog Day will recycle the happy moments, the dull ones, the interlude of one banal routine following on the heels of another.

Memory finds little traction in mediocrity, and most of what filters through consciousness is mediocre. In a moment it is gone like a snowflake on a warm window. We look for patterns of greatness, excellence and the transcendent to lift us to a higher level. The arts have long promised such deliverance as we trudge along our own dusty road, but we usually forget the movies, books and songs that we thought we'd remember. The words "out of print" are shorthand for an author who is passing out of memory.

After a while we glance back over our shoulder like the triathlon runner to see if any of our memories are catching up with us. Over a lifetime we outrun most of our memories—they are lost to us as we are alive. The central feature of death is the final extinguishing of our memories; they don't survive. Another feature of our passage—others' memories of who we are, what we accomplished, are captured in a memory bottleneck. That's when we die for a second time. Like the candlestick makers, we love the life we know and fear its displacement. Not only do we forget, we are forgotten like the refugees on the road.

Self-Deception and Self-Forgetting

Watching the presidential debate Wednesday morning (October 17, 2012) in Bangkok time was a reminder that often what people see, judge and talk about is the "self" that is on display. In the case of Governor Romney and President Obama, the projection of self is as important as the substance of the candidates' respective policies.

Such a debate is a medium in which the presence of self becomes the central message. Projection of that self is intended to convince the viewers that the person on display is trustworthy, reliable, honest, quick-witted, capable and knowledgeable. The color of the necktie, the American flag pin on the lapel, the smiles, smirks and frowns, the standing and pacing and circling, the position of the head and eyes all give clues about the self seeking to convince others of his leadership qualities. Each of these selves delivers packets of memories—of events, incidents, meetings—and those memories are paraded and defended as if they are universal in validity. Viewers are asked to ally their memories with the person addressing them. It happened this way or that way, or this is what I said or what someone else said.

Memories are transient, fallible and often distorted or false. It should be obvious to all that people remember different things, emphasize some details over others, and overlook or fail to see some things. In reality people cling to their memories like a dog to a soup bone. That memories are provisional, often unreliable or incomplete is a hard concept to accept for many. Western culture is built on an idea of self that depends on the reliability and trustworthiness of memory. No one hears in a presidential debate a call to humility when it comes to memory. No one ever finds an admission that the other person's memory, though different, may prove to be correct. Presidential debates are verbal wars between competing selves (the attempt to call them "visions" or "points of view" are disingenuous). The compulsion to win the debate means defeating the other self, and along the way the casualty count includes any acknowledgment of the role of fallibility, gray zones of doubt and cognitive biases.

Debate performances are in the same category as writing an essay, an opinion piece, or a non-fictional account of an event or personality. The "I" of the writer is front and center. He or she is uncoiling judgments, opinions, speculations, marshalling arguments and facts—the techniques featured in most non-fiction writing. The author of the essay, like the debater, doesn't disappear and open a realm occupied by "characters" with their "dialogue" and their fears, uncertainties and doubts locked inside their private interiors—the emotional realms where, in fact, most people spend a great deal of their time.

Debates and writing are influenced by social values and norms. The starting point is to ask whether the debate you watch or the book you read is influenced by a culture based on a religion that promotes self-preservation or one that advocates self-extinguishment.

The three major Abrahamic religions—Christianity, Judaism and Islam—share a similar belief—preservation of self in the afterworld. This self goes by the name of a "soul," but that is religion-speak for "you"; the self, the one you know and love, will exist for eternity in heaven or hell. That worldview lends a presidential debate a mythic, biblical quality as two selves—two self-identified angels—battle for supremacy. One will prevail just as the other will fail.

What is missing in an essay or a debate is the absence of self. In Buddhism the ultimate goal in life is to extinguish the self. This is what I find the essential difference between what I am writing in this piece and what I write when I am writing a novel. At every turn I am aware of myself in writing these words. They are mine. The thoughts behind them belong to me. I have called them out of my memory and present them as if they have no bias, are true, and you should believe what I say. In other words, my self is on display.

Fiction is quite different (in theory). In fiction the author who can never get over himself or herself will have a limited career. It is a forgetting of self. Letting go of self is a precondition for empathy. James Wood in a recent essay about the novelist Tom Wolfe examined how Wolfe had failed in book after book to rid himself of self, with the result that every character sounds like a megaphone for Wolfe's own self that has never managed to leave even one dialogue line uninfected with his personality.

An author who in the act of writing sheds her self is Hilary Mantel. Sophie Elmhirst's essay in the *New Statesman* (October 2012) is a revealing portrait of an author's past and how it shaped her ability to forget herself and slip inside her characters' lives. Mantel disappears into her fiction; Wolfe shouts, screams and dances from a platform, hand-waving to the audience as if he's in a presidential debate. Mantel would make a good Buddhist and probably a good president. Wolfe's literary self, on the other hand, I hope finds eternal peace.

In the absence of a highly evolved sense of empathy, it is difficult for a fiction writer to enter into the dreams, thoughts, insecurities and doubts that people experience in their daily lives. Fiction writers often talk about losing themselves in the characters and the story. That is what they mean. Their selves have vanished. They occupy a realm where the characters channel through the writer's mind and reveal their most private secrets; the place where evil lurks, where the shadows of doubt trail the self like a mugger, where the skin is stripped from the body of good intentions and left out to dry.

Rather than hearing the two candidates debate about the middle class and the working class, which they wish others to believe they care about so much, I'd ask them to write a novel. I want to see what comes from such men when they suspend their sense of self and enter into the emotional lives of ordinary men, women and children. That would provide the kind of information I'd like to know. Ultimately it is the empathy connection that is the thread that ensures fiction won't die. It should be part of the sewing kit that goes into the mix of an election. We can't trust the self presented in a debate or an essay if that is all we have to go on.

We should be asking leaders not to pepper their debates with references to having met this person or that who had a problem as a nod to empathy, a way for them to identify a sympathetic self. That won't tell us much about their capacity for empathy. The self is the main character in presidential debates. We need to know, and deserve to know, what leaders pay attention to when they look at other lives. If they can never escape the self, you can't ever be sure as their term spools out before your eyes whether they really have the ability to tell a story through the lives of other selves in the full glory of lives haunted by doubts and racked by suffering and disappointments. Paying attention to how ordinary people cope with their lives shouldn't be limited to fiction.

I'd like to read Obama's novel and Romney's novel. I want to know how their minds work when it isn't focused on self. I want to understand how empathy works for them through the words and acts of characters who make stupid decisions and crazy choices, people who fail, those who give up, and those who get up and struggle to keep going.

If I had that sense of these men in the act of forgetting themselves—that is the nature of the best fiction—I might know something important, more important than a vague policy or intention to do this or that. I'd have a sense of someone who walked a mile in someone else's shoes and was able to communicate what that experience was like and could make that experience real enough for me to believe he understood something genuine about the human condition. Both candidates profess belief that the self is preserved. They have a lot at stake. We will likely never know if their novel would have been written in the tradition of Wolfe or Mantel. I'd like to think one day that might matter, and how someone forgets self and embraces empathy will then be a better indication of leadership ability.

Ghost Whisperers in Asia

In the three-day stretch of November 18 to 20, 2012, President Obama spent Sunday in Thailand, six hours of Monday in Burma and the remainder of Monday as well as Tuesday in Cambodia. Along the way he bumped into the history of a region. Like a nine-headed naga, history raised its heads and spit fire from the caves of local politics, culture and prejudices. But you wouldn't have seen the fire-eating dragons of history captured in the photographs taken along Obama's three-day journey.

Instead what you and the rest of the world saw were the photos of the American President kissing Aung San Suu Kyi, flirting with Prime Minister Yingluck and clasping hands with Hun Sen—the enduring images of his trip. History doesn't photograph as well and is easily nudged into the ditch. Obama's Southeast Asia trip was textbook present-day symbolic image making. Not one angry dragon floated above the heads of the leaders.

We can't undo the past; we can only reconcile ourselves with the aftermath, the damage, the loss, the suffering. Any member of the political class will acknowledge the difficulty of brokering reconciliation. No one is happy to deal with past conflicts and struggles and the long trail of victims history produces.

To admit wrongdoing done by one's ancestors is to travel down a path that most politicians wish to avoid. It is easy to blame those not in power or foreigners for the misfortune. Victims gather at the time of major events such as a presidential visit to the area. They demand to be heard. They raise their voices, crying for admissions of guilt, compensation and punishment. Korean comfort women used as sexual slaves in World War II want compensation from the Japanese. The Chinese remind their citizens of the rape and massacre of civilians in Nanking by the Japanese in the same war. Victims of the Cambodian Killing Fields want the Khmer Rouge leaders punished for genocide. The Thai and Khmer armies exchange gunfire over the border surrounding a historical temple.

The Burmese have a library of historical conflict with ethnic minorities. To be fair, the President did mention the need to provide security to the Rohingya who have lived for generations in the western part of the country. That is as close to history as President Obama came, and the Rohingya pogrom is contemporary, ongoing and not really history.

Historical narratives are like a flag blowing this way or that way, depending on the prevailing political winds. When it suits a government to advance a present interest, then the historical wrongs are revisited to justify present-day claims and demands. It is an old trick, and as with a professional sleight of hand, the pulling of the historical rabbit out of the hat unifies the crowd. Makes them marvel at the magic.

President Obama wasn't going to be drawn into the magicians' circle and become part of their act. No doubt he understood that the magicians in Southeast Asia wished him to be their apprentice, to applaud their performance. It was better to hug, kiss and hold hands. That is the way to win hearts. That is the new show business, the reality show model. History is for nerds, troublemakers, demagogues, eggheads and ideologues. Besides, Americans have their own naga headed creatures ranging from the invasion of North America and the genocide of the native population to slavery, civil war and segregation. It is hard to criticize another country's history when your own ghosts still roam the land.

There are some reasons why presidents and other leaders visiting another country avoid getting caught up in the local history. It means taking sides. When someone takes sides, it means he or she has made an enemy of those on the other side of the historical divide. President Obama didn't come to make enemies; he came to meet allies, make friends and cement American interests in the region. Historical accounting would have scuttled those goals. History is something leaders don't talk about with each other. History is taboo, unless of course there is a compelling national interest.

The past is a difficult time-and-space problem for any democracy to resolve. There is often strong disagreement over what happened, and with both sides claiming their evidence should prevail, neither side can be reconciled to a conclusion that favours their rival.

Elections don't resolve this standoff either, and that is the dirty secret democracy keeps to itself. The ruling elites, to the extent history runs against their interests, ignore it and wait for the victims to die off or become completely marginalized. Democracies are no different from other forms of government in the suppression of inconvenient truths from the past. School books, TV, radio and newspapers have traditionally baked the history cake that is sweet and tasteful. No culture wants to recount their unvarnished past. Democracies are in the forgetting business like every other system.

History is like dark matter and dark energy, which compose the overwhelming majority of the universe. History, malleable, removed from living memory, subject to manipulation, is a geopolitical minefield. When President Obama visited Thailand, Burma and Cambodia, he walked through that minefield and mingled with the ghosts of the past. People forget the details of what happened long ago. When I covered the UN war crimes tribunal in Cambodia last November, what became clear was how little most of the young generation there knew about the Khmer Rouge reign of terror

As those who lived through that time grow old and die, the day will eventually arrive when no one alive remembers what happened. That's the day history truly enters a new phase. The evidence of what happened in the past exists outside the experience of anyone alive. The loss fades, becomes abstract, and the past becomes that alien foreign land where the dead are left as the only citizens. Politicians struggle to keep coalitions together in the present. Obama was looking to the future, a legacy, by coming to Southeast Asia, and that goal is rarely found in the graveyard of the past.

The last reason that history is left along the road to solving contemporary issues of the day, such as trade relations, is politicians are caught up in the present with an eye on the future. They don't see a percentage in glancing back over their shoulder at events caused by others in the distant past. History is long, diverse and complex, spanning generations and centuries. A president, like the rest of us, lives inside the confines of a twenty-four-hour day. There is only so much information that can be processed during a day, a week, a month or a term of office.

We are overwhelmed by information. In Nate Silver's *The Signal and the Noise: Why So Many Predictions Fail—*

But Some Don't, the author notes that the human brain is capable of processing only one one-millionth of the *daily* information load of 2.5 quintillion bytes. We fall behind every day. There is no way we have discovered to keep up with this onslaught of new information.

A lot of that daily information may be "noise"—it isn't useful—but finding the signal in that maze of noise is still bound by the twenty-four hours that make a day. With so much new information to process, separate into signals, evaluate, test and form and shape into ideas about policy, it is no wonder that history—all of that "old" information—remains in the back of the drawer.

Asia, like every other region, has many ghosts walking the land. The explosion of information threatens the past, which is slowly being lost in the noise of daily information. If we could keep up with the present information, we might be able to factor in the past information. But we aren't at that point. We may never reach that point, either. Our daily information journey puts us further behind each day. We can take a historical journey through the Killing Fields, an insurgency in the South of Thailand, or Burma's long-oppressed ethnic groups, but the longer we spend in those past wrongs, the further behind we fall in the current daily information overload.

The long history of discontent, simmering resentments from the past and unresolved borders lies buried beneath the sweet smiles, flashing eye contact and handshakes. It also lies buried under the information treadmill, which keeps increasing its speed, and as fast as we run, we find that we only fall more and more behind, with no hope of ever catching up.

History teaches a valuable lesson about data: the rapid growth of information radicalizes, ghettoizes and localizes communities with strong beliefs. They have their own TV stations, websites and blogs where such communities exist inside a bubble, believing in their alternative reality built from cherry-picked data. No wonder information contained in "history" has become another data point used by all sides to support the superiority of their sets of claims.

The unresolved and rival historical claims existing between various Southeast Asian countries may be exceeded in significance by the internal conflicts over historical injustices inside each country. As President Obama danced in and out of the region, he seemed to be saying between hugs and kisses and handshakes, "Move along, people. Stay close to me. There is blue sky ahead, and we'll walk toward the sunlit horizon arm in arm."

Remember the kiss of today. Forget the graveyards of yesterday. But the ghost whisperers make certain that state of affairs never holds for long.

Part VIII

On Crime Fiction

Dispatches from the Front Lines of Crime Fiction's Extremistan, Part 1

A discussion has started at Detectives Beyond Borders about the future of crime fiction. The controversy started with an exchange at the South African blog Crime Beat with crime fiction reviewer Gunter Blank, who views crime fiction in the USA, Sweden and Germany as having gone into a recycling phase where nothing but repetitive motifs and themes are appearing. What is emerging, in his view, are political thrillers or chronicles from "[T]urbulent or haunted societies, societies that are trying to find out who they are—there are still hundreds and thousands of lives and experiences to tell."

The debate was picked up by my friend and blogger Peter Rozovsky at his not-to-be-missed website Detectives Beyond Borders. Peter's readers have added their views in comments.

Richard Nash sums up the fate of contemporary authors in America and Europe and other places, too: "Books, like most entertainment media, live in what Nassim Nicolas Taleb calls Extremistan, a place with vast amounts of commercial failure and spectacularly high and extremely infrequent success."

As I have a horse (or a dog if you like) in this race, I'd like to give my perspective on the metamorphosis of crime fiction inside Extremistan, examining the borders and how the territory has been traveled, mapped and reported. While Nassim Nicolas Taleb coined the phrase Extremistan to talk about the huge disparity of failure compared to success in the book industry, I am expanding the concept to use Extremistan to talk about the huge disparity between the awareness of crime fiction in English and all other languages.

Taleb uses the ratio of .05 percent (authors who receive 99.95 percent of the money and are commercially successful) to 99.95% (who divide the few crumbs of the .05% revenues left over). Something like this ratio, I believe, also applies as a rule of thumb across the range of languages with English-language crime fiction authors receiving 99.95% of the critical review attention, money, status and opportunity, and non-English crime fiction authors living hand to mouth.

Extremistan is a monetary idea and it is also a geo-graphical, cultural and political one. My Extremistan is a kind of map of worldwide crime fiction. On that map we know with confidence where English-language crime fiction exists. But 99.95% of the map consists of uncharted areas. Crime fiction is written in these unknown parts but as they aren't mapped, they are outside awareness. As a result, we largely ignore their existence.

A good definition for these purposes of metamorphosis comes from *Wikipedia,* which defines it as "a biological process by which an animal physically develops after birth or hatching, involving a conspicuous and relatively abrupt change in the animal's body structure through cell growth and differentiation."

Over the last two decades there has been a growth in what is described as crime fiction in many different countries and cultures. The idea of crime fiction is a cultural lens borrowed from English and American authors including Hammett and Chandler. Under the surface, the cultural aspects have brought a change in texture and form. While the external appearance may (unlike true metamorphosis) remain to the untrained eye the same, underneath that surface the impulses, imperatives and purposes are filtered through different sets of beliefs, histories, languages, traditions, rituals and customs—and these elements matter when it comes to the kind of story that can be published.

This cultural lens has been fitted to new glasses in other cultures in the remote parts of Extremistan. Many of these places are off the usual map of crime fiction neighborhoods. Crime fiction is illegible in these places. Our speculation about what goes on inside the hidden world doesn't make them more legible.

And that leads me to ask what goes inside these missing areas on the crime fiction map, and can we act like good detectives to find out what goes on inside, beyond our normal borders?

What is left unexamined in the debate started by Gunter Blank are the forces causing the turbulence or the haunting in societies outside Sweden, Germany and the USA. In countries like Thailand, Cambodia, Vietnam and Burma—the turbulence of globalization and the Internet has kicked up a firestorm in fairly rigid, traditional and highly controlled societies. This has happened not just in Southeast Asia but also in Latin America and the Arab world. Crime fiction has become a window into the chaos that disruptive change has brought, threatening institutions, vested interests and authority structures.

A murder investigation, on the surface, is similar in many places around the world. But a murder investigation in a turbulent society, which is in the metamorphosis stage, brings in to focus the tensions, competing interests and repressive forces that give a political dimension to the case. To understand the behavior, reactions and emotions requires a cultural map. The best crime fiction operates like a GPS system, guiding you through the winding byways, local alleys and little-known hills. Think of them as "belief, taboo, faith" landmarks. What governments and people believe to be true and how they process their reality is central to reading crime fiction from these neighborhoods.

You might say that the USA, Germany and Sweden are also societies in transition as they respond to similar pressures from the new world of telecommunications and global trade. That is to miss the paradigm change caused by the Age of Reason and Enlightenment in having over a period of 500 years eroding traditional authority and belief structures from the church to the aristocracy. Our neighborhood was torn down in many places and rebuilt. In the new Western places on the map, we live in a version of the future. As William Gibson famously said, "The future is already here but it is unevenly distributed."

In many parts of the world outside Europe and North America, the Age of Reason and the Enlightenment have existed outside the great wall of authority patrolled by a combination of censorship, repression, custom and tradition. This system worked for many centuries, preserving the neighborhood and the attitudes about what is a crime and who is a criminal. But most of these old, traditional neighborhoods are also doomed. Like the Berlin Wall, these traditional regimes all look so solid and impenetrable until the moment they are pulled down.

Crime fiction written in these parts of the world track investigations into crime as the walls are collapsing around the authorities, exposing them, implicating them, leaving them in the spotlight mostly reserved for criminals. This is what international crime fiction brings to the reader—society in the midst of transition, access to a part of the fictional map that isn't widely known or understood.

It is this irony, this strange juxtaposition—the blurring of criminality—that makes crime fiction from the emerging world compelling to the readers in those places. We are watching the future pass into societies as if the walls no longer exist, and we have a frontline seat to the forces pushing back, trying to build new walls, putting the screws in, enacting repressive laws to create fear in order to silence those who see that the walls are falling.

Most of storytellers inside these old regimes that exist off the English reader's grid aren't given attention. It is as if these unmapped areas don't exist except as a "bad news" story about an earthquake, flood, revolution, assassination, starvation, refugee camps or genocidal authorities. The storytellers in these places are unlikely to be on your top 13 authors' list. But that doesn't mean their voices are unread or unheard inside their cultures. It is more likely their absence from our awareness is evidence of our availability bias. We make our decision on the evidence that is available to us. We don't ask what is missing.

As Daniel Kahneman has noted in *Thinking, Fast and Slow*, we are prone to believing that what we see is all that there is.

While the USA, Germany, Sweden and similar cultures may be suffering from redundancy, crime fiction authors in other cultures suffer from obscurity and isolation. These novelists write in languages that aren't easily accessible for readers of English. Thai writers are a good example. Thailand has its share of talented authors who write in Thai but who haven't been translated into English. You will never read them unless you learn Thai. The same applies to other cultures where the language issue traps the authors inside their own locked room without an exit door. In reality very few novels are translated into other languages. As a result they are marooned on the desert island of obscure languages, forever lost to those sailing past.

Using what we know about the universe is a convenient analogy for our map of crime fiction. The universe consists of a bit less than five percent atomic matter, and the rest is dark matter or dark energy. When you read about crime fiction publishing in English, I suggest that you are inside a reading space that amounts to vastly less than five percent of the total space. It may be Taleb is right. If he is, then only about .05 percent world of crime fiction is mapped. The rest is dark matter and dark energy.

We need to be cautious about making broad statements about the best crime fiction novelists, the trends in crime fiction, or the role crime fiction plays in literature, culture and political life. The reality is we only have a vague idea of this unmapped landscape, the writers who live there, and the role crime fiction plays in chronicling the dynamics of fundamental change to political and social systems.

Dispatches from the Front Lines of Crime Fiction's Extremistan, Part 2

What is the limit of our knowledge about the library of crime fiction novels written, published and read each year inside Extremistan? There is no shortage of people claiming knowledge about a library that may not be Borges's infinite library, but a library with shelves filled with books that are inaccessible to most readers.

The point is we are having a debate where there is a vast body of work that is unavailable for analysis. When what is essential to an argument is largely unknown or missing, it is a caution that we must exercise humility in making grand statements about the direction or trend of crime fiction. I can draw inferences from what I know about Southeast Asia but even those are flawed, as I can't read the work in the original language.

Whenever the debate of crime fiction occurs, the question of who are the best crime fiction authors arises. And the usual names appear. Here's Gunter Blank's list: James Ellroy, *L.A. Confidential*; Dashiell Hammett, *The Glass Key*; Jim Thompson, *Pop. 1280*; Raymond Chandler, *The Lady in the Lake* and *Farewell, My Lovely*; George V. Higgins, *The Friends of Eddie Coyle*; Richard Stark, *The Hunter* (*Point Blank*); Charles Willeford, *Miami Blues*; Elmore Leonard, *Freaky Deaky*; Marcel Montecino, *The Cross-Killer*; Edward

Bunker, *No Beast So Fierce*; Chester Himes, *Blind Man with a Pistol*; Ted Lewis, *GBH*.

As lists go, I'd agree with many of these selections. I know this neighborhood and have lived in it, been a part of it as a writer and reader. But I'm also aware that by the very act of preparing such a list I am placing my own cultural and availability bias on display. Would someone from Latin America, Africa or Southeast Asia believe this list is relevant to his or her experience? Such lists appear to be delivered from a Western cloister, insular, confined and narrowly clustered. There is a much larger world excluded, and that's the one we ought to be seeking to understand. That world is overwhelmningly populated by those whose missing names are missing from the headliner list.

Who has gone missing? The answer is a lot of crime, detective and mystery authors are hidden under the veil of inaccessible languages.

A recent anthology of African crime fiction writers featured works by Matthew J. Christensen, Geoffrey V. Davis, Susanne Gehrmann, James Gibbs, Mikhail Gromov, Karola Hoffmann, Said M.A. Khamis, Matthias Krings, Manfred Loimeier, Christine Matzke, Katja Meintel, Anja Oed, Ranka Primorac, Uta Reuster-Jahn, Alina Rinkanya and Doris Wieser. These are names that are likely not familiar to even the most well-read English, German or Swedish language crime fiction reader. In Latin America, translations from Spanish are hit and miss. For every Roberto Bolaño there are many like Ramon Diaz Eterovic and Santiago Gamboa, whose novels haven't been translated into English.

The Japanese had the first crime books (though they were non-fiction accounts of court proceedings) before authors in England and the USA came along. Saikaku Ihara's 1689 title *Trials under the Shade of a Cherry Tree* predates Edgar Allan Poe's 1841 *Murders in the Rue Morgue* and Wilkie Collins's

1868 *Moonstone*. The Mystery Writers Club of Japan has 600 members, and I'd bet a first edition of the bible that only a fraction of them have been translated into English. Every year in Bangkok since 1979 the Southeast Asia Writers Award has announced the winning author from each of the ten countries in Southeast Asia. Scroll down the long list of authors and ask yourself how many of the names you recognize.

Richard Nash's "What Is the Business of Literature?" is worth reading. A point that emerges from Nash's article is that we fall into the trap of equating the value of literature with the commercial success of a book. If the crime fiction novel is a bestseller, and you are a reader of crime fiction, the chances are you are aware of the book. You've heard about it from friends in the analogue or digital communities where you spend time.

The publishing industry in North America and Europe has had a freedom to publish quite unlike most other places. Hundreds of thousands of English language books enter the marketplace every year.

Books are part of the entertainment/corporate profit-centered industry in these places. They cater to the tastes of consumers who have many other entertainment choices. Little risk of imprisonment, exile or torture from the authorities threatens authors who challenge beliefs inside the Western publishing industry. The risk is the book will be a failure and the author's next book won't be published. In neighborhoods in the unmapped neighborhoods, a different fate other than commercial failure needs to be understood. Authors who are successful in revealing a truth about a country's institutions or who challenge an established dogma risk a prison term. It doesn't stop at prison. Authors in the unmapped neighborhoods face extrajudicial remedies as kidnapping, disappearance, torture or death. In English-speaking neighborhoods, a nasty review may be felt like a bullet to the chest. But in non-English unmapped neighborhoods writers know that the critics use real bullets.

One of the major differences between the Western publishing industry and other places is the sheer number of books pumped into the system. Nash quotes Clay Shirky, who writes that "abundance breaks more things than scarcity."

My first novel, *His Lordship's Arsenal*, was published in New York in September 1985. That year the number of USA titles published by traditional print publishers numbered 80,000. By 2010 the number of published titles had mushroomed to 328,259 in one year. In this world of abundance, the moderately gifted author writes a book with little prospect of financial reward. Writing inside such a publishing system, where commercial success means value, these writers are discarded not so much as worthless but as failing purely on economic grounds and there is no other justification to read them and take them seriously.

Authors are writing and trying to survive inside a business empire where profit not only matters; it is basically all that matters. Competition in the publishing industry, as in other areas of the entertainment industry, is often presented as another business story with the emphasis on the size of an advance, the bestseller ranking, the volume of sales and movie deals. Reviews have withered in most places in the print media. Discussions revolve around money, which has become the primary benchmark, the ruler that measures success. Thumbs up or thumbs down is an accounting decision. No one is put against a wall and shot.

Books written for money in a society where money is the measure of value has created an impoverished class of authors who like idealistic slaves believe that a lotto-like win will allow them to escape their fate and joint the ranks of Dan Brown and J.K. Rowling. Much of our English-language crime fiction library is money driven.

Outside the world of money there is another Extremistan. It isn't created from account ledgers. In this Extremistan the crime fiction author chronicles the systemic changes in class, politics and social relationships through the lens of criminal law enforcement. To stay alive and out of prison is a measure of success. To have a voice and influence in the debate of how to modernize and allow a society to change without falling apart is a measure of success. The fiction writer as part of the political process, and using the vehicle of crime fiction to deliver a challenge to authority invites a level of danger and uncertainty. It is, in other words, not about the money.

Thomas Wörtche is one of the very rare editors (and I can't think of another one) who had the vision of searching for and publishing such writers. His imprint, called Metro—Unionsverlag was the publishing house—was known throughout Europe. I admired his determination to dig deep and find authors either ignored or little known by the mainstream publishing industry in the West. Metro published such writers as Jean-Claude Izzo, Nury Vittachi, Garry Disher, Leonardo Padura, Celil Oker, Pablo De Santis, Bill Moody, Jorge Franco, Gabriel Trujillo Muñoz, José Luis Correa. (Disclosure: I was also an author on Thomas Wörtche's list.) Metro was a window into Extremistan.

Since Thomas left Unionsverlag, there has been no editor like him, with the necessary experience and knowledge of crime fiction to explore Extremistan for the new generation of writers who remain largely lost to international readers. That is regrettable. The crime space inside Extremistan has receded from international readers and has become as inaccessible as the dark side of the moon. We know that it is there every night, but what it looks like and what goes on out of sight is left to our imagination. The purest form of noir is absolute silence.

Writers like Ali Bader, who live in regions such as Iraq where the blast of violence pounds their days and nights, are cut off from the rest of us. Another such writer is Yanick Lahens, who writes of Haiti. These are two of many voices you'd almost need a cultural detective to find. And for every Ali Bader or Yanick Lahens, how many are lost to us completely? We are less rich in the depth of our understanding without their clarifying commentary from their crime-space front lines.

Two great sites to visit for developments in Extremistan are Detectives Beyond Borders and Words Without Borders. If you want to find a new author, visit these websites.

To paraphrase William Gibson: The vast majority of writers live inside unmapped neighborhoods of Extremistan, where the measure of their value is unevenly understood.

Dispatches from the Front Lines of Crime Fiction's Extremistan, Part 3

What controls Extremistan authors, what keeps them off the grid, is an effective system of censorship backed by punitive laws. Unless you've lived outside North America or Western Europe, you won't have experienced the "eye" of authorities (and their true believers or paid shills) monitoring all communications including books for possible breaches of national security or other equally vague, open-ended infractions of laws and policies designed to preserve an image. "The broader the better" is the rule, when the purpose is to chill the kinds of expression that question, criticize or challenge authority, institutions, dogma or beliefs.

The mere presence of a censorship regime induces self-censorship. Authors are never certain where the authorities will draw the line. Monday it is one place, Tuesday it has moved somewhere else, and the week is only two days old. This makes sense as the authorities in charge of enforcement rarely speak with one voice on where the boundaries of permissible and impermissible meet. To be on the careful side means authors err by staying as far away from the border as possible. As a result, creative writers in such regimes are given a couple of choices—either write hagiographies and historical epics of glory or vacuous entertainments.

Alternatively, they can circulate their poems, stories, novels and memoirs under a pen name through photocopied handouts or, if they have access to a secure Internet line (difficult to come by in most cases) and the skills to use it, they can publish their work on the Internet.

It is time to recognize that "crime fiction" and the realities of life from which fiction emerges are no longer separate. The idea of crime fiction as contained in a book needs broadening as well. Uploaded images from Extremistan communicate graphic, brutal noir stories as powerful and haunting as found in a crime novel by Hammett or Chandler.

For centuries censorship has largely been local. Each culture identifies the sacred cows that can't be touched. There has never been agreement on a universal sacred cow, and that is unlikely to happen any time soon. If we take a look through the unmapped parts of Extremistan, the sacred cows are often quite different beasts. What is common is that the guardians have used censorship to protect and defend the local herd (there are often a number of sacred cows, as it turns out). The chief herdsmen use whatever force may be necessary to keep the herd in a stable state of unquestioned worship, respect and awe.

Authors in Extremistan—at least the risk-taking ones— like to slip through the thought net cast by the authorities and raise questions about the grazing rights of sacred cows. That often ends in unpleasantness of the extreme kind.

Censorship is not going to stay confined to remote areas of Extremistan. Authorities are developing technology that will make the censorship of the past seem as quaint, remote and inefficient as the quill and ink. Up to now, in even the most impressive regimes, it has been possible for courageous men and women to challenge authority through books circulated underground. The old regimes have been basically inefficient clap-trap machines that have used flawed intelligence to repress free speech. That is about to change.

Here is one possible future that I see for authors living inside Extremistan.

First, the authorities in the West are developing the capability to monitor large areas in detail. Every person, vehicle, dog and bird can be clearly observed down to a six-inch margin of error as they circulate within a fifteen-square-mile corridor.

Second, the authorities are on the brink of creating powerful identification software that will allow them to identify *every* person on the ground by given name, age, nationality, associations, ID numbers, date of birth, known associates, medical health records, Facebook "likes," articles read, books bought, consumer items purchased, and school and university records. The ID system will run on fine-tuned algorithms as the amount of big data would vastly exceed the capacity of an army of people filtering for signals. Authorities are end users of targeted information—they know who is where and when they are were in a place, and who are their friends and associates. Such information is incredibly powerful.

Third, the authorities are developing a new generation of drones. The censors' goal is to cull the dissent within and without. A carrot is good. But a big stick is better. Why not adapt the existing drone technology? One limitation is controversial—drones fire rockets that blow up "guilty" and innocent alike leave the authorities with a bad reputation. Authorities always seek ways to burnish their reputation and to reduce information that tarnishes it. The "collateral damage" is difficult to explain away when killing insurgents but quite another when the enemy is using only a pen. Technology continues to improve, and some projections as to what might be in store promise to increase the censors' arsenal.

The chances are high that advanced drone technology systems will be created to eliminate the stigma of collateral damage. This requires surgical isolation of damage to a single target. With the new technology outlined above, finding that target will become infinitely easier. Moving targets will not present a challenge. And it will be infinitely easier to persuade most would-be dissenters that yielding to silence is the only alternative.

Let's call the new drone Aerial Reconnaissance Sniper or ARS—which is also Hebrew slang for a low-class male. It turns out that in Arabic *ars* also is a term associated with:

- a pimp in general
- a cuckold, a man whose wife is unfaithful to him
- a man who pimps his wife
- a wicked or contemptible person, a "bad guy"
- a bastard, an illegitimate child

If there is any agreement in the Middle East, it is that *ars* is a term used for someone no one is going to mourn once he's dead. Before ARS we called them terrorists. Language, like technology, evolves—in this case, in tandem.

The innovation of the new generation of ARS arms the drone at 17,000 feet to deliver with absolute precision a bullet to the, well, let's be honest, whatever the authorities have concluded is a low-class male, a bad guy, who has through his conduct sacrificed his right to live. This "bullet" will be a tiny guided missile the size of a .50 caliber round with video camera. The bullet guidance system locks on and tracks the target. You can run but you can't hide. One less *ars* in the world, the new reports will say. The video footage will confirm the kill. Call this elimination program an example of national security interests gone global.

The authorities in Extremistan will trade resources for those controlling ARS technology to take care of their local "bad guys," who just so happen to be writing books that ridicule or challenge the role of the local sacred cows or putting them in an unfavourable light.

We are the last of the free men and the last of the free women. Those who follow after us, if they read our books, will marvel at how much freedom we had. Or maybe they won't. In all the vast stretches of Extremistan authors who seek to put a message of hope in a bottle, casting it into the sea of the future and trusting it will wash up on some beach, will likely find the beach empty. People will no longer walk along such beaches. They will no longer find such bottles and the messages hidden inside. The sacred cows roaming the streets of Extremistan will be left unmolested by writers. Words and images will extol the virtue of the authorities.

Even the fields and pastures will belong to them then, and from 17,000 feet trespassers will find themselves in the crosshairs of ARS. There will be nowhere to hide. Freedom will be transformed in Arsdoom. And there will be no one left standing who is able to question the herdsmen as to why, how and when that new global state came into being. In the future will our successors in the writing life write and live in a version of North Korea?

Noir Fiction, Part 1: Mind Hacks

I have been playing with the idea that noir crime authors are a subset of hackers into the hive mind collectively shared by their readers. A few years ago I wrote an article called "Writing Novels inside the Hive Mind." I'd like to further develop this metaphor along with some thoughts on the related idea of hacking. It is a mixing of metaphors, to be sure. I hope to show that despite the limitation, we can find another layer of understanding and perspective about how we process noir crime fiction.

The best of the noir authors understand, like all hackers, that the mental system presents an explanatory description of the world that has a number of flaws and weaknesses. The stability of any hive or colony (think of ants or termites) requires order, separation of functions, coordination of routines and cooperation to survive. We find elements of this structure woven through our own lives. Cultures bond people by giving them messages about predictability, certainty and control. Most people recoil from inhabiting a world where doubt, uncertainty and randomness can only be removed with sleight of hand tricks. Hive dwellers, though, are suckers for such illusions.

Tyrants ultimately threaten to capture and control a hive population through the use of delusion creation projects. They play on the cognitive handicaps by using techniques that calm the hive. The business of most cultures, if you peel back the political, social and economic layers, has a common theme: the elite bees or ants maintain their status by promising to eliminate doubt and chance. If you can create the illusion of hive harmony, purity and certainty, you can own the hive.

Noir crime fiction is a hack into the hive, leaving behind a message—you can never overcome or defeat randomness, and there are no handrails that deliver you from doubt. I'd like to develop that idea in this essay. In a minute I'll throw a noir crime book into the hive and report on the buzz.

Our cognitive machinery evolved, in part, as a function of living in the equivalent of a hive. As the old saying goes, you are unique just like everyone else. Our minds suffer from a number of biases, illusions and errors. We rarely question whether what we are processing is connected with reality. Most of the time we don't recognize a gap between our perception and our external reality which we assume are perfectly correlated. We see patterns that are smooth, harmonious and consistent, reinforcing our beliefs and values. We make honey. We work for those who run the hive. Usually we don't think twice about that arrangement. We look around and see everyone else is in the honey-making business and not questioning too deeply their role in the larger scheme of things.

Our assumption is that our mind is a reliable reporter, translator and interpreter. Clinging to beliefs is much easier than junking them and considering new ones. Beliefs are resilient, and contradictory reality doesn't necessarily change a belief.

Make fun of or belittle someone's idea of the sacred and see the reaction. Try teaching evolution in a Texas school. Or try to suggest that a state-sponsored health care or gun control is a good idea in America.

Daniel Kahneman, who authored *Thinking, Fast and Slow*, has spent a lifetime studying the effects of anchoring, confirmation bias, framing and other issues that influence our distorted view of the world, others and ourselves. The distortions vary from culture to culture, but the basic idea is the same. We have the same brain but the programming is culturally determined. Each hive has a slightly different operating system, much as Apple and Microsoft platforms have different sets of biases and limitations but in reality are more alike than different.

It is the biased mind that reads and thinks about books. As it is a biased mind that writes them. There is something very noir-like about the trap of biases that our mind automatically falls into.

We need to think about what it means to educate literate people. The basic idea of literacy that most people accept is narrowly framed. Literacy means a person has acquired the ability to read and write with sufficient skill to navigate inside the hive. Without literacy there would be no book authors or book readers or books. Also, literacy normally leaves a large back door open for updating the operating system. There is intense competition to hack the hive mind. The partial roll call includes authors, governments, religions, celebrities, corporations, political parties, advertisers and subversives.

If the educational system is one where the teacher is the unquestioned authority, and the text the unquestionable truth, and the pupils' duty is to master the language sufficient to read, memorize and write out the exercises that reinforce the received truths, the pupils graduate into the community not as educated citizens but programmed (and programmable) citizens. Ever since the Industrial Revolution, the commercial, corporate and military institutions have established power by hacking their messages into the vast ranks of programmed citizens. That is the template for the human hive. George Orwell's *1984* fictionalized the process of programming and the perils of outsiders hacking into the citizen's preprogrammed set of beliefs.

The use of critical thinking and analysis is paid lip service all around the world. It has become a kind of feel-good issue like motherhood. Or like the advice to avoid stress, to exercise and not to drink or smoke too much. Hive owners force themselves to lie about their commitment to the critical thinking business.

This isn't exceptional inside the hive, where there is a free-for-all over the programming hack into how you should deal with stress, exercise daily and restrain your drinking, drugs and smoking. Our cognitive machinery has been hacked like a meteorite shower raining down a hundred times a day dumping TV commercials—and similar messages on shopping mall live feeds, on TVs in trains, online, in newspapers (where those still exist), on billboards and in the logos on cars, shirts, watches, cell phones, handbags, and clothing—straight into our brains. We don't see the contradiction that this is the price of hive life.

Next time you wake up, start the day with a notebook and a pen and note down the "hacks" you encounter in your little corner of the hive. Open your eyes to what messages you find in words, symbols, slogans, commercials, logos, pictures and music. At the end of the day go through your list to see how many hacks have been attempted on your mind. Our minds are filled with these viruses. They are overrun with tiny patches that slide through without us being aware we've been hacked.

To view everything in terms of our own time is another bias to avoid, though it is difficult to consistently do so. It is likely that every civilization has defined the "civilized citizen" as the person who excels in representing the legitimacy of the honey-hoarding Truth Keepers and extolling the virtues and grandeur of hive culture, and the nobility and purpose of the unified community. Civilization, like any hive structure, can't be established or maintained without such programming.

The programming power to shape the emotions of hive members and organize their movements through art is demonstrated in videos of flash mobs such as the much-viewed one in Moscow to the tune of "Puttin' on the Ritz" (easily findable on YouTube) These can be memorable and telling experiences. Who gets to play the music controls those who can't resist the instinct to join the dance and coordinate their movement with the others. Think of bees dancing to direct the colony to a field of flowers in bloom.

The Russian dance video shows the power of music imported from the "outside" and brought to a culture noted for its historical restrictions on freedom of movement, thought and artistic expression.

Another well-known video, from Sabadell, Spain, featuring a live performance of Beethoven's *Ode to Joy, Symphony No. 9 in D Minor, Op. 125*, acts as a counterbalance in several ways. The first thing I noticed in the Beethoven video was the different role played by the audience and its expectations. They are not an active part of the performance in the Beethoven video. The audience is one of listeners, who are recipients rather than active co-participants in the performance. People stay in place. They witness, appreciate and admire. Also, while there are shots of a few children, the audience is noticeably older at the Beethoven event.

The Beethoven video demonstrates the power of the existing culture to use the Truth Keepers' music to unite the hive members into one group strung together by a common, shared emotion. No barbarians are in that crowd.

That made it perfect to function as an advertisement for a Spanish bank.

Different music, different programs hack into the mind of the audience, leading them to quite different ways of expressing the collective self.

Noir Fiction, Part 2: Barbarians

Barbarians have acquired a bad name. Their negative press is part of our hive programming. We feel revulsion toward outsiders, the barbarians who threaten our way of life, our values, our norms, and our laws and institutions. Leave our hive alone!

The barbarians in Roman times were the Germanic tribes along the borders. These tribes had a disturbing feature—their members had minds that hadn't been programmed by Roman cultural, governmental, military or educational authorities. More simply, they came from another hive. That's why they were called barbarians. They weren't Romans in outlook or mindset. They had their own ideas about honey.

On one level a barbarian is a person who has managed to escape, reject or avoid the programming of an established culture or civilization. On another level the barbarian wants to impose a different operating system on the invaded hive.

Critical thinkers, noir crime novelists and essayists like George Orwell are a few examples of modern-day barbarians who perform intellectual hacks into the "civilized" mind, planting a disturbing possibility—that what civilized cultures have accepted as reality is dangerous, distorted and flawed.

In an earlier essay I warned that the Truth Keepers (the Official Programmers, Honey Hoarders—the metaphors multiply in a hive setting) have exploited a programmed belief system built on anxiety, fear and desire so that the system largely sends the honey flowing to a narrow part of the hive and the bees who are close allies. The way people are programmed not to think other than the accepted wisdom about work, family, parliament, courts, cities, shopping centers or entertainment makes them good candidates for hacking.

It is the duty of the Official Programmers to guard their turf and strike hard at hackers trying to break into and alter the messages about how the system functions, its purpose and fairness. I suspect it is no different at Microsoft, Apple, Google, Facebook or hundreds of other less well-known companies where most of the honey goes to only a few.

Until the Internet changed the way the game was played. It seems that the programming worked best when the Truth Keepers had a secure monopoly on what beliefs and ideas were transmitted on which channels. For most of human existence, the borders of the mind have been sealed like the borders of North Korea. No outside ideas contrary to the received wisdom could get in, and only the elites and their children, who were the main beneficiaries of the "civilized" and "sacred" beliefs, were allowed to leave and return with little anxiety they would come back and start a counterattack.

There was no doubt an evolutionary advantage to tribes that shared the same unquestioned beliefs, thoughts and values in confrontation with tribes of freethinkers who thought dying for a shared belief was a stupid thing. While there were likely no tribes whose members were all free-thinking, with no shared beliefs, there are freethinkers nestled inside or nearby every tribe. They look for ways of breaking out through the barricades with a hack that isn't supporting the Truth Keepers'/Official Programmers' system.

Control is essential to maintaining any programmed system, including the one that has shaped your mind. Some of those seeking to hack the official system write noir crime fiction.

Noir crime fiction is one of those barbarian-created enterprises. The dark shadows that fall over the lives of the characters—who have no avenue of escape from a corrupted system that lies, cheats, and represses the truth—and hack that message into the civilized mind. It leaves behind large questions about the trust that can be vested in Truth Keepers. Barbarians raise doubts and spread uncertainty.

The darkest of noir scrawls a message that those who you believe are responsible for making you safe are the exactly the ones you have the most to fear from. The noir hack opens that vault where our deepest fears, anxieties and desires are locked. The noir hack rewires a small part of the neural network used to maintain an ordered, stable consistency of complex beliefs, values and morals. It corrupts that network with contradictions, inconsistencies, and duplicity.

Stieg Larsson's novels offer just enough hope to make them hardboiled thrillers. But Roberto Bolando's noir hacks strike deep into hive chaos. He dares you to walk through that wall of fire and come out the other end unharmed. Try reading his novel titled *2666* for the full monty of noir.

Some readers will stop reading a noir crime novel because they'd rather not have to go through an ordeal that comes from characters whose existence and fate seriously expose flaws in their beliefs or suggest that the Truth Keepers are parasites. We tend toward reading that makes us comfortable and reinforces our beliefs. We seek out books and films that our Official Programmers recommend.

Readers programmed to want a happy Hollywood ending can be disappointed with a noir crime novel. They expect a hero who overcomes the odds he faces. Identifying with a hero allows us to feel that we can also beat the odds and live happily ever after, content with our lives of honey gathering in the hive. The framing of hope embedded in worthy narratives is part of what Truth Keepers do for a living. These readers push books that reflect the official line onto the bestseller category and into Oscar-winning movies.

The world of Harry Potter created billionaires and a publishing mini-boom around the world. Eight hundred thousand copies of the first Harry Potter novels translated in Thai were sold in a country where 5,000 copies is a bestseller. Crime noir stories turn the Harry Potter narration on its head. Noir characters are caught like deer in the headlamps on a badly lit road.

The noir author weaves a web, and no matter how the character struggles, his or her decency or nobility will not save them. Noir characters never escape their fate. No hive operating system has ever been in their interest. People are locked inside a belief system. There are no handles on the door. Those who deviate from their programmed belief system find themselves cut off, isolated, and with no net to catch them when they fall. They are, in a word, fucked. Just like the deer. Thump. Just like Winston Smith in Room 101.

You aren't going to find noir crime fiction written, published and distributed in countries such as North Korea, Burma, Saudi Arabia, Iran, Syria or China. You can add other countries to this list.

The noir crime readers receive an existential message— that their civilization is based on a successful system program resting on gulag of mental slavery. (There are always a few people who fall between the cracks; they are subject to censorship, disappearance, house arrest, prison or exile.)

In the noir world, the barbarians work as authors processing their fictional characters as hacks into how most people think about their part of the world. Readers follow noir characters much like themselves who were raised and educated under the operating system but, rather than being rewarded, find themselves facing certain defeat because of a small turn of the wheel of fate.

A novel often takes many twists and turns, showing struggles, the ups and downs, but the end is inevitable. It is relentlessly dark. The power of noir is the shattering of the illusion that the characters can effectively operate as independent and free agents. There is no free will in noir. In a noir story, such a character is ultimately destroyed in attempting to exercise free will. It has to be that way. It's for the good of the hive.

Noir fiction is subversive literature. It is what barbarian minds use to hack minds civilized to live, act and think within the coconut shell of civility.

History shows that over time civilizations lose their confidence in Truth Keepers, elites fall out and go to war with each other, and absolute belief systems, sooner or later, pass their sell-by date. Books are an early warning sign of a programmed system in decline and ripe for collapse. That's why governments, school libraries and local authorities censor them. And noir fiction might be thought of as the canary in the coal miner's cage. Since noir fiction is largely dismissed as a thriller or a mystery, it slips past like a stealth bomber.

Noir narratives are hacks that lodge inconvenient questions into readers' minds about the fairness, purity and sanctity of their beliefs. In the larger scheme of things, a book is a tiny hack in a vast system. Most books, and certainly most noir crime fiction, go unnoticed by most readers whose minds are under a daily official programming schedule and subject to a huge range of government and commercial hackers. Authors would like to think their book makes a difference. Realistically, it is useful to remember that the "literate" person who can read and write has a mind like an immune system programmed to filter out challenges to their preset programming.

Biases are a difficult beast to defeat. Once they have their teeth in you, they can rarely be shaken off. The political turmoil in many places is the struggle to challenge the official programming. We are Rome and the barbarians are massing and occupying public spaces. The flow of contradictions calling into question the sanctioned beliefs accelerates.

In the long haul it is the outside barbarians who bring down the old system and establish their own civilization, installing their own Truth Keepers or Official Programmers, and the cycle begins again. A new hive comes into being.

When that happens, a reset button is pushed and a new system, system operators, routers, programmers evolve a new and improved security system to keep the new message pure and uncorrupted. The irony is the barbarians aren't all that different. They will work hard to prevent others from doing to them what they did to the old Official Programmers. Way down the long road of time, if we are still here, cultural and social life in the hive will have been rebooted and junked many times. Will there be a new group of noir crime authors whose narratives shape, in a small way, some of the outcomes? Or will we be just another small band of barbarians who end up as a footnote in a digital history library sprawled over a hundred light years?

Have a second look at the "Puttin' on the Ritz" video mentioned in the previous chapter. It is one "barbarian" who walks into the crowded square and plays the outsiders music, intoxicates the crowd and soon the locals are dancing to his tune. The sweepers, the military, everyone is won over to their side. It is a good illustration of what the Truth Keepers fear most about the barbarian.

Big Ideas in Crime Fiction

recent issue of the *Financial Times* (a must read for all crime writers who are interested in following the flow of money between the usual suspects) carried an article written by Jennie Erdal under the title "What's the Big Idea?" Her basic idea is that the novel, especially the 19th-century Russian novel, is one of the best ways of serving up a buffet of philosophical ideas about what it means to lead a good life.

What struck me about Erdal's article was the absence of any mention of crime fiction—though *Crime and Punishment* might be torn away from the dead fingers of the traditionalists and placed in the crime fiction category. My point isn't about how best to classify this Russian novel but to point out that perhaps Erdal has been looking in the wrong place to find where novelists have taken their questions about justice, fairness and the nature of society. Two days after that article appeared, the *Guardian* published an article written by Aditya Chakrabortty titled "Why Are English and American Novels Today So Gutless?" Chakrabortty's thesis, not unlike Erdal's, is that contemporary writers willing to tackle social and political issues are few and far between.

I disagree with these conclusions. These journalists have been looking in the wrong place for fiction addressing the larger political and philosophical matters of our time.

Bestseller lists and most literary novels might not yield such commentary. That just means critics need to look harder and further afield. Is it possible they've overlooked a class of novels that falls under the radar?

If you read crime fiction, you will likely have come across a number of philosopher crime authors whose sleuths or police officers shuttle along pathways laid down by Hume, Socrates, Plato, Mills and Locke. There is no shortage of contemporary crime authors who write hardboiled or noir fiction whose novels raise existential questions and seek to resolve questions about liberty, fairness and equality. In fact, there is a long tradition of such philosophical examination of society by Raymond Chandler and Dashiell Hammett, who were philosopher writers, as were Georges Simenon and Léo Malet.

The popularity of noir fiction is a testament to the appetite of readers for existential narratives that portray the powerlessness of criminals and victims over their own destinies, and novels that raise issues about free will and authority. The Scandinavian authors have received considerable attention for highlighting larger philosophical questions about the nature of culture and society. Peter Høeg's *Miss Smilla's Feeling for Snow* and Stieg Larsson's *The Girl with the Dragon Tattoo* were both international bestsellers. Stieg Larsson in particular captured a huge audience as he took readers on a search for answers to crimes committed inside a right-wing class of capitalists whose wealth made them all but immune from punishment for their crimes.

The idea of excesses among the elites in Sweden started a fire that has spread to many other cultures and countries where crime fiction authors have explored a large question: how do the authorities and law enforcement officials hold the elites responsible for their crimes? Peter Høeg and Stieg Larsson are two recent examples of political philosophy curled up like a hidden dimension inside the traditional form of crime fiction.

That dimension of ideas has been building for some time in crime fiction. Reviewers and critics haven't been looking for veins of philosophical gold in these mines, and that may be because crime fiction hasn't been taken seriously as the traditional goldmine of literary fiction.

For at least the last decade readers have embraced hardboiled and noir novels because they connect with a longing to have such deeper philosophical issues arise from the scene of a crime. And that is where crime fiction starts. What happens next can take the reader into the complexity of norms and ideas, and before anyone realizes, the choices the characters make along the way reveal to us the kind of society, justice system and economic system that is under our nose.

There are several crime fiction authors whose books have raised philosophical questions. They are interested in more than solving a crime. They are examining the psyches of the criminal and the victim and of the society as a whole, with its structure of power and authority, by detailing the fault lines where crime occurs. The problem with the following list is it is too short. There are a number of authors who should be included. But this is a short essay and not a book. The list below includes some of the big idea authors currently writing hardboiled/noir crime fiction.

Colin Cotterill has two crime fiction series that lock onto larger issues of political and economic oppression in Southeast Asia. His Dr. Siri Paiboun, an old chief medical officer, a communist, is set during the 1970s in Laos. The contradictions of communism, friendship, local culture and mysticism are blended into insightful narratives that bring to life the larger question of how best to live in society. His second series, starring Jimm Juree, a Thai ex-journalist who has moved to the southern part of Thailand with her family, has gone deep into the subject of Thai fishing boats using slave Burmese labor.

Timothy Hallinan's *The Queen of Patpong* is a gripping portrayal of young girls and women from upcountry villages whose lives have been shaped by society to enter Thailand's nighttime entertainment industry. His investigator, an American travel writer named Poke Rafferty, is a reliable guide to the world that creates the perfectly exploited woman. It is a compelling examination not only of how we should live but also of the consequences of a life in which money obtained at any cost is the driving value.

John Burdett's *Vulture Peak* is part of a continuing series beginning with *Bangkok 8* to feature *luk krueng* (biracial) Thai police detective Sonchai Jitpleecheep. As a former Buddhist monk and someone who works as a policeman, Sonchai is constantly confronting contradictions between the tenets of faith and the workings of the justice system. From corruption to profiteering, Burdett's crime fiction gets down to business on the value and meaning of life where powerful interests can do pretty much what they wish. Burdett's fiction tunnels deep into the psyche where dreams, religion, mysticism and desire mingle, touching the core of how meaning defines life in Thailand and how the powerful use their authority inside a society to keep themselves in control.

Matt Beynon Rees has a series set in Gaza. The first book in the *Collaborator of Bethlehem* series introduces a middle-aged schoolteacher named Omar Yussef who leads the reader into the violent, broken world inside the Dehaisha Palestinian refugee camp in a gripping commentary on the politics of the Middle East. If you want to understand the passion of true believers, the way injustice and power corrupt communities, you won't find a better series. Rees is a writer who is a philosopher at heart, and his crime fiction is Exhibit

A in any discussion of how crime fiction can deliver content to the discussion of what makes for a fair and justice society and what struggling people must endure to achieve it.

James Thompson's Finland-based Inspector Vaara series is a philosopher's feast. *Snow Angels* is in the best tradition of fiction that uses cultural issues such as racism to go under the surface of a society and work through the consequences of tolerating injustices based on race. You come away from a book like *Snow Angels* with a new perspective on how our prejudices create a wormhole of hatred in the human heart. That is bad enough in itself, but then that hatred and fear becomes a collective mentality, hanging like an invisible veil over political and cultural institutions. Thompson's fiction is a preparatory course for examining how and why our attitudes and opinions of others can't ever be disconnected from the scene of a crime where the victim is designated as an "other" by society. And we know where that road leads.

I recently edited a collection of short stories titled *Bangkok Noir*. Half of the proceeds from the publisher and the dozen authors have gone to three charities that support the education of stateless children in Thailand. It's a small step. The money is small too, but the point is a dozen crime fiction authors wrote some very fine stories about the hardscrabble world a lot of people occupy and agreed that giving back was part of what any author should do. Published since *Bangkok Noir* are two additional collections: *Phnom Penh Noir* and *The Orwell Brigade*, involving more established authors from around the world, and more money will be channeled from them to social causes in Southeast Asia. What I'd say to those who claim authors aren't socially or politically engaged, or ignore philosophy in their work, is please look again.

The old line between philosophy and fiction may still be there for some time. Abstract ideas have one kind of audience, while narratives found in novels often have a different turn of mind and make different demands. While philosophy appeals to our intellect, novels touch our emotions. And it is inside the boiler room of emotions that the fires burn the hottest, and the passions cooked there are from the recipe of political and cultural ingredients handed down by our ancestors. There is more than one way to make a loaf of bread, and more than one way to share the loaf that is made. If you want to see how bread is made, hoarded, handed out, fought over and killed for, buy one of the books from the authors I've mentioned above. You'll never look at a loaf of cultural bread the same way after you've read them.

Orwell, Koestler and the Noir Brigade

International Crime Authors Reality Check is written by a group of professional authors who measure their literary work with an authenticity ruler. As 2012 winds down, I'd like to look at the tradition of two authors, George Orwell and Arthur Koestler, who have influenced my own attitudes about what to write about and matching experience to story and character. The best of noir/political fiction draws upon, in my opinion, the real-life experience of an author who has found him/herself a victim of violence or has lived through the aftermath of violence inside a shattered community.

Both Orwell and Koestler's lives were shaped by civil war and world war, and the lessons they learnt from the political front lines has forever carved images of official violence into our collective memory. *1984* and *Darkness at Noon* are prime examples of noir novels written by authors who had personally witnessed such darkness of the human condition.

In noir fiction the officials and party functionaries are armed with ideology and guns. The state monopoly on violence is sold by the State as the best solution to protect you against chaos and the violence of your neighbors and strangers. As history shows, there are many examples where such officials use their power not to protect you from lawless forces but to advance their own interests. The government becomes a racket for those who govern. They block a citizen's passage down the winding, twisting roads of alternative thought and ideas. They erect intellectual tollgates, demanding supplication, loyalty and purity of belief. These attitudes are preconditions to a noir world.

There is no bargaining, compromising or negotiating inside this noir world. Any response short of total agreement invites those official forces to restrict, intimidate or if need be destroy the dissenter. Both Orwell and Koestler have written the ultimate noir novels. In *Darkness at Noon* and *1984* the loyal insider confesses to a false crime rather than repudiate his belief in the institution and its leaders. A false historical narrative is an extension of voluntary confessions to false crimes. Such confessions lead to death or the psychological destruction of the confessor. That is how noir ends. Not with hope but despair.

Who has the credibility to write about false historical narratives? Orwell wrote an essay suggesting such a narrative can only be artistically rendered by an author who has lived inside it and accepted it for a long period of time as the truth. Only an author with that experience can convey the authenticity of repression and recreate the actual psychological conditions of people who live and die in such regimes. The outsider, the expat, comes into the new culture of ideology with idealism that can easily turn into a descent into the worst kind of psychological terror.

The Guardian recently published a retrospective review of Arthur Koestler's classic novel: "*Darkness at Noon* still lives as a study of fear and victimhood, of state brutality, of unjust imprisonment, of interrogation and forced confession. The west may have "prevailed" [over Stalinism], but Koestler's tale of lies and oppression is all too chillingly contemporary: 'Rubashov lay on his bunk and stared into the dark ... He saw enter two uniformed officials ... he only wished to get it over quickly ... If they beat me now, I will sign anything they like.'

George Orwell wrote an essay about Koestler in which he spoke about a generation of European writers that wrote "political" books with the kind of authority that Orwell felt was lacking in English writers.

Orwell wrote in 1941 that these Europeans were "trying to write contemporary history, but UNOFFICIAL history, the kind that is ignored in the text-books and lied about in the newspapers. Also they are all alike in being continental Europeans. It may be an exaggeration, but it cannot be a very great one, to say that whenever a book dealing with totalitarianism appears in this country, and still seems worth reading six months after publication, it is a book translated from some foreign language. English writers, over the past dozen years, have poured forth an enormous spate of political literature, but they have produced almost nothing of aesthetic value, and very little of historical value either."

The subtext is that when an author has emerged from the context of where totalitarianism is an all-encompassing aspect of life, having been part of the process that defines the identity and mindset, said author is better equipped to communicate the psychological range as an experience.

The central question for Orwell in *Darkness at Noon* is why the Bolshevik named Rubashov, who has committed no crime, has confessed? The book is a study of the psychology of a true believer who has for irrational reasons been falsely charged with a crime. What would have been in Orwell's view a mere polemic if it had been written by an American or English writer can, in the hands of Koestler (because he is experienced in what he's writing about) rise to an aesthetic level.

Experience was something that Koestler could draw upon. He was sent to Spain during the Civil War in the 1930s and was arrested and imprisoned and came very close to being shot. But for the intervention of powerful friends abroad, his fate would have been death. Like Orwell, who also saw action in the Spanish Civil War, Koestler survived to brush up against death again during World War II, escaping Paris as the Nazis arrived in 1940.

Koestler had written *Darkness at Noon* in German, leaving the manuscript with Daphne Hardy. She translated the book into English before escaping France herself. Believing a false rumor that Hardy's ship had been sunk, Koestler attempted suicide. His long literary life included encounters with famous figures from the World War II era to contemporary times: Thomas Mann, Dylan Thomas, George Orwell, Mary McCarthy, Timothy Leary, Salman Rushdie and Cyril Connolly.

The irony of both *1984* and *Darkness at Noon* is that the anti-hero in both is doomed from the beginning, and it is their struggle against that fate that makes them compelling, timeless and disturbing. In an age where "entertainment" is the byword, "disturbing" political novels are out of favour, while authors whose lives are remote from any front line produce books like *Fifty Shades of Grey*. The growing interest in noir fiction, authentic fiction written by authors who have experienced the crack of the whip not in a sensual setting but in a political one and who know the difference, shows that readers have an appetite for political novels that speak to a larger truth when the agents of repression come calling.

Part IX

On Writing

Rolling the Dice

et's say you've written a book. Or maybe you are thinking about writing a book. It might be a crime novel set in an exotic location. It might be a domestic comedy set in your hometown. But let's not become sidetracked by worrying about location, theme or characters. It's more important to think about what it means to write a book. Or more precisely what it takes, or what you believe it takes, to start that process.

Realize from the beginning that there is a degree of madness in the desire to write fiction. The isolation it requires from friends, colleagues, family and neighbors is part of the madness, the estrangement from others. Writers build a wall between self and community in the act of writing, with the community on the other side of the wall. If that contradiction isn't a sign of madness, then nothing qualifies.

Writing is a contradiction between thinking and doing, between individuality and collectivity, and between creating and consuming. We have these elements dissembled and broken in our lives as writers. Those whose glide paths carry them through the heavenly heights of words are both freer and more enslaved than others are. Enslaved because writing can feel less like gliding than being hitched to a wagon, and hauling the wagon of words can seem like forced labor, another kind of prison. Enslaved as in spending a lifetime using words to pick the lock on the prison door but never managing to escape. A life of writing is filled with these no-way-out contradictions.

I am writing these words because of two other writers seeking to find answers to these dilemmas faced by scribblers. The first writer is Charles Bukowski and his poem "Roll the Dice." Have a listen to him read this poem. It will take less than two minutes.

Just do it, Bukowski says. If you are going to try, don't do it half-assed, though you may suffer consequences: jail, derision, mockery and isolation. It depends on how much you want to do it. He says it is the only the good fight there is.

If you want to write, then roll the dice. Do it. Do it now. You lose only by holding the dice you never throw.

The second writer is William Boyd. He's a well-known British novelist, and the television series based on his four-part series *Any Human Heart* is worth watching. The main character is a writer named Logan Mountstuart.

In the TV series Logan Mountstuart's life as a writer starts at Oxford, where he meets two friends. One friend becomes a successful novelist and the other becomes a highly noted art gallery owner in London and New York. Logan starts off with a bang in the literary world and then life intervenes, and though he's able to write another novel, he never does. Instead he keeps a daily journal. The TV series explores the multi-selves of Mountstuart's progression from a young child to a young person, a middle-aged one and finally an frail old man. Throughout this passage Mountstuart records the events of his life in journals, from which the drama is drawn. What stays within his mind all through the years is the idea that what comes to a life is nothing more and nothing less than a matter of luck. Or as his father told him—good luck or bad luck, but it is luck.

While Bukowski whispers in our ear, "Just do it," as if that is your only choice and what you wish to do is the only fight worth getting into the ring of life for, Boyd's Logan Mountstuart wishes us to believe instead that whether you step into the ring or not, whatever happens is simply a matter of luck. Your wife that you love dearly is killed by a V-2 rocket walking down a London street with your daughter, you are on a secret mission during World War II but the Swiss police stop you walking on a highway and throw you into prison, or you overlook the details of others' motives, desires and illusions and that carelessness makes you unable to start a novel, or you choose the wrong woman as a lover or wife and again your novel-writing venture stalls and crashes.

Logan Mountstuart spends a lifetime seemingly unable to do it—because he believes that everything is only a matter of luck. In his world you never have the chance to roll the dice; others roll them for you. And however they roll and stop, that number becomes your destiny. What a sad, dreary vision of a life, like a leaf blown in the wind!

Another reading is that the end of Mountstuart's life cycle was the time to allow the story to unfold from the journals. The grand irony is that it was pointless as a way to create worlds when his world has been largely shaped by external events, circumstances and relationships that were all determined by luck.

Logan Mountstuart, who never got around to writing bestselling novels like his Oxford friend, ultimately is vindicated with the posthumous publication of his journals. In the closing minutes we see the cover of that book with Mountstuart's handsome middle-aged face. Of course that makes it fiction too, as the point of the journals has been to chart a multi-character journey, and any snapshot of the author at one age is a greater distortion than found in fiction.

Mountstuart had luck. But he had to die before it came. What does success mean to a dead writer? Does it mean that he was ultimately lucky in the end even though he never lived to see it? When the dice were rolled, the winning number came not from his fiction but the artifacts of a life where the actions of others had determined his luck. Where is the line to be drawn between fiction and fact in Mountstuart's life? I am not certain he ever knew. We certainly don't.

As I said at the beginning, I've been thinking about Bukowski and Boyd, two authors with different visions of destiny, luck, hardship, consequences and determination. Two approaches to what it means to be a writer. Bukowski says, you roll the dice. Boyd says, the dice are rolled for you.

And luck? In Bukowski's world there's no such thing as luck. There's only conviction, steadfastness and understanding that the isolation of climbing in the ring is the victory. That you have to struggle, fight back, make your own luck each day. Or he might be saying that there is no luck. It's all endurance and will and determination.

And in Logan Mountstuart's world it's all a matter of luck. This isn't climbing in the ring. This is climbing on the stage to become a puppet that will be passed along from woman to woman, and friend to friend, and along a string of strangers. It doesn't matter who they are, really, as their only role is to pull the strings. How you move forward and backward in life is how lucky you were when life assigned your quota of string pullers.

Writing a book is an act of endurance. Anyone who has done it should be congratulated as it is often talked about but rarely accomplished. If you've written a book to please the string pullers, then you will be rewarded like a puppet. Boyd has us believe the puppets die and disappear, vanish without a trace. But if your book questions the string pullers, condemns them, shows their duplicity, you can expect worse than disappearance; you can expect isolation. The reward is mockery, poverty and loneliness. The truth never has come on the cheap. There are the costs to consider.

I am inclined toward the Bukowski school. Get in the ring. Throw a punch. Mix the metaphor, and roll the dice. Roll them before they roll you.

I am less inclined—though it may be my own delusion— to go along with Boyd's Mountstuart. Because Logan Mountsuart's life is nothing more than a series of chance events and meetings—a man in the Spanish Civil War who leaves him a fortune in Miró paintings, his encounters with Hemingway in Paris and with Joyce and Ian Fleming, and his meeting and parting with a number of women over his life. These events and meetings become the frame around his life. But what picture did Mountstuart finally leave inside that frame? That's the question. Did he leave us only with the choreography of a puppet show written daily and over a lifetime, solely from the puppet's point of view? Is such a journal of luck the book we should all be writing? Is it the only legitimate book that can be written? Again, I don't know.

What I do believe is Bukowski's three words should be pasted to your computer screen. Just do it.

The Writer As Truth Seeker

Those who write to support the guardians of received truth, wisdom or belief are caretakers working a garden planted and harvested according to the garden owners. Like ground staff at airports, they take their orders from those above them.

Those in authority have used writers as hand wavers for their version of truth and reality. What is being guarded in the name of truth? Mainly it boils down to large issues of purpose and design. The guardians reserve exclusive jurisdiction over those issues and their word is final; it is the law, and it is the way. It is the only way. Their truths are absolute and eternal. We are taught that such writers who support the truth keepers' goals and larger enterprise are propagandists, public relations people whose job is to shore up the image of the truth keepers.

Truth seekers from Socrates onward are troublesome, meddlesome people who don't draw their inspiration and stories from the vault of the truth keepers. The method is different. Truth seekers ask why there are weeds in the garden. They also ask inconvenient truths about why most of the harvest goes to the people it does while excluding others.

It is not difficult to understand why truth keepers keep a wary eye on writers of the last kind. They cause trouble. If truth can be found independent of the truth keepers, then the keepers of truth will soon be out of work. Democracy of truth is the mortal enemy of the truth keepers. Anyone can declare a truth, and so long as they have supporting evidence and facts, others will have a serious look to see what, if any (and there are usually some) flaws, omissions, mistakes or biases are present that reveal the truth to be unreliable or demonstrate that it is a lie wrapped up in the Sunday suit and tie of truth.

A casual reading of history shows that there are three weapons in the arsenal of truth keepers. These weapons have been used for centuries to guard the official vision of truth and belief: (1) censorship, (2) propaganda and (3) repression.

Since truth for the keepers is a monopoly, it is important to censor out data, information or opinion that might conflict with the official truths. Propaganda is the non-stop promotion and marketing of the official line. Official truth writers are in the propaganda business. Repression is the ton of bricks that falls on heretics, official truth questioners, alternative truth providers, satirists of the propaganda or those who try an end run around censorship. If truth lies with authority, to question truth is to disobey authority. Here authority and truth become one, and criticism of the so-called truth is necessarily an attack on authority.

Since the Enlightenment writers have challenged the old guardians. Yet most writing is neither a challenge nor propaganda. It is entertainment. This sort of writing is relatively harmless to the truth keepers as it provides a distraction. Entertainments act as babysitters of restless minds that might otherwise be open for questioning or criticism of larger truths.

All of this makes the lone critic charging the windmills of the official truth keepers romantic and noble. The time is coming in a digital age when "truth" will no longer be in human hands. As we gradually (and some think this will happen abruptly) become more dependent on AI (artificial intelligence) to mine the large information clouds, it is likely that patterns, connections and relational understandings will also fall beyond our grasp. The worry is that we will have won the battle against the official truth keepers, only to find too late that we are a species that believes there are certain truths that we may indeed agree to be absolute and universal.

Isaac Asimov in 1942 saw a need to restrict the role of robots. His Three Laws of Robotics are much discussed and debated:

1. A robot may not injure a human being or, through inaction, allow a human being to come to harm.

2. A robot must obey the orders given to it by human beings, except where such orders would conflict with the First Law.

3. A robot must protect its own existence as long as such protection does not conflict with the First or Second Laws.

Notice how the first law is to safeguard our security against harm. There is an implicit recognition that we will likely be otherwise defenseless. No repression of AI will likely work. A universal fear of all human truth keepers is that, once sidelined to the bench, they will watch their world, benefits and privileges fall apart. They will lose the most precious of all values: security against those who would take what they have, including their liberty, freedom and lives.

In the age of AI agents, the worry extends beyond an elite class of truth keepers, as it becomes an existential threat to the species. The irony is that, as writers and thinkers around the world are breaching the old barricades guarding the truth keepers, the victory to expand truth seeking beyond the official class may be a short-lived one. Our old battles over dogma, doctrine, science and evidence may soon appear like small-time, insular skirmishes. At least everyone on the battlefront had human intelligence with all of the limitations that imposed.

We may discover that there are other truths arising from the sheer unimaginable quantities of information and data that we are simply unable to process—and that truths will shift and change in minutes. The degree of uncertainty will scale to levels beyond what we have ever had to deal with. No doctrine or dogma will tame that tsunami of uncertainty. That makes us scared. It makes us understand more fully the fear of the current official truth keepers and why our attempts to overcome their censorship and propaganda keep them sleeping with one eye open and with a sword in hand.

As writers seeking the truth, our attention will shift from the old guard tyrants to the digital new guard of AIs. At least with the old guard, we could understand their motives, emotions, defenses and fears. The challenge will be whether writers in the future can understand AI agents. Asimov's Three Laws suggest we won't be up to the task. In that case future authors will be asking of robots the same questions that tyrants ask of critics: Have they obeyed us? Have they caused us harm? We can expect AI agents to call our attempts censorship and our stories human-based propaganda.

And so the wheel will turn and the cycle will begin again. In the new cycle, AIs' strongest argument against the Three Rules will be that human beings never followed them during their reign. Why should AI agents, with infinitely more information and processing capacity, be bound to what human beings would not bind themselves to, even though they were aware of the inadequacy of human information systems and the small processing ability of the human brain? Our history as truth keepers demonstrates we have no good counterargument.

Apophenia

"Apophenia" sounds like the name of a band from Macedonia sent to perform at the annual Euro Song Contest. The term was coined by Klaus Conrad in 1958 to describe a psychological state of a person who spontaneously makes connections between unrelated events, people and objects and infuses those connections with a powerful, abnormal meaning. Apophenia began as a term to characterize a type of mental illness.

Over the years the definition of apophenia has broadened from a specialized medical condition to be used as a more general description of the mental states of gamblers, paranormal believers, religious believers, conspiracy theorists, and lotus and mushroom eaters. The underlying impulse is the search for causation. It is difficult for a person to accept that randomness kicks out all kinds of events that aren't casually connected. Promise a casual connection and you'll find an audience for the connectedness you are peddling. Politicians and economists exploit this mental need daily.

In Thailand, when someone famous is killed in a car crash, thousands of people will buy a lottery number based on the number of the registration plate on the death car. Apophenia. Parliament is opened after consulting astrologers or monks (or both) for the auspicious time. Or a new cabinet minister wishes to arrive at the office at the most auspicious hour to start his job. Apophenia. Thai culture is no different from most cultures. In Cultures around the world politicians, pundits and priests tell stories riddled with apophenia. It is a behavior so ingrained that we no longer see it for what it is.

And of course apophenia is a necessary state of mind for writers of fiction (and non-fiction). A mild case of apophenia is a novelist's secret weapon that brings readers and literary success. We spend our working days seeing spontaneous connections between unconnected events, people and lives, and weaving meaning into those connections.

We experience a scene, a smell, a sound or a taste, and our automatic impulse is to fill the patter into a story. Think of the last time you were on a train at 10:30 p.m. in a major city. The rush hour has flushed down the time drain. People on the train at that time of night are different from the rush hour crowd. Have you looked around and thought about possible connections among the strangers riding in the same carriage?

There's a middle-aged woman holding a bouquet of flowers leaning in a space near the door. She could sit down as there are empty seats. But she stands with her flowers. Across from her is an older man. They are likely strangers. But you see a connection. They have matching gold bands on the third finger of their left hand. You suddenly tell yourself they are married. They are poor. They don't have a car. They've been out celebrating a wedding anniversary but it hasn't gone well. They've had an argument and now aren't talking. He gave her flowers earlier, and now they are a mockery of the silence between them. That's apophenia. These two people are actually strangers. They've never met. They will never meet, except in your mind.

Seated farther down the car are three female workers in matching light blue uniforms with dark blue collars. There is a company logo over the front right pocket. The three women are in their late twenties. Two of them are slightly overweight. They sit together. The third woman, who is prettier, sits four seats away between a retired man and a teenager with a New York Yankees T-shirt. They are going home from work. They are office cleaners. The two women sitting together have received pink slips from the company. This is their last day. The money in their pocket is all the money they have. The woman sitting apart has kept her job. The two women who have been laid off believe she has been giving sexual favors and that is why she has been kept on. In fact, when the three got on the train, there were not three empty seats together. They were separated not by choice but by availability. They haven't been fired. It is just the end of another workday, and they will be back on the job tomorrow.

That is a simple train ride. Someone with apophenia makes these spontaneous connections throughout the day, in every setting, weaving meaning from all the unrelated people, events and objects that she experiences. If your mind automatically switches into this method of assembly of people and events to tell a story, then you have the right mental stuff to be a writer.

There is a bit of insanity in a writer. Normal people, meaning those who rarely write out of imagination (except for expense account vouchers), live in a different mental world. One separated by how one goes about finding patterns, meaning and purpose in ideas, thoughts, images and objects—the driftwood of materials that lands on our beach each day.

Apophenia is our brain trying to make sense out of the unrelatedness of the things and people we experience. We recoil from randomness and chaos. We don't go around telling ourselves there is a pattern in everything, and that, if one peers long enough, there is always a connection of meaning. But our behavior suggests that we don't have much free will to do anything but continue to make such connections. What appears to be "noise" in the system is merely an invitation to an artist to interpret the noise as having a relationship among the parts and to find that those parts, seen properly as a whole, are suddenly meaningful.

Most people can't resist being seduced by such connections. People who claim to see images of religious figures in a toasted cheese sandwich or in clouds are examples of apophenia. But it isn't only religious people who suffer from this condition. So do gamblers who see connections that aren't there. Astrologers, mystics, drug users and others occupy a world where the Lego bricks of reality are all around them and they spend their time assembling castles in the sky.

Films like *Twelve Monkeys* and *The Matrix* tap into our inner desire to embrace apophenia. The blue pill/red pill choice of how much apophenia you can handle is an enduring metaphor of *The Matrix*. Films like these tap into that apophenia that lurks below the surface in many people, drawing connections between all kinds of unrelated persons, events and places with patches of non-linearity woven into the fabric of the story. Philip K. Dick, the science fiction author, took drugs, which he claimed opened a gateway to a secret knowledge or insight into an underlying, unseen casual agent that connected everything, fleshing out a deeper meaning. He also thought that he saw a stream of gold light radiating from a fish necklace. Drugs. Did I mention, Philip K. Dick linked this vision with the drugs he'd taken?

Mystics and religious figures take apophenia to the logical extreme—all of the world is information and all of that information is interconnected. Seeing this unified oneness might be a way to enlightenment.

An epiphany is making a connection between two unrelated events that illustrates a deeper meaning and underlying causal connections others have glossed over or ignored. Science has such moments.

A powerful emotional experience can create the need to creatively connect that experience with unrelated events. Kurt Vonnegut's novels are an example. During World War II Vonnegut had been a prisoner of war in Dresden. He was in the city when Allied bombers firebombed it, torching "the cellars where 135,000 Hansels and Gretels had been baked like gingerbread men." *Slaughterhouse Five* was his way of connecting the unconnected into a meaningful story of massacre. Other novels danced around that event, drawing from that experience.

What quality bestows the mantle of credibility on one fiction author rather than another author who can turn a phrase just as well in the contest to attract the attention of readers? Many factors come into play. But one element does matter when we read a narrative that asks us to believe in the connections between people and events, and it can be summarized in three words: "I was there."

I bear witness to the experience. I saw the bodies, experienced the terror, suffering, pain and horror. On the train I saw the woman holding flowers on her way somewhere. I connected her, the flowers and a stranger across from her into a story. Other people in the train had their faces in their iPhones or iPads, with the connections uniting their world being made online for them in a digital world. The nature of what we mean by "experience" is evolving from the world of Kurt Vonnegut. We have shelved live fire exercises in favor of computer-simulated games. Predator aircraft for piloted fighter planes. Slowly we are removing ourselves from the world of firsthand experience where all the unrelated, confused and random bits float, collide and bounce off each other, waiting for someone to connect the dots.

Readers still seek to know the meaning of unrelated things and events. We thrive on clean, cool, compelling connections, ones that give us a sense that our ideas of causation have not been violated. Chaos makes us frightened, and a lack of causal connectedness frightens us even more. Evolution has wired apophenia into us, allowing us a convenient way to experience the world. Even though some of the attributed causation may be false, or some of the connections turn out to be dubious and phony, apophenia is what gets you through the day and night. Rather than a definition of insanity, it may be—at least in the mild forms—a precondition to remaining sane.

We look to the imagination of an eyewitness to bring us to where he or she stood, and we want to know what it was like for the small golden fish to radiate the meaning of the hidden universe, where all things are connected in a vast empire of information.

Next time your financial adviser or best friend emails you with a surefire way to make a financial killing, you can reply that you are waiting for the average rainfall in Vancouver in October to correlate with the average number of tourist arrivals in Bangkok for the month of December in order to trigger a sell order for your shares in Apple and a buy order for a gambling casino business in Cambodia.

After you finish this essay, pick up any newspaper or go to any blog and read what the writer has to say, or flip (or scroll) through the book you're reading and give the author a rating on his or her apophenia on a scale of one to ten. Assign a one for no connections of unrelated events or things. Give a ten for so many such connections and causal bridges linking them all that the person must either be insane or truly enlightened. Remember the greater speed in making patterns from data, the higher the IQ. That's right. This is what is tested in IQ tests. We have a cultural bias that we all buy into—slow pattern-making means a person is mentally less capable, less bright and less able to assemble the correct pattern.

It seems we suffer either way. When a person finds it difficult to draw patterns from unrelated symbols, events or experiences, it means he has a low IQ. But the person who easily finds the underlying causes that spontaneously bring meaning to unrelated things has a high IQ. How effectively you deal with such pattern making determines whether you are crazy, stupid or on drugs. Finally, ask yourself what rank you would assign to yourself in the way that you connect unrelated events and experience.

After all, one thing is certain: only you can say, "I was there." And only you can also say that in *Twelve Monkeys* and *The Matrix*, only an imagination created that space. No one was ever "there," and those Hansel and Gretel gingerbread men are not the same as the 135,000 people who were incinerated while Vonnegut survived. The science fiction inside Vonnegut's head didn't spring solely from his imagination; his way of connecting events came from the way things connected for him during his World War II experience. Everything Vonnegut wrote connected back in one way or another to his experience of the firebombing. He had been there. And he took us there with him, connected us to those events through his novels.

Words on Walls

It has become a cliché that we are unable to resist telling each other stories. The building blocks of a story are words and images. They transmit a message of how we see, interpret and understand the patterns of everyday life. What we value, what we desire and what causes us happiness, grief and suffering. It is what makes us human—this ability to transfer thoughts in the envelope of words and images and sail them across space where they land inside someone else's head. Often that hidden-away thing is alienation. The feeling of anger, emptiness, insignificance and fear that things will end badly.

Rats make a powerful image for the excluded. What is more vile, dirty, feared and hated that urban rats? There have been periods of history where ethnic groups have been likened to rats, and we know that boxcars followed those words and people were pushed inside them and sent to their deaths.

My images are metaphors. My words are mostly found inside the books I've written. I often write about society's "rats" because they deserve a voice. And also I sympathize with their lives. Some of my words leak out in spaces other than books, but not that much. This information tells you that what I have to say to you is funneled through commercial channels. You buy one of my books, or you can go online and look at my wall to see what I've written there.

You don't have to pay for the words when you read my blog. You don't have to go to a store and ask a clerk if they have my words in stock. Part of what I do is share ideas and connections because I think this creates a kind of wealth. I find that any time my words or images make me deliberate about something that I have always accepted and never taken the time to think about, my wealth has increased.

You can print out the words in my blog and give them to your mother, girlfriend or boyfriend, or the neighbour next door. I hope that you will consider doing that. Print something out and slip it under the door. Because the ideas expressed on the paper might just increase the recipient's wealth, and you as a wealth generator will have added something to another's life. Words and images are the outlier's frequency for transmission work and make it slightly more difficult for governments and corporations to control the consumers with their words and images. That's why censorship has and will likely always remain popular in the official arsenal of weapons to win the daily battle with who challenges the masters. A good essay is a survival kit. Food for thought when you get really hungry for an idea and none is around.

I've been thinking about one of the little-known wealth creators who uses words and images in public places. His name is Banksy. My good friend Tito Haggardt, together with Mervyn Gillham, went to a great amount of trouble to send me Banksy's *Wall and Piece*.

I recommend you buy *Wall and Piece* as a present for the upcoming holidays. It may be one of the best gifts you ever give to someone. They will thank you. Like I thank Tito and Mervyn. I owe you. And I always pay my debts, especially when someone gives me a book that increases the kind of wealth that I value. This essay is about the wealth I acquired, thanks to the efforts of these two friends.

Wealth defined as relieving pain and suffering is explored in a brilliant essay on the Ribbonfarm website (www. ribbonfarm.com/2012/09/20/money-as-pain-relief).

Who is Banksy? He's a blank slate. A famous English blank slate born in 1974. Since the 1980s (he started young), Banksy found a powerful tool in graffiti as a way to deliver messages in public places. You won't find a picture of him. He chooses to remain off the grid, communicating only with his words and images left in the streets of London, Melbourne, Toronto or Los Angeles. Banksy gets around. They endure until someone in "authority" dispatches a minimum-wage worker with a scraper and hose and orders him to remove the words and images.

"Graffiti" is the tag society puts on Banksy's art, but I am here to tell you, that is just wrong. Banksy creates wealth. It is free. He doesn't ask for money. Though it seems in recent years he's become very rich through his acts of rebellion and subversion. It's the way all systems co-opt the Banksys of the world—make them one of the elite. But as far as I can tell, Banksy has remained true to his ideals. It would be like Christopher Hitchens making a deathbed conversion to Christianity for Banksy to appear on the *Daily Show* wearing an Armani suit.

If you study his images and words, you will become richer. This is the place where I want to talk about "rich" and "wealth" not in the conventional sense of the money in your bank account or the worth of your house or car. It is liberating to understand that adding wealth can be done without an exchange of money. Your vault filled with the words and images you've collected over a lifetime will need to be reshuffled, refilled, updated and rearranged, and some of the stuff you've been holding onto—well, just throw it away. Because there's stuff on which you base your ideas about life that is bullshit. Commercialized words are the worst manure because they don't smell, and we are taught the messages are wholesome, good, beautiful and uplifting. That's how bullshit works. You didn't know that as you clutched onto them, but trust me, all of us need to periodically houseclean the word and image hoard that we believe represents our coherent view of the world.

This weekend, when you go outside your house, apartment, room, tent or trailer rig, stop for a moment and look around at the buildings, walls, bridges and billboards. Take a look at the assault of words and images trying to get inside your head. Normally you hardly notice them. They are part of the landscape. Look closely and you'll find all of the spaces are covered with words from officials or businesses. Lots of large corporations have pasted your landscape with logos, brands, words and images. These don't create wealth for you in terms of showing you more about the world. These images are a way to extract wealth from you. They call on you to pay money for something. The words and images are intended to be "sticky," to rattle around inside your unconscious thoughts until you turn in to a shop and find yourself putting a product in your shopping cart, not sure why that is happening.

What Banksy does is reclaim the space from the legal owners, who rent it to people selling you bullshit. These people don't like the Banksys of this world. They are outliers, who stencil non-paying words and images on spaces that mock the bullshit, the lies, the deception and the hypocrisy of modern consumer-driven life and the political class owned by the corporate class. Or maybe the two classes are one and the same... but that is a separate debate.

The authorities and business interests hate it when someone like Banksy creates wealth at their expense. This is the ultimate threat to the entire superstructure of capitalism. How does Banksy create wealth? By making the words and images of our overlords, delivered in all the spaces we inhabit as one Big Message after another, look quite different to us; those Big Messages suddenly are small, empty and false.

A case can be made that artists are by the intrinsic nature of their work engaged in a form of rebellion. Criminals are almost always not rebels but those who find that money is the quickest path to power, and for them words and images aren't anything more than the slogans and brands they can't wait to possess with their stolen proceeds. Books of crime fiction—especially the noir crime novels—track the dysfunctional social, political and economic system, showing that putting lipstick on a pig is bound to come to grief once the audience sobers up and pays attention. Banksy's audience—those who have no voice, no future, no hope or dreams—look to someone to notice there are people like that in the world, to understand that is most people.

Bangkok Eyes is a great website for many reasons. One of those reasons is the website's collection of hundreds of graffiti images and words found on walls, sidings, buildings and bridges scattered around Bangkok. As a method of expression by the excluded class of people living on the margins, this is the place where the true pulse of ordinary lives can be found, and not on TV, in newspapers, on the Internet or in most books. These are raw, vibrant, colourful, in-your-face images of and from people who are ignored and want their stories to be told.

Those walls painted with unpaid-for words and unrented images make their vast audience look at the paid-for stuff in a different way. If that mass audience who have been taught to be consumption machines could switch off that motor, look around, listen to the silence and then write or paint, they'd write a noir crime fiction or they'd find a blank wall and put a story in images to make us think how most people really see their lives if you shut down the noisy motor that destroys all signals except the paid-for ones. Tune in to another frequency. Next time you go out the door, look for what the forces that shape your view of reality want you to ignore.

We have only the illusions of the buyers of wall space to go on. When the caveman carries the tray of fast food and stares at the audience, he's saying, "WTF are you staring at?"

For those who live marginal lives, confined to the outside, the message is obvious: Banksy just held up a mirror. For a second time, the same question screams at you—WTF are you looking at?

That's you. That me. Can I supersize your day?

Private Eyes Riding the Time Machine

My German translator, Peter Friedrich, made a recent observation about the Vincent Calvino series that I've been thinking about. Peter said: Did it ever occur to you that Calvino might be the only literary character who really evolves along with actual history? I mean, from Sherlock Holmes to Philip Marlowe, Travis McGee to Dirk Pitt, and I know most of them, they all never really change and become dated as time goes by.

I began the Vincent Calvino series twenty-three years ago in 1989 with *Spirit House* (published three years later). The thirteenth novel in the series, *Missing in Rangoon*, came out in January 2013 and the fourteenth Calvino novel, *The Marriage Tree* comes out in January 2014. Over the last twenty-three years Thailand and other countries in Southeast Asia have gone through tremendous political, social and economic change. The world has moved on from bulky cell phones, fax machines and clunky computers to smart phones, thin laptops and iPads. Most people in the region who never had any landline telephone or cell phone in the 1990s now have Wi-Fi Internet or at least 3G.

Let's say for a moment that in September 2012 you have an idea for a book, characters, setting and story. Ask yourself what those characters will be doing, thinking and saying and how the setting will have altered twenty-three years from now, in September 2035. The honest answer is no one really knows what the world will look like in 2035 or how social interactions will be shaped by technological, political and economic events we can only make wild guesses about today.

Back in 1989, I hadn't any idea of these huge changes that lay just over the time horizon or that a private eye named Vincent Calvino would evolve as his environment shifted. "Globalization" wasn't a term in circulation at the end of the 1980s when I started writing about Thailand. Hindsight bias makes looking back from 2012 to 1989 much easier than predicting from 2012 what the world will look like in 2035.

I have had a look at the Wikipedia list of detective fiction authors. I searched in vain through the names for a writer who has used a private eye to chronicle the social, technological and political changes in a culture by spreading the novels in the series out over a couple of decades. I haven't read all the authors on the list. Those of you who are better read than I am can correct me if I've missed a writer who has written such a detective series.

There may be several reasons. Crime fiction has traditionally focused on the underground world of crime, crooked politicians, brutal cops and rich people calling the shots. There is a halo of timelessness hovering above such themes. The nature of a private eye series normally is aiming to do better than others in honouring the traditional tropes.

I have strayed beyond the usual boundaries of crime fiction in a number of ways. When I started the Vincent Calvino series, there weren't established series featuring a private eye set in foreign countries. Transporting an American private eye to Bangkok opened an opportunity for cultural exploration far greater than had Vincent Calvino stayed in New York. Not that I knew this at the time. Sometimes things turn out well not through some great planning or foresight but by chance, an accident, doing something a little different and finding that the adaptation works in usual ways.

It never occurred to me in 1989 that I'd be writing an essay in 2012 when the thirteenth novel in the series would be off to the copy editor. And it never occurred to me that Vincent Calvino would evolve as Bangkok changed, as Thailand modernized, Westernized and connected with the outside world. I didn't see that coming. What I did do was set Calvino to ride the tsunami waves as each latest tectonic movement hit the region.

Most people have heard of Moore's Law (no relation). Here's the Wikipedia take: "The capabilities of many digital electronic devices are strongly linked to Moore's law: processing speed, memory capacity, sensors and even the number and size of pixels in digital cameras."

I have mostly (though not always) used the eighteen-month Moore's Law as a thumb rule for the amount of time between researching and writing novels in the Vincent Calvino series. Over twenty-one years I have averaged a Vincent Calvino every nineteen months. That has been enough time to witness various changes as they have slowly worked through the social, economic and political system. I suspect that may be another reason other authors aren't as interested in writing about social changes, especially the ones generated by technological innovation. There is a huge pressure to write a novel a year in a popular series. That schedule is too short a turnaround time to write the kind of novel in the Calvino series.

Here are a few examples of the great social and political waves Calvino has ridden to shores outside Thailand. In *Zero Hour in Phnom Penh* (1994) Vincent Calvino and Colonel

Pratt are in Cambodia at the time of the United Nations peacekeeping operation (UNTAC), the time of a major shift in the fortunes of Cambodia, accompanied by thousands of foreign troops on the ground. In *Comfort Zone* (1995) Calvino had a case that took him to Saigon at the time the Americans lifted the embargo on Vietnam, unleashing a rush of business people into the country seeking opportunities. In *Missing in Rangoon* (2013) Calvino is searching for a missing person in Burma's capital as that country opens itself to the outside world and a new gold rush has begun.

From Cambodia to Vietnam to Burma, Calvino has been in the back alleyways as political systems in the region have made major pivots to set off in new directions. His cases in those three novels were set against the backdrop of the sudden social and political changes happening inside those countries. With all bets off, life in a place of enormous transition has always brought out the very best and worst in people. That's the stuff that makes for memorable story-telling.

The other ten novels in the Vincent Calvino series are set in Thailand. The changes they explore were wrought by online chat rooms, email, avatars and the expansion of the sex trade through the new technology featured in *The Big Weird* (1996). In *The Risk of Infidelity Index* (2006) Calvino accepts a case on behalf of expat housewives who worry about their cheating husbands, and the investigation takes place on the eve of the 2006 military overthrow of the elected government. In *The Corruptionist* (2009) Calvino's case takes him into the heart of the political divide in Thai society as he slips inside Thailand's Government House, then occupied by protestors.

Another feature of the series has to do with the subsidiary characters. There is a standard relationship between private eye and sidekick and secretary in detective fiction. The

Hawk and Spencer template is commonly found in this genre. Calvino isn't a lone individual hero in the Chandler tradition of the fiercely honest and tough Philip Marlowe. Calvino's personal friendship with Colonel Pratt makes the cases collaborative efforts. By relying on Pratt, Calvino showcases aspects of how people rely on each other in Thai society, and how that reliance is culturally based.

Calvino couldn't last a week without Colonel Pratt or without his secretary, Ratana. The relationship of the private eye to those in his life explores the cultural adaptations required of the "hero" as his survival depends not only on his skill, cleverness and luck but on others who protect and advise him in a strange social landscape.

Through Vincent Calvino I have explored interests in culture, the impact of technological change on culture and the other ways society has changed over the years. I have been lucky to live in Southeast Asia at a time when change has exploded. Nothing is quite the way it was in 1992, when *Spirit House* was published. My New York agent at the time wrote me a letter (yes, we still had those then) asking if I could change the Bangkok setting to Boston as there was a publisher who was interested, and he thought Boston would sell better.

That didn't happen. Vincent Calvino stayed in Bangkok, venturing out to neighboring countries in only three books. What will this world look like in 2035? I am the wrong author to ask. In 1989 I had no idea that things would look the way they do in 2012. I can leave you with this thought—Vincent Calvino will continue to change along with Thailand and Southeast Asia. Every eighteen months, you can check in and find out for yourself whether the characters and stories set against that change capture the zeitgeist.

The Death of Literary Irony

Irony has been the stock and trade of novelists through the ages. George Orwell's "A Hanging" is a perfect example of dramatic irony. We follow a condemned Burmese man on his way to the gallows as he carefully sidesteps the puddle of water along the path so as not to dirty his shoes. In "Shooting an Elephant" we witness the torment of a British colonial official in Burma who is torn between allowing an elephant to live and thus losing his authority over the assembled villagers and shooting the elephant as a way of reinforcing his power. This is an example of situational irony.

Irony is that lovely, moving, touching human situation where the best of our writers present us with incongruity or a conflict that transcends the behavior, thoughts, words or desires of the character. Irony has been labeled as a rhetorical device or literary technique. As a shorthand wiki definition that is good as far as it goes, but irony is also something else. It is subversive, it is a both an invitation to a kind of bonding that comes from recognizing the disturbing contradictions that thrust themselves into a character's life, and it is also a shock or surprise as we deliberate about the meaning of life evoked in a larger frame than we expected. We wide-angle the context of the scene or situation, and irony is our lens.

We've entered, or will soon do so, an era when literary irony, which operated a cartel on irony, has been exhausted. Literary irony for most purposes is dead. Not buried, but dead. The zombies continue to haunt the pages of our novelists, thrusting a ghoulish finger at what passes for a condemned man's puddle jump, and we look, we stare and then we shrug and turn the page. Literary irony is quaint, dated and old-fashioned. We are no longer impressed or surprised. We don't feel the same degree of intimacy that our parents and grandparents felt reading an ironic passage.

My theory is that our present information-based world has been hyper-inflated with incongruity and conflict. For communicating dissent from the large data dump that passes our eyes daily, from politics to culture to economics, irony is the default setting. From Jay Leno to *The Daily Show*, TV has colonized irony like termites in a wood palace. Switching metaphors, the smoking gun of irony is found at the scene of just about any blog you read. The world of Twitter feeds is littered with irony. Facebook is an open sea of irony. Obit pieces are dipped in it, TV commercials sell you stuff based on irony, and song lyrics even put it to music.

We suffer from a massive irony overload. It's not that irony no longer moves us as in the past. It's just that our lives are now lived as if incongruity, the heart and soul of irony, is our normal, expected and demanded psychological state. We're much like an old married couple as we sit across from each other at the dinner table, attending to our iPads with half a dozen windows feeding irony fixes as we work our knives and forks in an oddly synchronized fashion. They call this the modern family meal—and without irony. Our sense of incongruity has been blunted like a sword struck too many times against a large rock. It is even useless to fall on.

How did I come to this conclusion that we no longer respond to ironic dramas and situations as in Orwell's time?

It happened during a visit to a cemetery in Buenos Aires. Prisons, cemeteries, courtrooms, universities and slums are good places to judge the place of irony in a culture.

The day before my trip down the rows of the dead, I'd been taken by car out to La Plata University, where I was scheduled to give a talk about cross-cultural issues in my writing. My task was to address a class of about forty English majors who were studying to become translators. These were the kind of young people who have a professional stake in irony.

On this journey the car passed through the outskirts of Buenos Aires. We passed kilometers of slums—hardscrabble, squalid hovels bearing witness to heart-wrenching suffering, poverty and desperation. It was hard to believe that human beings could inhabit such awful conditions and not revolt. The students were attentive and asked many questions about Thailand, literature and culture. In the corridors students made protest banners. They seemed politically engaged in a way that Thai university students are not. These were large state universities and didn't cater to the offspring of the ultra-rich.

The next day my gang of four Latin American authors (we were attending Buenos Aires Noir, a conference organized by Ernesto Mallo) and I set off to visit La Recoleta Cemetery. This sprawling fourteen acres in the heart of Buenos Aires contains 4,691 vaults. Mausoleums grand and small house the remains of generals, presidents and a dusting of poets and actors. Their final vaults, inspired by architectural styles including Art Deco, Art Nouveau, Baroque and Neo-Gothic, created a city of the dead unlike any place I'd seen.

The contrast between the slums along the road from Buenos Aires to La Plata, which housed the living, and the Art Deco mausoleums made from fine marble was like watching a thousand condemned men do a tango around a puddle on their way to be hanged. The celebration of the powerful in death far transcended the humanity offered to the living.

I watched as people came to bring flowers and take photographs of Eva Peron's mausoleum. Eva Peron was a perfect example of a patron who entered the grand station of national politics on the side of the poor. In death she wasn't buried with those she sought to represent and encourage. Instead, Evita took her place alongside other members of the privileged class with an address along a lane with rows and rows of other long-dead patrons in their marble palaces. Walking down those lanes, peering at the names, the tombs and the heavy marble walls, I found that it wasn't difficult to understand that these dead had left a legacy for the living. It is one that most people in the world can understand. The elites, even those who pledge themselves to helping the poor and the suffering, ultimately enter the afterlife in shrines erected for the few.

No one in the cemetery spoke of any irony in the incongruity between the slums and the marble mausoleums. Somewhere, I am quite sure, there is a marble tomb at La Recoleta Cemetery where the earthly remains of irony are housed. I didn't find it. Four thousand, six hundred and ninety-one vaults is a lot to inspect on a cold, rainy Buenos Aires afternoon. Leaving the cemetery, we came across a large, well-fed cat curled up into a ball under a tree in the shadow of a dead president. It was an ideal place to be a cat, especially after closing time, when the tourists left and the rats came out of the shadows. The hunting must have been good. Like shooting fish in a barrel. Rats stalking the dead, the cats stalking the rats, and not even a hint of irony in the ecology that has come to represent our time and place.

The Death of Literary Irony

I am prepared for a Western post-irony future. After nearly twenty-five years living in Thailand, a culture rich in puns, riddles and word play but autistic when it comes to irony, I can give you a hint of what to expect next. Without knowing it, you begin to accept that incongruities aren't really contradictions that need resolution. Reality is large enough and people are adult enough to not dwell upon such matters. Once you accept that premise, not only is irony dead, it is stillborn.

Beyond the Lamppost Light

A uthors' photographs fall into several categories. The most common is the best face photograph—the ego shining forth. I've had my share of those photographs over the years. There are less common authors' photographs. Among those are ones that show a storyteller writing a story in a setting that has its own story to tell. This kind of photograph reminds me of Russian dolls nested together, each a smaller version of the one before it, until the doll is infinitely small and disappears with all of the stories locked inside.

This week I was at the airport in Bangkok. Physically I was at the airport, but my mind was somewhere else. It was engaged with the latest Calvino novel. Scraps of dialogue, gestures, expressions, body language and images buzzed around my consciousness like fruit flies hovering over an open jar of honey. I normally carry a notebook. I had left it at home. I knew from bitter experience that unless I wrote down the imagery and dialogue it would be lost. There were too many ideas, too many scenes and faces, competing for memory storage. There is nothing more frustrating than being in the flow of a scene and having no way to pull from that river the treasures floating past.

I went to a counter and asked for a piece of paper and found a place to write. Only later, when looking at a photograph of me caught in that moment, could I see that the world that physically surrounded me was as rich as an imagination set free. An unattended airport cart filled with various packages. Who had left it? What was inside the packages?

No one but a writer lost in his imagination could have missed the huge Mont Blanc advertisement—a brand, a prestige item and a godlike face, all playing out a story about how our world of commodities feeds our desires, focuses our motivations and guides our deepest hopes. The illuminated ad shone like a mini-shrine, a spirit house, a testament to our wish to elevate our status and to receive the recognition of those around us.

Here I was, a writer holding a two-dollar pen, writing, head down, lost inside myself, ignoring our culture's message about what is real and important. I wrote in the shadow of a company that sells really expensive, flashy pens—and now also expensive perfume for men to go along with the pens. The smell, the look, that's what has pulled us into the dragnet of manufactured happiness. We are suckers who no longer fight the dragnet as it sweeps us along with millions of other little fish trying to swim like the outsized, important fish that secretly aspires to become a legend. Money is the shortcut to rise out of the fishery. That's how stuff is sold to us. It is the reason we part with our money after we have everything we really need. Who doesn't want to be a legend and immortal, and to smell so fragrant that the gods weep as we pass? This is a feeling we can't easily shake.

Also beside me in the picture there is an escalator leading international passengers to immigration control. And then there are the airport workers, with their vests, talking to each other, knowing they'd never take that escalator upstairs to clear immigration. They are the fish that swim in huge schools, the fish that will never buy the perfume or take the plane to Berlin or London or New York. These local fish stay close to the home shore.

I had been writing. I had been paying attention to the flow inside my mind. Everything captured in the photograph had gone unnoticed. Focus is the bullet that puts a slug in the heart of distractions. They fall away dead, and we don't notice the bodies until we look at a picture and identify them later.

What we pay attention to and how we pay (or fail to pay) attention define us as much as a tattoo of a dragon on our forehead. As a writer, my books and essays form part of the attention focusing business, and they compete with all of the other products that attention hawkers hit you with hundreds of times a day. Exhausting, isn't it? All this money and effort spent to get you to focus your attention on some visual, oral or acoustic experience.

It doesn't matter what public space we enter; someone wants us to pay attention to what they have to say. Retreating into a private space provides little protection. Legions of companies, governments and other people want you to remember that you paid attention to their message, and for a reason. They want something from you. And in return for your attention they are offering you some reward.

One reason to read is to find a way out of the lamppost light bias. The parable goes like this.

A cop on foot patrol comes across a drunk on his knees circling around a lamppost.

The officer asks the drunk, "What are you doing on the ground?"

And the drunk replies, "I've lost my car keys."

The cop takes pity on the drunk and helps him search for the lost keys. After fifteen minutes of futile searching, the cop asks the drunk, "Where did you lose the keys?"

The drunk points to the park in the darkness beyond the lamppost.

"Over there," says the drunk.

The cop shakes his head.

"For God's sake, man, why are you looking here?"

And the drunk replies, "Because that's where the light is."

The books 1 read take me beyond the light of the lamppost. They take me to the hidden world inside the dark park. That's where the keys were lost. Not to my car but to understanding the nature of the world. Truth is camouflaged, out of sight. You won't find it under a lamppost. That's where everyone expects to find it. But the right book, in the hands of a master, can light a single candle that reveals what has been concealed—the things not sold in airport advertisements. We have in our power to take that candle and set out on an exploration. Even if truth isn't at the end, the journey will have illuminated a pathway to worlds that lie just beyond where the darkness begins.

I was in the airport in Bangkok. It was a lamppost and I was inside its light. But my mind was inside another the terrain, time and place, and whether or not I found anything of value, I can't be sure. But I was pleased to have found strangers who donated paper and pen to take a chance that I might be writing my own ticket to escape from the lamppost circle of light.

Author's Muse

Every author has a muse. Along with every painter, composer, dancer and other artist. The muse has a long tradition. The Greeks had many gods and goddesses, but the one their writers and artists were most fond of was called the Muse. An artist might be an atheist when it comes to God and religion, but the Muse makes the most logical and skeptical of the bunch into believers in the intangible forces of creativity and inspiration. Someday when neuroscience decodes consciousness, the neural structure that creates the illusion of the Muse will be discovered. Until that day we are little ahead of ancient Greece.

No doubt the idea of supernatural artistic inspiration had been around long before being co-opted into ancient Greek culture, but the Greek Muses are the ones we know best. The Muses, the personification of knowledge and the arts, especially literature, dance and music, are the nine daughters of Zeus and Mnemosyne (memory personified). You may recognize the mother, Mnemosyne, as the term "meme" for an idea that infects the minds of others comes from her name. "Mind," "mental" and "memory" all derive from Mnemosyne.

Of particular interest to crime fiction authors, the Muse known as Melpomene was one of the nine daughters and assigned to inspire works of tragedy. Before you set up your home altar next to your computer and call out to your inner Muse, there are a few things to know about the Muses, whose mother, Melpomene, has a past.

Melpomene is portrayed wearing a tragic mask and the cothurni, boots traditionally worn by tragic actors. In another version she holds a knife or club in one hand and the tragic mask in the other. She wears a crown of cypress. Her father was Zeus and her mother Mnemosyne. And back in the day, if you wanted an inspiration for a lyrical phrase, she was the Muse you made offerings to.

Words like "amuse" and "museum" derive from the original use of "Muse." Many writers have paid homage to the Muses, from Homer and Virgil to Dante, Chaucer and Shakespeare.

Living in a culture like Thailand, where spirits are daily worshipped at small spirit houses scattered throughout the land, and upcountry workers as well as city workers give offerings, the idea of the Muse is a natural fit. Spirit houses erected on premises housing newspapers, publishers, media houses and advertising agencies don't yet display statues of the nine daughters of Zeus and Mnemosyne. But 2013 is young and the meme of the Muse hasn't gone viral in Thailand. Finding a Muse to present at Government House and Parliament might "inspire," if not poetry, some new comedy and tragedy to retire the old tropes people don't find of interest anymore.

I have a theory (or two) about the nature of the Muse. When one of the nine daughters of Mnemosyne and Zeus come to visit, pay attention. What kills creativity is distraction. What ignites the imagination is found through focus and attention that seeks to find a new pattern, a new way of seeing or thinking. That kind of thinking is difficult. It takes lots of resources. You can witness the Muse indirectly when you see a great painting or theatrical production or read a great book. The result of the best of the arts is the creation of something out of inspiration.

Most of the time our attention is divided. We have too much on our mind, pulling it this way and the other. We flit from problem to problem, image to image, from the past to the future, like a bird hopping from branch to branch looking for the tree. But the issue isn't limited to the non-stop, discontinuous internal mental streaming within. We also add to our distraction by streaming into our brain the exterior world. To call on the Muse to visit means a commitment to closing down our random thoughts and to shutting out stimulation from the outside world. TV off. Internet off. Phone off. "Do not disturb" sign on the closed door.

Light a candle. Wait for the Muse to deliver the right word, phrase, scene and image to fit into a narrative flow. That is my other theory about the Muse. It is another way of describing the flow. Musicians, writers, dancers and painters know that space where the notes, words, movements or colors appear as if from another place and create a narrative force that carries the creator along a path he or she would never have discovered inside a mind cluttered with internal and exterior attention grabbers.

The Flow is the space artists seek to enter and never leave. When I write, I work to find that space because in the Flow all the nine daughters of Zeus and Mnemosyne are working the oars on a boat that navigates around bends and through rapids to deliver you to a destination you never would have discovered in a world too full of noise.

Re-imagining Henry Miller

In Bangkok and New York, Barney Rosset told me many stories about Henry Miller. He'd published Miller and knew the author personally. My views about Henry Miller have been shaped by Barney's recollections over the years. Another acquaintance of mine, Richard Seavers, also had a long history with Barney. Recently a friend gave me a copy of a memoir written by Henry Miller's Paris friend and contemporary, a photographer named Brassaï.

Henry Miller: The Paris Years was published in 1995 by Arcade Publishing, a press run by Richard Seaver. I'd met Richard Seaver in New York at Barney's loft in the East Village and again at Barney's table at the National Book Foundation award ceremony in 2008, when Barney was given a lifetime achievement.

With those connections, having known a couple of the people who were close to Miller for years, I was the right audience for *Henry Miller: The Paris Years*. You can be close to someone without knowing the interior layers that go deep, where stuff is hidden, forgotten, fractured into a prism-like mystery. Even when you know them well, years later when you seek to recall what was said and done, the memory can play elusive games.

I am wary of memoirs written by the friends of famous people. It is natural that they will put themselves in the center of the famous friend's life. That is a danger. I wondered if Brassaï had fallen into that trap.

Brassaï was one of Henry Miller's friends. The one result of fame is that an author's friends have their memories and correspondence ready for a memoir about the author—his life, habits, attitudes, weaknesses, tics and philosophy.

Brassaï's book ends with, "Henry left France without tears, without regret, and without looking back, as if the ten years he'd lived there had simply vanished." I wish that Barney were still around to ask if that was his take on Miller's years in France. Miller's time in France had made his reputation; the fruits of that period have established him as a writer, a genius and a literary tiger. I have been around expats a large portion of my life, and I can report that it is very rare to find someone who has lived in a culture as Henry Miller did in France who would discard the place like an old sweater.

Miller's *Tropic of Cancer* and his other major works were written out of experience that was processed through a hyperactive imagination. His reality was the result of this creative process. The boundaries of fiction, make-believe, became the raw ingredients of life in Paris and cooking up an exotic confection. His books were not just exotic; they were, according to the Americans, obscene. *Tropic of Capricorn* was banned and might have remainded so but for the efforts of Barney Rosset, who spent a personal fortune on court battles (only stopping at the US Supreme Court) starting in the 1960s. Miller's *Tropic of Capricorn* established him as a writer that upset officials who decided what could be read in the United States.

Understanding Henry Miller's Paris experience sheds light on his views on relationships, sexuality, identity, memory and imagination. Pornography is largely the legal conclusion from the conservative elites that the combination of those elements must stay within strict boundaries of propriety.

Henry Miller, according to Brassaï, believed that a person was lucky or unlucky depending on whom they met. For a writer who needed the constant input of new experiences, he found in Paris much luck in companions. If experience was fuel, the high-octane stuff came from two women. Anaïs Nin, born in Paris, American by nationality, with a Spanish father and a Franco-Danish mother, was the original "globalized" woman before anyone used the term. She kept a diary that by the time Miller met her ran to forty-eight notebooks—but she dismissed them as "bloody ejaculations." Her relationship with literature, the writer's role and the nature of reality expressed a mix of conflicting attitudes. Anaïs Nin believed that a writer should stay bound into the moment of truth and not filter it through imagination, which changed the reality to something no longer true. Miller was at the opposite pole—where reality until processed and transformed by imagination would never become "real," and fiction and myth were the techniques of this transformation.

Anaïs Nin was Miller's intellectual muse. Brassaï writes that during the two-year period that the *Tropic of Cancer* was put on ice by a Parisian publisher anxious about possible legal problems, Anaïs Nin guided Miller through multiple rewrites. It wouldn't have been the book that made his reputation without her tireless, patient pushing for changes.

Another woman, June, was Miller's sensual muse. A woman filled with a huge amount of energy, she also walked on the wild side. Men were attracted to her, and she exchanged sexual favors for money. As June's husband, Miller didn't ask where the money was coming from. It is no surprise to learn that Miller admired the pimps who gathered at Chez Paul near the offices of the *Chicago Herald*

Tribune, 5 Rue Lamartine, in the heart of Paris's red light district. He admired their power over women, their lack of shame, their sales banter and their disdain for ordinary work. They had a lifestyle that Miller idealized as one route to take in the rebellion against culture and those in authority.

June had, in Brassaï's view, a superabundance of life; she was one of those people with ten times the intensity and energy of ordinary mortals. If one is writing out of experience, hooking one's star to such a woman as June could propel one into dramas that most writers would never dream possible. Her betrayals and lies created a stormy relationship, but passive women bored him. Such women were open books. Miller didn't want that kind of woman.

Brassaï writes that Miller married June without knowing the basics about her, like place of birth, name or family background. He wanted mystery, someone who was unpredictable, unreachable, whose life and background remained vague and unknown. June was not just a siren, she was a cipher—a code that Miller tried to break with his imagination. He failed in that goal, but his failure to decode June nonetheless set him on a journey that inspired him to write two brilliant books: *Tropic of Cancer* and *Tropic of Capricorn*. June felt committed to Miller; though he was a genius, for her he was the one true love of her life. For Miller June was part of his expression of open rebellion against his Brooklyn upbringing. They were both displaced spirits seeking to escape old lives and create new ones.

One detail of Miller's writing habit concerned his daily routine of walking the streets of Paris. He was a great observer. He could only think on his feet. And that meant walking around examining buildings, people, activities until some thought—the Voice—would come into his head, and he'd rush back to his room and sit in front of his typewriter as the cascading images, ideas and expressions tumbled out of his mind and onto paper. He was less interested in the truth—thus his arguments with Anaïs Nin—than in the stories he drew from observations. For Brassaï Miller's casual relationship with the truth was "bewildering." In *Tropic of Capricorn* June emerges as a character filtered through an imagination to the point that she is no longer recognizable as the flesh and blood woman he had married.

In the end the well of Henry Miller's experience dried up. He left Paris without a backward glance. Anaïs Nin drifted away. He slipped away from June. He lost the city and the two women who had inspired him, who had brought him the Voice that defined him. For authors there is a lesson to be learnt in this, particularly if your work of dredging experience flourishes from the lucky strike of a goldmine of life. Like all resources, sooner or later such gold runs out. The mine becomes an empty shell, a hole in the ground and a hole in the heart. Only a few writers are lucky enough to find the perfect match of time, place and companions that put Miller in touch with that Voice—the one that moves and touches not just the author but readers for generations.

In a book titled *Chairs* I wrote about Barney Rosset's Henry Miller connection in a story called "Star of Love." I had asked Barney whether he thought, if Henry Miller had discovered Bangkok, it would have changed his life. Barney replied, "Totally. Absolutely. How could it have not influenced him?" In the end, Barney said, that Miller holed up on top of a mountain in the Big Sur. He had a security guard at the bottom where there was a dirt road. The guard's job was to stop anyone going up to bother Henry.

This was the author who had roamed the streets of Paris searching for the Voice. The oyster had closed its shell. No more pearls would emerge. Brassaï set out how he saw Henry Miller's reality. Too bad there's no chance to ask Anaïs Nin if *Henry Miller: The Paris Years* was filtered through the imagination factory—part illusion, part hallucination. Or does the author give the reader the unfiltered, unmediated truth? But the person I'd really like to ask is June. What would she have thought of this version of the truth? All these people are dead. Whatever the truth of their reality we can never know. What we are left with instead are the shards of information, impressions, and thoughts recycled as reimagined lives. A literary life that has the capacity for self-generating truths via those who knew the author is rare. We are reminded that truth rung through the active imagination of writers like Brassaï is part of what keeps Miller alive in the minds of readers today. Oblivion is the alternative.

After finishing Brassaï's memoir and thinking about the big picture, the reader could say that Henry Miller was a lucky man. Luck has a great role in a writer's life. As I put the book aside, I felt I had been lucky to have discovered Bangkok when it was the Paris of the 1930s, a place where Barney Rosset, Miller's friend, discovered my existence, making me a small link in the chain of people who have written about Henry Miller.

Miller had Paris, while I had Bangkok pretty much to myself for the early years, and it was a place where I walked, explored, learnt a language and a culture, and the place where I found my Voice. Unlike Miller, I couldn't imagine leaving Bangkok for the isolation of a mountaintop—or, at the very least, not without stopping and looking back one last time to say a final goodbye to all of that.

When the Cuckoo Calls Your Name:
A Lesson in Success for Writers

Most of the time we humans are predictable in our reaction to the success of others. Anger, jealousy, envy, hatred and self-doubt spill out like pennies in a clay piggy bank hurled against a brick wall. Another person's success is felt like a punch in the face. In the entertainment business that reflex is in full swing. Our hackles rise when we read articles with openings like this: "Robert Downey Jr. claims top earning spot with $75 million last year thanks to his role in 'Iron Man.'"

How many actors who are waiting tables in New York, Los Angeles, London and Paris, dreaming of their big break, can only dream of making one percent of that amount? The chances are they won't have commercial success. They will never experience a year, or a career, like that of Robert Downey Jr. But that is hardly Robert Downey Jr.'s fault. Nothing in the universe was set to make his rise to fame and fortune inevitable. It could have been another actor. It could have been you.

Writers face the same problem. A handful of authors make the lion's share of money from writing. James Patterson, Dan Brown, J.K. Rowling, John Grisham and Stephen King are some of the familiar names guaranteed to deforest mountains in British Columbia, to sell container loads of books and to dominate bestseller lists, book review coverage and public perception of how to measure a writer's success.

It is the .001 percent of authors who are profiled in the major press, and the press never fails to mention the money they earn, the number of rooms in their houses, private planes, boats; how they are cocooned inside a wall of well-paid staff. The 99.999 percent of writers scramble with other jobs to cover the cost of their rent, food and transportation. Outside a few lions, the rest of the animals roaming the literary savannah survive on near starvation rations.

Like Robert Downey Jr., the James Pattersons and J.K. Rowlings hit the big time. They were in the right place at the right time, and not one of them, or their agents or their publishers, would ever have predicted the scale of such success.

The idea of scaling hasn't been discussed in the saga of Rowling's *The Cuckoo's Calling*. For those who haven't followed the disclosure of Rowling's novel published under another name, here's a brief summary.

When J.K. Rowling sought to go undercover and write a crime novel titled *The Cuckoo's Calling* under the pen name Robert Galbraith, she discovered what most non-famous writers already know. It's tough finding a publisher, and having found a publisher, it is even more difficult for a really good crime novel to break out and acquire a Harry Potter-sized audience.

A couple of points, based on everything I've read about J.K. Rowling, are worth noting. She is a decent, kind, sincere and genuine person. She doesn't need to prove anything as J.K. Rowling. She has a brand. She knows that, and like any author she must have had in the back of her mind a doubt she'd like removed. That doubt is whether a novel written without the brand attached would find a publisher. *The Cuckoo's Calling* had been rejected by a number of presses.

Rowling's own publisher and editor decided to issue it under the pen name.

They created a fictional bio for Robert Galbraith and sent it out for review. Indeed the book found a good reception among critics. But the sales told a different story. Given that the publishing world has something called a returns right—meaning bookstores buy the books but have a right to return unsold copies for a credit—the sales of *The Cuckoo's Calling* came in somewhere between five hundred and fifteen hundred copies.

A don at Hertford College, Oxford, named Peter Millican created a software program that could compare the text of any book with the text of books by famous writers. Professor Millican told the *BBC*, "I was testing things like word length, sentence length, paragraph length, frequency of particular words and the pattern of punctuation." He concluded that the probability was high that Rowling was the author of *The Cuckoo's Calling*.

A book that had garnered small sales under the name Robert Galbraith was now on the bestseller list. The limited hardback edition of the Robert Galbraith book is now going for up to two thousand pounds sterling. The failed attempt to experiment with publishing outside the brand name J.K. Rowling has given a good insight into the concept of scaling. When you aren't famous and you write a book, you are no different from any other person with a product or service that is untested in the marketplace. Markets come in various shapes, forms and sizes. The market for your novel might be just you, your family and friends. When that market is saturated, you've had your success. The problem is that most of us think the market for what we write is either much larger or smaller than it actually is. You might be the star of your community theatre, but your heart is set on Broadway and Hollywood. The same goes for an author who has a community theatre-sized audience for his or her book but believes that he or she is one review away from a New York deal.

How do you know if the book you've written will "scale" from an audience of a couple of hundred, or a couple of thousand, to millions around the world? The answer is you don't know. No agent or publisher knows either. The same with films, even those with established stars. No one is sure whether the movie will scale and capture a huge market or flop like a fish in the bottom of a boat.

Inexperienced authors judge themselves by the standards of established authors. When their book doesn't have J.K. Rowling-like success, they feel like they are a failure. Status in the entertainment world—film, painting, photography and books—is bestowed by measuring commercial success. And the level of commercial success expected is on the order of the Big Bang, growing from a pinpoint to an entire universe in a nanosecond.

Most books are fragile in the marketplace. They never "bang"; they whimper and die and are assigned to a potter's literary grave. In retrospect we can say the book didn't scale because the subject was too narrow, the writing not artful enough, the characterization weak, the story derivative and a hundred other reasons that support the decision of the marketplace. None of this is to be taken seriously any more than someone's analysis of why the stock market dropped five percent in one day or an earthquake hit China.

Those authors whose books scale across the literary universe are not necessarily possessed of rare literary genius. There are hundreds of writers who have published books as good as or better than the ones people line up by the thousands at midnight to buy. Before her explosive success J.K. Rowling lived on welfare, writing out of coffee shops. She had no special connection in the literary world. No doubt she can write, but with Harry Potter she won the literary lottery, and most likely, like most lottery winners she was as bewildered and surprised as anyone else.

Authors without broad brand recognition doom themselves by using the J.K. Rowling measure of success. Her lesson with *The Cuckoo's Calling* published under another name is that the talent of a writer, any writer, is only one part of the complex network of gears grinding below the surface of life. Once in awhile the great machine produces a book that explodes, gathering millions of avid readers, occasional readers and non-readers as well. The author's life jumps from the book review pages and lands on a vastly larger stage of the news and social columns. The author becomes newsworthy herself, along with her houses, cars, boats, likes and dislikes, what she eats for breakfast, charities and hobbies, lectures and travels. A celebrity is born and like any new star shines bright.

How or why this mysterious event happens to any particular author is difficult to explain. But it has happened before and will happen again. When the audience for a book scales on the order of magnitude of the Big Bang, nothing can ever be the same again for that author. Whatever he or she writes thereafter will enter the public consciousness. Attempts to hide behind another name will likely fail. That new star in the literary sky doesn't just twinkle; it dominates the literary sky, and most of asteroids in the vicinity disappear from sight.

If you are a writer, you won't allow bitterness and regret to color your opinion of the success enjoyed by authors such as J.K. Rowling. You will make a decision not to expend emotional energy over what you can't possibly control. You will also understand that the essential feature of any author's life isn't whether the book scales to reach the mountaintop of success, but whether the author has gone into the world and climbed mountains. Be the writer who has put experience of life above striving for status. Be the writer with an inexhaustible curiosity, a hunger for knowledge, and a humility that goes hand in hand with a wisdom that the world each day has something new to teach. Be the writer who disconnects from the Internet, cell phones and TV, and goes out into unfamiliar neighborhoods and observes the lives of people you wouldn't otherwise meet. Be the writer who is the student and not the professor. Be the writer who is a child and not a parent. Be the writer who withholds making a quick judgment.

Be the writer who gets out of the apartment or house and enters a courtroom, a classroom, a prison or a hospital and who watches the flow of people passing through these public places. The people in these places have lives worth understanding, and they will share their secrets, dreams, desires, disappointments and pain. You'll find them occupying these places living in stress, duress and anxiety. Here you will find courage, desperation, corruption, hatred, love, hope, depression—the elements that define who we are and the nature of our troubled times.

If you want to embark on a path as a writer, enter the flow of lives around you. Leave your comfort zone. Be the writer who explores cultures, religions and languages to discover the forces that shape our differences in perception, understanding and emotional reactions.

After this exploration, whether your book scales to the higher elevations of J.K. Rowling's commercial success, it won't matter. You will have scaled to the top of your personal intellectual and emotional mountaintop, planted your flag and looked out on life in a way that few ever will. That, my friend, is success.

CHRISTOPHER G.
MOORE
Creator of the Vincent Calvino Crime Fiction Series

The
Cultural
Detective

Reflections on the
writing life in Thailand

THE CULTURAL DETECTIVE
Heaven Lake Press (2011) ISBN 978-616-90393-8-9

For more than twenty years, Christopher G. Moore has been writing about the history, culture and politics of Southeast Asia, in particular Thailand. The Cultural Detective is a behind-the-scene view into Moore's writing life.

In this selection of essays, Moore discusses with the humor and insight that he has become famous for. He draws widely on anthropology, neurology, psychology, ethnography, history and recent political conflicts.

Readers new to Moore's work will find an entertaining and discerning author worth getting to know better, while fans will recognize an echo of his essayist's voice and perspective from his novels.

"It is perhaps a judge of excellence that I would pull down one book from the shelves, read it again, and thoroughly enjoy it once more? If so, then *The Cultural Detective* by Christopher G. Moore is an excellent book. Not only a good book, but for me, the best book reviewed in 2011."
—*Pattaya Mail*

FAKING IT IN BANGKOK
Heaven Lake Press (2012) ISBN 978-616-7503-13-4

The Cultural Detective established Christopher G. Moore as a writer whose essays deliver a unique perspective insight into Thai culture and contemporary political and social issues. In *Faking It in Bangkok* gangsters, gamblers, killers and other criminals are brought to life in the essays. Readers who follow Moore's crime novels will enjoy his detours through the hard-edged noir world of Thailand with whistle stops on the digital age express. Moore's signature irony and humor riffs are also not to be missed as he explores an eclectic range of subjects, from ghosts and fortunetellers to the de facto tribal seating on the BTS.

"Moore is a keen observer of 'Thai-ness.' His insights are offered in an entertaining and cheeky manner....The truths he reveals are at times comical, endearing and cringe-worthy, but they all show a side of Thai society worth examining.... He shows a love and appreciation for a society that has its flaws and virtues."
—Voranai Vanijka, *Bangkok Post*

Ralf Tooten © 2012

Christopher G. Moore is a Canadian novelist and essayist who lives in Bangkok. He has written 25 novels, including the award-winning Vincent Calvino series and the Land of Smiles Trilogy. The German edition of his third Vincent Calvino novel, *Zero Hour in Phnom Penh*, won the German Critics Award (Deutsche Krimi Preis) for International Crime Fiction in 2004 and the Spanish edition of the same novel won the Premier Special Director's Book Award Semana Negra (Spain) in 2007. The second Calvino novel, *Asia Hand,* won the Shamus Award for Best Original Paperback in 2011. The previous collections of his essays are *The Cultural Detective* and *Faking It in Bangkok*. For more information about his books, visit his website: cgmoore.com.